The Library of:

Name:

Address:

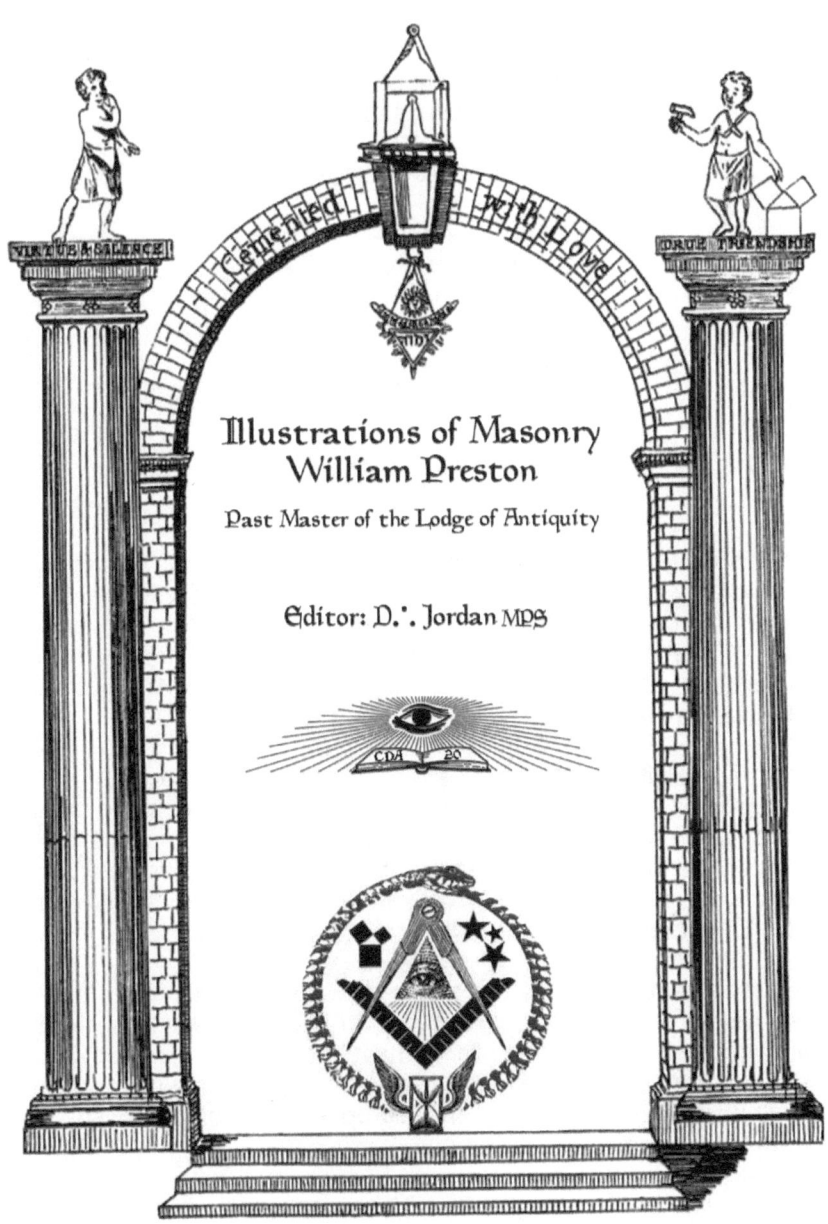

Illustrations of Masonry
William Preston
Past Master of the Lodge of Antiquity

Editor: D∴ Jordan MPS

Illustrations of Masonry
Original Publication 1772

© 2017 FLVTAA Publishing 1st Edition
All Rights Reserved

Author: William Preston

Editor/Compiler/Cover Designer:
Bro. Darrell Jordan MPS

ISBN: 978-0-9728825-7-6

$21.99

A Seat of Knowledge Series

Note: Print is in 12 point font for ease of reading and study. <u>Definitions</u> are included immediately after the word in question and indicated in 10 point *(Italic font and parenthesized)*. All other parenthesized words in 12 point font are those of the original author. Pictures were added for the reader's reading pleasure and old English verbiage has been modified to current American English spelling.

Disclaimer: The Editor made every attempt to provide an accurate and as concise a work as possible. *On the level*, there may be some mistakes hereon and whereas it is admitted that no matter how often one proofs a publication of this size, there will always be a mistake not detected prior to publication; to wit; I apologize in advance for any errors and for any inconvenience it may cause the reader.

In an effort to further the good cause of Masonry, as the information contained herein is of primary importance to Masonic research, therefore; the Editor coupled with the Publisher have no issues with copying said material by corporate or private individuals and utilizing said information in a private or public forum for educational purposes. The only proviso; please indicate whence it came.

"Employ your time in improving yourself by other men's writings so that you shall come easily by what others have labored hard for." ~ Socrates

Dedicated to:

The Brothers of CDA 20

"You must understand that knowledge cannot be turned into words. That knowledge is there for everyone. It is there to be felt, to be used, but not to be explained. One can come into it by changing levels of awareness, therefore, heightened awareness is an entrance. But even the entrance cannot be explained. One can only make use of it." ~ Carlos Castaneda

And to:

B∴ Becker 33°

"From time to time there appear on the face of the earth men of rare and consummate excellence, who dazzle us by their virtue, and whose outstanding qualities shed a stupendous light. Like those extraordinary stars of whose origins we are ignorant, and of whose fate, once they have vanished, we know even less, such men have neither forebears nor descendants: they are the whole of their race."
~ Jean de La Bruyère

A Glossary of Antiquated Words in the foregoing Manuscript

<u>Antiquated Word</u>   <u>Translation</u>

Albein.....................Only
Alweys....................Always
Beithe ....Both

Commodytye............Conveniency
Confrerie..................Fraternity

Façonnynge..............Forming
Fore-sayinge ....Prophesying
Freres.....................Brethren

Gude......................Good

Headlye..................Chiefly
Hemplese................The / they / please
Hemselfe.................Themselves
Her.......................There / their
Hereynne................Therein
Herwyth..................With it
Holpynge.................Beneficial

Kunne....................Know
Kunnynge................Knowledge

Maçonne..................Mason
Make gudde.............Are beneficial
Metynges................Measures
Middlelonde..............Mediterranean
Myghtylye................Mightily
Mote......................May
Myghte...................Power
Occasyonne.............Opportunity
Odher.....................Other
Onelyche.................Only

William Preston

Pernecessarye............Absolutely necessary
Preise ....Honor

Antiquated Word   Translation

Recht.........................Right
Reckenyngs..................Numbers

Skylle.........................Knowledge
Sonderlyche..................Particularly

Wacksynge....................Growing
Werck ....Operation
Wey............................Way
Whereas.......................Where
Woned..........................Dwelt
Wunderwerckynge............Working miracles
Wylde..........................Savage
Wynnynge....................Gaining

Yf...............................If
Ynn.............................Into

William Preston

Philosophy of William Preston
Bro. Roscoe Pound DGM
Excerpt from Philosophy of Masonry

PHILOSOPHERS are by no means agreed with respect to the scope and subject matter of philosophy. Nor are Masonic scholars at one with respect to the scope and purpose of Freemasonry. Hence one may not expect to define and delimit Masonic philosophy according to the easy method of Dickens editor who wrote upon Chinese metaphysics by reading in the Encyclopedia upon China and upon metaphysics and combining his information. It is enough to say at the outset that in the sense in which philosophers of Masonry have used the term, philosophy is the science of fundamentals. Possibly it would be more correct to think of the philosophy of Masonry as organized Masonic knowledge-as a system of Masonic knowledge. But there has come to be a well-defined branch of Masonic learning which has to do with certain fundamental questions; and these fundamental questions may be called the problems of Masonic philosophy, since that branch of Masonic learning which treats of them has been called commonly the philosophy of Masonry. These fundamental questions are three:

1. What is the nature and purpose of Masonry as an institution? For what does it exist? What does it seek to do? Of course for the philosopher this involves also and chiefly the questions, what ought Masonry to be? For what ought it to exist? What ought it to seek as its end?

2. What is and this involves what should be- the relation of Masonry to other human institutions, especially to those directed toward similar ends? What is its place in a rational scheme of human activities?

3. What are the fundamental principles by which Masonry is governed in attaining the end it seeks? This again, to the

philosopher, involves the question what those principles ought to be.

Four eminent Masonic scholars have essayed to answer these questions and in so doing have given us four systems of Masonic philosophy, namely, William Preston, Karl Christian Friedrich Krause, George Oliver and Albert Pike. Of these four systems of Masonic philosophy, two, if I may put it so, are intellectual systems. They appeal to and are based upon reason only. These two are the system of Preston and that of Krause. The other two are, if I may put it that way, spiritual systems. They do not flow from the rationalism of the eighteenth century but spring instead from a reaction toward the mystic ideas of the hermetic philosophers in the seventeenth century. As I shall try to show here-after, this is characteristic of each, though much more marked in one.

Summarily, then, we have four systems of Masonic philosophy. Two are intellectual systems: First that of Preston, whose key word is Knowledge; second, that of Krause, whose key word is Morals. Two are spiritual systems: First that of Oliver, whose key word is Tradition; and second, that of Pike, whose key word is Symbolism. Comparing the two intellectual systems of Masonic philosophy, the intrinsic importance of Preston's is much less than that of Krause's. Krause's philosophy of Masonry has a very high value in and of itself. On the other hand the chief interest in Preston's philosophy of Masonry, apart from his historical position among Masonic philosophers, is to be found in the circumstance that his philosophy is the philosophy of our American lectures and hence is the only one with which the average American Mason acquires any familiarity.

WILLIAM PRESTON

PRESTON was not, like Krause, a man in advance of his time who taught his own time and the future. He was thoroughly a child of his time. Hence to understand his writings we must know the man and the time. Accordingly I shall divide this discourse into three parts: (1) The man, (2) the time, (3) Preston's philosophy of Masonry as a product of the two.

First, then, the man. William Preston was born at Edinburgh on August 7, 1742. His father was a writer to the signet or solicitor- the lower branch of the legal profession - and seems to have been a man of some education and ability. At any rate he sent William to the high school at Edinburgh, the caliber of which in those days may be judged from the circumstance that the boy entered it at six-though he was thought very precocious. At school he made some progress in Latin and even began Greek. But all this was at an early age. His father died while William was a mere boy and he was taken out of school, apparently before he was twelve years old. His father had left him to the care of Thomas Ruddiman, a well-known linguist and he became the latter's clerk. Later Ruddiman apprenticed William to his brother who was a printer, so that Preston learned the printer's trade as a boy of fourteen or fifteen. On the death of his patron (apparently having nothing by inheritance from his father) Preston went into the printing shop as an apprentice and worked there as a journeyman until 1762. In that year, with the consent of the master to whom he had been apprenticed, he went to London.

He was only eighteen years old, but carried a letter to the king's printer, and so found employment at once. He remained in the employ of the latter during substantially the whole remaining period of his life. Preston's abilities showed themselves in the printing shop from the beginning. He not merely set up the matter at which he worked but he contrived in some way to read it and to think about it. From setting up the great variety of matter which came to the king's printer he acquired a notable literary style and became known to the authors whose books and writings he helped to set up as a judge of style and as a critic. Accordingly he was made proof reader and corrector for the press and worked as such during the greater part of his career. He did work of this sort on the writings of Gibbon, Hume, Robertson and authors of that rank, and presentation copies of the works of these authors, which were found among Preston's effects at his death, attest the value which they put upon the labors of the printer.

Preston had no more than come of age when he was made a Mason in a lodge of Scotchmen in London. This lodge had attempted to get a warrant from the Grand Lodge of Scotland, but that body very properly refused to invade London, and the Scotch petitioners turned to the Grand Lodge of Ancients, by whom they were chartered. Thus Preston was made in the system of his great rival, Dermott, just as the latter was at first affiliated with a regular or modern lodge. According to the English usage, which permits simultaneous membership in several lodges, Preston presently became a member of a lodge subordinate to the older Grand Lodge. Something here converted him, and he persuaded the lodge in which he had been raised to secede from the Ancients and to be reconstituted by the so called Moderns. Thus he cast his lot definitely with the latter and soon became their most redoubtable champion. Be it remembered that the Preston who did all this was a young man of twenty-three and a journeyman printer.

At the age of twenty-five he became master of the newly constituted lodge, and as such conceived it his duty to make a thorough study of the Masonic institution. His own words are worth quoting: "When I first had the honor to be elected master of a lodge, I thought it proper to inform myself fully of the general rules of the society, that I might be able to fulfill my own duty and officially enforce obedience in others. The methods which I adopted with this view excited in some of superficial knowledge an absolute dislike of what they considered as innovations, and in others, who were better informed, a jealousy of preeminence which the principles of Masonry ought have checked. Notwithstanding these discouragements, however, I persevered in my intention."

Indeed one cannot wonder that the pretenses of this journeyman printer of twenty-five were scouted by older Masons. But for the present Preston had to contend with nothing more than shakings of the head. Unlike the scholarly, philosophical, imperturbable, academic Krause, Preston was a fighter. Probably his confident dogmatism, which shows itself throughout his lectures, his aggressiveness and his ambition made more enemies than the supposed innovations involved in his Masonic research. Moreover we must not forget that he had to overcome three very serious obstacles namely, dependence for his daily bread upon a trade at which he worked twelve hours a day, youth, and recent connection with the fraternity. That Preston was not persecuted at this stage of his career and that he succeeded in taking the lead as he did is a complete testimony to his abilities.

Preston had three great qualifications for the work he undertook: (1) Indefatigable diligence, whereby he found time and means to read everything that bore on Masonry after twelve hours of work at his trade daily, six days in the week; (2) a marvelous memory, which no detail of his reading ever escaped; and (3) a great power of making friends and of enlisting their enthusiastic co-operation. He utilized this last resource abundantly, corresponding diligently all with well-informed Masons abroad and taking advantage of every opportunity to interview Masons at home. The results of this communication with all the prominent Masons of his time are to be seen in his lectures.

It was a bold but most timely step when this youthful master of a new lodge determined to rewrite or rather to write the lectures of Craft Masonry. The old charges had been read to the initiate originally, and from this there had grown up a practice of orally expounding their contents and commenting upon the important points. To turn this into a system of fixed lectures and give them a definite place in the ritual was a much-needed step in the development of the work. But it was so distinctly a step that the ease with which it was achieved is quite as striking as the result itself.

When Preston began the composition of his lectures, he organized a sort of club, composed of his friends, for the purpose of listening to him and criticizing him. This club was won't to meet twice a week in order to pass on, criticize and learn the lecture as Preston conceived it. Finally in 1772, after seven years, he interested the grand lodge officers in his work and delivered an oration, which appears in the first edition of his Illustrations of Masonry, before a meeting of eminent Masons including the principal grand officers. After delivery of the oration, he expounded his system to the meeting. His hearers approved the lectures, and, though official sanction was not given immediately, the result was to give them a standing which insured their ultimate success. His disciples began now to go about from lodge to lodge delivering his lectures and to come back to the weekly meetings with criticisms and suggestions. Thus by 1774 his system was complete. He then instituted a regular school of instruction, which obtained the sanction of the Grand Lodge and thus diffused his lectures throughout England. This made him the most prominent Mason of the time, so that he was elected to the famous Lodge of Antiquity, one of the four old lodges of 1717, and the one which claimed Sir Christopher Wren for a past master. He was soon elected master of this lodge and continued such for many years, giving the lodge a pre-eminent place in English Masonry which it has kept ever since.

Preston's Masonic career, however, was not one of unbroken triumph. In 1779 his views as to Masonic history and Masonic jurisprudence brought him into conflict with the Grand Lodge. It is hard to get at the exact facts in the mass of controversial writing which this dispute brought forth. Fairly stated, they seem to have been about as follows: The Grand Lodge had a rule against lodges going in public processions. The Lodge of Antiquity determined on St. John's Day, 1777, to go in a body to St. Dunstan's church, a few steps only from the lodge room. Some of the members protested against this as being in conflict with the rule of the Grand Lodge, and in consequence only ten attended. These ten clothed themselves in the vestry of the church, sat in the same pew during the service and sermon, and then walked across the street to the lodge room in their gloves and aprons. This action gave rise to a debate in the lodge at its next meeting, and in the debate Preston expressed the opinion that the Lodge of Antiquity, which was older than the Grand Lodge and had participated in its formation, had certain inherent privileges, and that it had never lost its right to go in procession as it had done in 1694 before there was any Grand Lodge. Thus far the controversy may remind us of the recent differences between Bro. Pitts and the Grand Lodge authorities in Michigan. But the authority of Grand Lodges was too recent at that time to make it expedient to overlook such doctrine when announced by the first Masonic scholar of the day. Hence, for maintaining this opinion, Preston was expelled by the Grand Lodge, and in consequence the Lodge of Antiquity severed its connection with the Grand Lodge of Moderns and entered into relations with the revived Grand Lodge at York. The breach was not healed till 1787.

Upon settlement of the controversy with the Grand Lodge of Moderns, Preston, restored to all his honors and dignities, at once resumed his Masonic activities. Among other things, he organized a society of Masonic scholars, the first of its kind. It was known as the Order of the Harodim and included the most distinguished Masons of the time. Preston taught his lectures in this society, and through it they came to America, where they are the foundation of our Craft lectures. Unhappily at the Union in England in 1813 his lectures were displaced by those of Hemming, which critics concur in pronouncing much inferior. But Preston was ill at the time and seems to have taken no part whatever in the negotiations that led to the Union nor in the Union itself. He died in 1818, at the age of 76, after a lingering illness. A diligent and frugal life had enabled him to lay by some money and he was able to leave 800 pounds for Masonic uses, 500 pounds to the Freemason's charity for orphans - for which, left an orphan himself before the age of twelve, he had a natural sympathy - and 300 pounds to endow the so called Prestonian lecture - an annual lecture in Preston's words verbatim by a lecturer appointed by the Grand Lodge. This lecture is still kept up and serves to remind us that Preston was the first to insist on the minute verbal accuracy which is now a feature of our lectures. It should be noted also that in addition to his lectures, Preston's book, Illustrations of Masonry, has had great influence. It went through some twenty editions in England, four or five in America, and two in Germany.

So much for the man.
Now as to the time.

Three striking characteristics of the first three quarters of the eighteenth century in England are of importance for an understanding of Preston's philosophy of Masonry: (1) It was a period of mental quiescence; (2) both in England and elsewhere it was a period of formal over-refinement; (3) it was the so-called age of reason, when the intellect was taken to be self-sufficient and men were sure that knowledge was a panacea.

1. In contrast with the seventeenth century, the eighteenth century was a period of quiescence. Society had ceased to be in a state of furious ebullition, nor was there a conflict of manifestly irreconcilable ideas as in the time just gone by. On the surface there was harmony. True, as the events of the end of the century showed, it was a harmony of compromise rather than of reconciliation-a truce, not a peace. But men ceased for a time to quarrel over fundamentals and turned their attention to details and to form. A common theological philosophy was accepted by men who denounced each other heartily for comparatively trivial differences of opinion. In politics, Whig and Tory had become little more than names, and both parties agreed to accept, with little modification, the body of doctrine afterwards known as the principles of the English Revolution. Political ideas were fixed. Men conceived of a social compact from which every detail of social and political rights and duties might be deduced by abstract reasoning and believed that it was possible in this way to work out a model code for the legislator, a touchstone of sound law for the judge and an infallible guide to private conduct for the individual. In literature and in art there was a like acquiescence in accepted canons. A certain supposed classical style was assumed to be the final and the only permissible mode of expression. In other words acquiescence was the dominant tendency and finality was the dominant idea. For example, Blackstone, a true representative of the century, thought complacently of the legal system of his

time, with its heavy load of archaisms, almost ripe for the legislative reform movement of the next generation, as substantially perfect. Nothing, so he thought, was left for the completion of five hundred years of legal development but to patch up a few trivial details. In the same spirit of finality the framers of our bills of rights undertook to lay out legal and political charts for all time. Indeed the absolute legal philosophy of our text books which has made so much trouble for the social reformers of yesterday and of today, speaks from the eighteenth century. In this spirit of finality, with this same confidence that his time had the key to reason and could pronounce once and for all for every time, for every place and for every people, Preston framed the dogmatic discourses which we are content to take as the lectures of Freemasonry.

2. For the modern world, the eighteenth century was par excellence the period of formalism. It was the period of formal over-refinement in every department of human activity. It was the age of formal verse and heroic diction, of a classical school in art which lost sight of the spirit in reproducing the forms of antiquity, of elaborate and involved court etiquette, of formal diplomacy, of the Red Tape and Circumlocution Office in every portion of administration, of formal military tactics in which efficiency in the field yielded to the exigencies of parade and soldiers went into the field dressed for the ball room. Our insistence upon letter perfect, phonographic reproduction of the ritual comes from this period, and Preston fastened that idea upon our lectures, perhaps for all time.

3. The third circumstance that the eighteenth century was the era of purely intellectualist philosophy naturally determined Preston's philosophy of Masonry. At that time reason was the central idea of all philosophical thought. Knowledge was regarded as the universal solvent. Hence when Preston found in his old lectures that among other things Masonry was a body of knowledge and discovered in the old charges a history of knowledge and of its transmission from antiquity, it was inevitable that he make knowledge the central point of his

system. How thoroughly he did this is apparent today in our American Fellowcraft lecture, which, with all the abridgments to which it has been subjected, is still essentially Prestonian. Time does not suffice to read Preston in his original rhetorical prolixity. But a few examples from Webb's version, which at these points is only an abridgment, will serve to make the point. The quotations are from a Webb monitor, but have been compared in each case with an authentic version of Preston.

"The Globes are two artificial spherical bodies, on the convex surface of which are represented the countries, seas, and various parts of the earth, the face of the heavens, the planetary revolutions, and other particulars. "The sphere, with the parts of the earth delineated on its surface, is called the Terrestrial Globe; and that with the constellations, and other heavenly bodies, the Celestial Globe. "The principal use of the Globes, besides serving as maps to distinguish the outward parts of the earth, and the situation of the fixed stars, is to illustrate and explain the phenomena arising from the annual revolution and the diurnal rotation of the earth around its own axis. They are the noblest instruments for improving the mind, and giving it the most distinct idea of any problem or proposition, as well as enabling it to solve the same."

It has often been pointed out that these globes on the pillars are pure anachronisms. They are due to Preston's desire to make the Masonic lectures teach astronomy, which just then was the dominant science. Note particularly the purpose, as the lecture sets it forth expressly: "or improving the mind and for giving it the most distinct idea of any problem or proposition as well as enabling it to solve the same." In other words, these globes are not symbolic; they are not designed for moral improvement. They rest upon the pillars, grotesquely out of place, simply and solely to teach the lodge the elements of geography and astronomy. We must remember that Preston, who worked twelve hours a day setting type or reading proof, would look on this very differently from the Mason of today. What are commonplaces of science now were by no means general property then. To him the teaching of the globes was a perfectly serious matter.

Turn to the solemn disquisition on architecture in our Fellowcraft lecture. As we give it, it is unadulterated Preston, but happily it is often much abridged. You know how it runs, how it describes each order in detail, gives the proportions, tells what was the model, appends an artistic critique, and sets forth the legend of the invention of the Corinthian order by Callimachus. The foundation for all this is in the old charges. But in Preston's hands it has become simply a treatise on architecture. The Mason who listened to it repeatedly would become a learned man. He would know what an educated man ought to know about the orders of architecture.

In the same way he gives us an abridgment of Euclid: "Geometry treats of the powers and properties of magnitudes in general, where length, breadth and thickness are considered, from a point to a line, from a line to a superficies, and from a superficies to a solid. A point is a dimensionless figure, or an indivisible part of space. A line is a point continued, and a figure of one capacity, namely, length. A superficies is a figure of two dimensions, namely, length and breadth. A solid is a figure of three dimensions, namely, length, breadth and thickness."

But enough of this. You see the design. By making the lectures epitomes of all the great branches of learning, the Masonic Lodge may be made a school in which all men, before the days of public schools and wide-open universities, might acquire knowledge, by which alone they could achieve all things. If all men had knowledge, so Preston thought, all human, all social problems would be solved. With knowledge on which to proceed deductively, human reason would obviate the need of government and of force and an era of perfection would be at hand. But those were the days of endowed schools which were not for the many.

The priceless solvent, knowledge, was out of reach of the common run of men who most needed it. Hence to Preston, first and above all else the Masonic order existed to propagate and diffuse knowledge. To this end, therefore, he seized upon the opportunity afforded by the lectures and sought by means of them to develop in an intelligent whole all the knowledge of his day.

Now that knowledge has become too vast to be comprised in any one scheme and too protean to be formulated as to any of its details even for the brief life of a modern text, the defects of such a scheme are obvious enough. That this was Preston's conception may be shown abundantly from his lectures. For instance: "Smelling is that sense by which we distinguish odors, the various kinds of which convey different opinions to the mind. Animal and vegetable bodies, and, indeed, most other bodies, while exposed to the air, continually send forth <u>effluvia</u> *(An unpleasant or harmful odor, secretion, or discharge.)* of vast subtlety, as well in the state of life and growth, as in the state of fermentation and putrefaction. These effluvia, being drawn into the nostrils along with the air, are the means by which all bodies are smelled."

This bit of eighteenth-century physics, which makes us smile today, is still gravely recited in many of our lodges as if it had some real or some symbolic importance. It means simply that Preston was endeavoring to write a primer of physiology and of physics. He states his theory expressly in these words: "On the mind all our knowledge must depend; what, therefore, can be a more proper subject for the investigation of Masons? By anatomical dissection and observation we become acquainted with the body; but it is by the anatomy of the mind alone we discover its powers and principles." That is: All knowledge depends upon the mind. Hence the Mason should study the mind as the instrument of acquiring knowledge, the one thing needful.

Today this seems a narrow and inadequate conception. But the basis of such a philosophy of Masonry is perfectly clear if we remember the man and the time. We must think of these lectures as the work of a printer, the son of an educated father, but taken from school before he was twelve and condemned to pick up what he could from the manuscripts he set up in the shop or by tireless labor at night after a full day's work. We must think of them as the work of a laborer, chiefly self-educated, associated with the great literati of the time whom he came to know through preparing their manuscripts for the press and reading their proofs, and so filled with their enthusiasm for enlightenment in what men thought the age of reason. We must think of them as the work of one imbued with the cardinal notions of the time-intellectualism, the all-sufficiency of reason, the absolute need of knowledge as the basis on which reason proceeds, and finality. How, then, does Preston answer the three problems of Masonic philosophy?

1. For what does Masonry exist? What is the end and purpose of the order?
Preston would answer: To diffuse light, that is, to spread knowledge among men. This, he might say, is the proximate end. He might agree with Krause that the ultimate purpose is to perfect men-to make them better, wiser and consequently happier. But the means of achieving this perfection, he would say, is general diffusion of knowledge. Hence, he would say, above all things Masonry exists to promote knowledge; the Mason ought first of all to cultivate his mind, he ought to study the liberal arts and sciences; he ought to become a learned man.

2. What is the relation of Masonry to other human activities? Preston does not answer this question directly anywhere in his writings. But we may gather that he would have said something like this: The state seeks to make men better and happier by preserving order. The church seeks this end by cultivating the moral person and by holding in the background supernatural sanctions. Masonry endeavors to make men better and happier by teaching them and by diffusing knowledge among them. This, bear in mind, was before education of the masses had become a function of the state.

3. How does Masonry seek to achieve its purposes? What are the principles by which it is governed in attaining its end? Preston answers that both by symbols and by lectures the Mason is (first) admonished to study and to acquire learning and (second) actually taught a complete system of organized knowledge. We have his own words for both of these ideas. As to the first, in his system both lectures and charges reiterate it.

For example: "The study of the liberal arts, that valuable branch of education which tends so effectually to polish and adorn the mind is earnestly recommended to your consideration." Again, notice how he dwells upon the advantages of each art as he expounds it: "Grammar teaches the proper arrangement of words according to the idiom or dialect of any particular people, and that excellency of pronunciation which enables us to speak or write a language with accuracy, agreeably to reason and correct usage. Rhetoric teaches us to speak copiously and fluently on any subject, not merely with propriety alone, but with all the advantages of force and elegance, wisely contriving to captivate the hearer by strength of argument and beauty of expression, whether it be to entreat and exhort, to admonish or applaud." As to the second proposition, one example will suffice: "Tools and implements of architecture are selected by the fraternity to imprint on the memory wise and serious truths." In other words the purpose even of the symbols is to teach wise and serious truths. The word serious here is significant. It is palpably a hit at those of his brethren who were inclined to be mystics and to dabble in what Preston regarded as the empty jargon of the hermetic philosophers.

Finally, to show his estimate of what he was doing and hence what, in his view, Masonic lectures should be, he says himself of his Fellow Craft lecture: "This lecture contains a regular system of science note that science then meant knowledge demonstrated on the clearest principles and established on the firmest foundation."

One need not say that we cannot accept the Prestonian philosophy of Masonry as sufficient for the Masons of today. Much less can we accept the details or even the general framework of his ambitious scheme to expound all knowledge and set forth a complete outline of a liberal education in three lectures. We need not wonder that Masonic philosophy has made so little headway in Anglo-American Masonry when we reflect that this is what we have been brought up on and that it is all that most Masons ever hear of. It comes with an official sanction that seems to preclude inquiry, and we forget the purpose of it in its obsolete details. But I suspect we do Preston a great injustice in thus preserving the literal terms of the lectures at the expense of their fundamental idea. In his day they did teach-- today they do not. Suppose today a man of Preston's tireless diligence attempted a new set of lectures which should unify knowledge and present its essentials so that the ordinary man could comprehend them. To use Preston's words, suppose lectures were written, as a result of seven years of labor, and the co-operation of a society of critics, which set forth a regular system of modern knowledge demonstrated on the clearest principles and established on the firmest foundation. Suppose, if you will, that this were confined simply to knowledge of Masonry. Would not Preston's real idea (in an age of public schools) be more truly carried than by our present lip service, and would not his central notion of the lodge as a center of light vindicate itself by its results? Let me give two examples. In Preston's day, there was a general need, from which Preston had suffered, of popular education--of providing the means whereby the common man could acquire knowledge in general.

Today there is no less general need of a special kind of knowledge. Society is divided sharply into classes that understand each other none too well and hence are getting wholly out of sympathy. What nobler Masonic lecture could there be than one which took up the fundamental of social science and undertook to spread a sound knowledge of it among all Masons? Suppose such a lecture was composed, as Preston's lectures were, was tried on by delivery in lodge after lodge, as his were, and after criticism and recasting as a result of years of labor, was taught to all our masters. Would not our lodges diffuse a real light in the community and take a great step forward in their work of making for human perfection?

Again, in spite of what is happening for the moment upon the Continent, this is an era of universality and internationality. The thinking world is tending strongly to insist upon breaking over narrow local boundaries and upon looking at things from a world-wide point of view. Art, science, economics, labor and fraternal organizations, and even sport are tending to become international. The growing frequency of international congresses and conferences upon all manner of subjects emphasizes this breaking of local political bonds. The sociological movement, the world over, is causing men to take a broader and more humane view, is causing them to think more of society and hence more of the world society, is causing them to focus their vision less upon the individual, and hence less upon the individual locality.

In this world-wide movement toward universality Masons ought to take the lead. But how much does the busy Mason know, much less think, of the movement for internationality or even the pacifist movement which has been going forward all about him ? Yet every Mason ought to know these things and ought to take them to heart. Every lodge ought to be a center of light from which men go forth filled with new ideas of social justice, cosmopolitan justice and internationality.

Preston of course was wrong-knowledge is not the sole end of Masonry. But in another way Preston was right. Knowledge is one end - at least one proximate end-and it is not the least of those by which human perfection shall be attained. Preston's mistakes were the mistakes of his century-the mistake of faith in the finality of what was known to that era, and the mistake of regarding correct formal presentation as the one sound method of instruction. But what shall be said of the greater mistake we make today, when we go on reciting his lectures-shorn *(Shear- past participle: shorn)* and abridged till they mean nothing to the hearer-and gravely presenting them as a system of Masonic knowledge? Bear in mind, he thought of them as presenting a general scheme of knowledge, not as a system of purely Masonic information. If we were governed by his spirit, understood the root idea of his philosophy and had but half his zeal and diligence, surely we could make our lectures and through them our lodges a real force in society. Here indeed, we should encounter the precisians and formalists of whom lodges have always been full, and should be charged with innovation. But Preston was called an innovator. And he was one in the sense that he put new lectures in the place of the old reading of the Gothic constitutions. Preston encountered the same precisians *(A person who adheres punctiliously to the observance of rules or forms, especially in matters of religion.)* and the same formalists and wrote our lectures in their despite. I hate to think that all initiative is gone from our order and that no new Preston will arise to take up his conception of Knowledge as an end of the fraternity and present to the Masons of today the knowledge which they ought to possess.

BIOGRAPHICAL NOTE

Nathan Roscoe Pound was born on October 27, 1870, in Lincoln, Nebraska. He was the son of Stephen B. Pound, a lawyer and judge, and Laura Biddlecome Pound, a native of New York. Roscoe Pound earned his B.A, M.A. and Ph.D. degrees in botany at the University of Nebraska and was one of Dr. Charles E. Bessey's first serious botany students at the university. Pound began studying law at Harvard in 1889 but stayed only a year before returning to Nebraska to begin his own practice. He was admitted to the Nebraska Bar without a law degree, and from 1899 to 1907, Pound taught law at the University of Nebraska, serving as Law School Dean during his final four years. He was also Commissioner of Appeals of the Nebraska Supreme Court from 1901 to 1903 and later taught at Northwestern University and the University of Chicago before becoming a law professor at Harvard in 1910. In 1916, Pound became Dean of the Harvard Law School, a post he held until his retirement in 1936, at which point he agreed to stay on as a professor. This appointment made him Harvard's first professor with a license to teach any subject in the university, not only law. At the age of 76, Pound resigned from teaching to accept an invitation from Chiang Kai-Shek to codify Chinese Laws. During his long career Pound held many posts of legal prominence, including the presidency of the Association of American Law Schools, membership in the standing advisory committee for the jurist section of the International Institute of Intellectual Cooperation, and membership on the Wickersham Commission which reported to President Hoover in 1931 on the prohibition law. Pound held some 200 honorary degrees from universities in this country and abroad. In 1940 he was awarded the Golden Medal of the American Bar Association for "conspicuous service to the cause of American jurisprudence." Roscoe was a past master of Lancaster Lodge 54 AF&AM in Lincoln and grand orator of the Grand Lodge AF&AM of Nebraska, of which he was an honorary past grand master. He received the 33rd degree of the Scottish Rite in 1913 in Philadelphia. Roscoe made his last appearance in Nebraska in March 1960 when he delivered a lecture at the University Of Nebraska College Of Law, where in 1950 the Roscoe Pound Lectureship was established.

His first wife, Grace Gerrard of Columbus, Nebraska, died in 1928. In 1931, he married Mrs. Lucy Miller of Washington, D.C. who died in 1959. Roscoe Pound died on June 30, 1964 at the age of 93 in Cambridge, Massachusetts. He left no survivors.

Illustrations of Masonry

Preface

The favorable reception this Treatise has met within the several Editions through which it has passed, encourages the Author to hope that its appearance on a still more enlarged scale, will not render it less deserving the countenance of his Brethren. He would be wanting in gratitude to his friends, not to acknowledge his obligations to several gentlemen for many curious extracts, and the perusal of some valuable manuscripts, which have enabled him to illustrate his subject with greater accuracy and precision.

This Tract is divided into Four Books. In the First Book, the excellency of Masonry is displayed. In the Second Book the Lectures of the different degrees are illustrated, with occasional remarks; and a brief description is given of the ancient ceremonies of the Order. This part of the Treatise, which the Author considers most essential for the instruction and improvement of his Brethren, is considerably extended in the present edition. The Third Book contains the copy of a curious old Manuscript, with annotations, the better to explain this authentic document of antiquity. The Fourth Book is restricted to the history of Masonry, from its first appearance in England to the present time, in the course of which are introduced the most remarkable occurrences of the Society, both at home and abroad, with some account of the principal patrons and protectors of the fraternity at different periods.

The progress of the Society on the Continent, as well as in India and America, is also traced, while the proceedings of the Brethren of Scotland particularly claim attention. Throughout the whole are interspersed several explanatory notes, containing a variety of interesting and well authenticated particulars. At the end is given a collection of Anthems and Songs; some of which have never appeared in any of the former editions. These being occasionally introduced in our assemblies must tend to greatly enliven the proceedings.

Thus having endeavored to put the finishing stroke to his Treatise, the success of which has far exceeded the its merit, the author can only observe, that should the additions be considered real improvements, he will be amply gratified for any pains he may have taken. Dean Fleet, Fetter Lane, Dec 1 1795

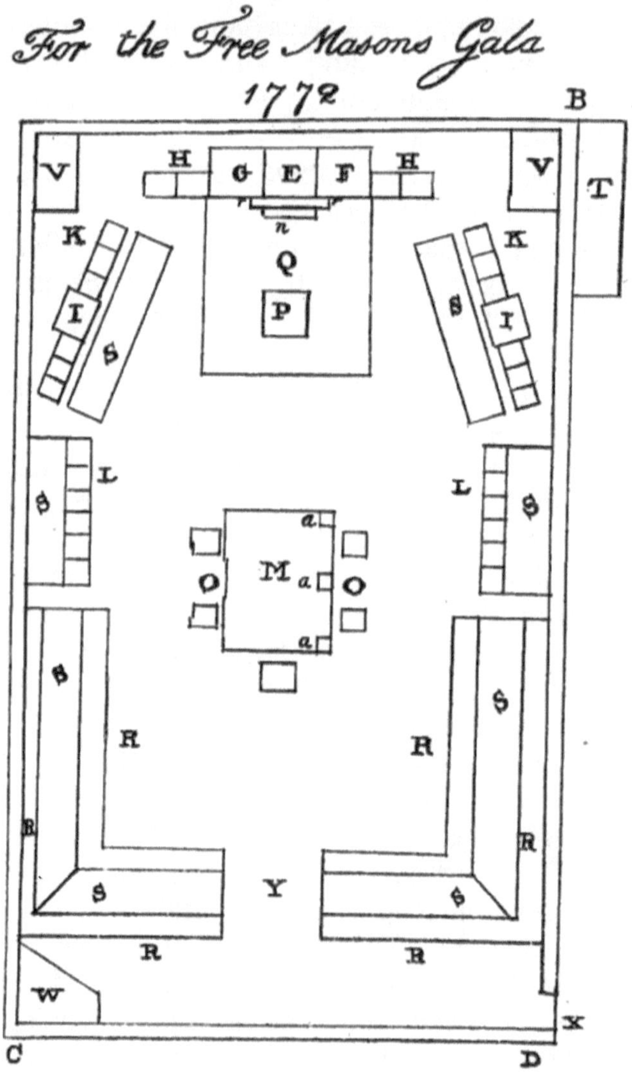

Introduction

hoever, attentively considers the nature and tendency of the masonic institution, must readily perceive its general utility. From an anxious desire to display its value, I have been induced to offer the following sheets to the Public. Many reasons might have with-held me from the attempt; my inexperience as a writer, my attention to the duties of a laborious profession, and the many abler hands who have treated the subject before me; yet, under all these disadvantages, the persuasion of friends, added to a warm zeal in the cause, have stimulated me to risk my reputation on the fate of my performance.

When I first had the honor to be elected Master of a lodge, I thought it proper to inform myself fully of the general rules of the Society, that I might be able to fulfill my own duty, and officially enforce a due obedience in others. The methods which I adopted with this view, excited in some of superficial knowledge, an absolute dislike of what they considered as innovations; and in other, who were better informed, a jealousy of pre-eminence which the principles of Masonry ought to have checked. Notwithstanding these discouragements, however, I persevered in my intention of supporting the dignity of the Society, and discharging with fidelity the trust reposed in me.

As condor and integrity, uninfluenced by interest and favor, will ever support a good cause, many of my opponents (pardon the expression) began to discover their error, and not only applauded, but cheerfully concurred in the execution of my measures; while others, of less liberality, tacitly approved of what their former declared opinions forbad then publicly to adopt.

This success exceeding my most sanguine wishes, I was encouraged to examine with more attention the contents of our various lectures. The rude and imperfect state in which I found them, the variety of modes established in our lodges, and the difficulties which I encountered in my researches, rather discouraged me first attempt; preserving, however, in the design, I continued, I continued the pursuit; and assisted by a few friends, who had carefully preserved what ignorance and degeneracy had rejected as unintelligible and absurd, I diligently sought for, and at length happily acquired, some ancient and venerable landmarks of the Order.

Fully determined to pursue the design of the effecting a general reformation, and fortunate in the acquisition of the friends which I had made, I continued my industry till I had prevailed on a sufficient number to join in an attempt to correct the irregularities which had crept into our assemblies, and to exemplify the beauty and utility of the masonic system.

We commenced our plan by enforcing the value of the ancient charges and regulations of the Order, which inattention had suffered to sink into oblivion, and we established those charges as the basis of our work. To imprint on the memory of a faithful discharge of our duty, we reduced the more material parts of our system into practice; and to encourage others in promoting the plan, we observed a general rule of reading one or more of these charges at every regular meeting, and of elucidating such passages as seemed obscure. The useful hints afforded by these means enabled us gradually to improve our plan, till we at last succeeded in bringing into a connected form the sections which now compose the three lectures of Masonry.

The progress daily made by our system pointed out the necessity of obtaining the sanction of our patrons; hence several brethren of acknowledged honor and integrity united in an application to the most respectable members of the Society for countenance and protection and so far happily succeeded, as not only to obtain the wished for sanction, but to secure the promise of future support, Since that time the plan has been universally admitted as the basis of our Moral Lectures; and to that circumstance the present publication owes its success.

Having thus ventured to appear in vindication of the ceremonies, and in support of the privileges, of Masonry, I shall be happy to be considered a feeble instrument in promoting its propriety. If I am honored with a continuance of the approbation of my brethren, and succeed in giving the world a favorable idea of the institution, I shall have attained the full completion of my wish; and if my hopes are frustrated, I shall still indulge the not unpleasant reflection, of having exerted my best endeavors in a good cause.

William Preston - January 18, 1788

Reflections on the symmetry and proportion in the works of Nature, and on the harmony and affection among the various species of beings.

hoever attentively observes the objects which surround him, will find abundant reason to admire the works of Nature, and to adore the Being who directs such astonishing operations: he will be convinced, that infinite wisdom could alone design, and infinite power finish, such amazing works.

Were a man placed in a beautiful garden, would not his mind be affected with exquisite delight on a calm survey of its rich collection? Would not the groves, the grottoes, the artful wilds, the flowery <u>parterres</u> *(A level space in a garden or yard occupied by an ornamental arrangement of flower beds.)*, the opening vistas, the lofty cascades, the winding streams, the whole variegated scene, awaken his sensibility; and inspire his soul with the most exalted ideas? When he observed the delicate order, the nice symmetry, and the beautiful disposition of every part, seemingly complete in itself, yet reflecting new beauties on the other, and all contributing to make one perfect whole, would not his mind be agitated with the most bewitching sensations; and would not the view of the delightful scene naturally lead him to admire and venerate the happy genius who contrived it?

If the productions of art so forcibly impress the mind with admiration, with how much greater astonishment and reverence, with how much greater astonishment and reverence must we behold the operations of Nature, which presents to view unbounded scenes of utility and delight, in which divine wisdom is most strikingly conspicuous? These scenes are indeed too expanded for the narrow capacity of man to comprehend; yet whoever contemplates the general system, form the uniformity of the plan must naturally be directed to the original source, the supreme governor of the world, the one perfect and unsullied beauty!

Beside all the pleasing prospects that everywhere surround us, and with which our senses are every moment gratified; beside the symmetry. Good order, and proportion, which appear in all the works of creation, something further attracts the reflecting mind, and draws its attention nearer to the Divinity, the universal harmony and affection among the different species of beings of every rank and denomination. These are the cements of the rational world, and by these alone it subsists. When they cease, nature must be dissolved, and man, the image of his Maker and the chief of his works, be overwhelmed in the general chaos.

In the whole order of beings, for the seraph which adores and burns, down to the meanest insect, all, according to their rank in the scale of existence, have, more or less, implanted in them, the principle of association with others of the same species. Even the most inconsiderable animals are formed into different ranks and societies, for mutual benefit and protection. Need we name the careful ant, or the industrious bee; insects which the wisest of men has recommended as patterns of unwearied industry and prudent foresight? When we extend our ideas, we shall find, that the innate principle of friendship increases in proportion to the extension of our intellectual faculties; and the only criterion by which a judgement can be formed respecting the superiority of one part of the animal creation above the other, is by observing the degrees of kindness and good-natured in which it excels.

Such are the general principles which pervade the whole system of creation; who forcibly then must such lessons predominate in our assemblies, where civilization and virtue are most zealously cherished, under the sanction of science and the arts?

The advantages resulting from friendship

No subject can more properly engage the attention, than the benevolent dispositions which indulgent Nature has bestowed upon the rational species. These are replete with the happiest effects, and afford to the mind, the most agreeable reflections. The breast which is inspired with tender feelings, is naturally prompted to a reciprocal intercourse of kind and generous actions, as human nature rises in the scale of beings, the social affections likewise arise. Where friendship is unknown, jealousy and suspicion prevail; but where that virtue is the cement, true happiness subsists. In every breast there is a propensity to friendly acts, which being exerted to effect sweetens every temporal enjoyment; and although it does not remove the disquietudes, it tends at least to allay the calamities of life.

Friendship is traced through the circle of private connections to the grand system of universal benevolence, which no limits can circumscribe, as its influence extends to every branch of the human race. Actuated by this sentiment, each individual connects his happiness with the happiness of his neighbor, and a fixed and permanent union is established among men.

Nevertheless, though friendship, considered as the source of universal benevolence, be unlimited, it exerts its influence more or less powerfully, as the objects it favors are near or more remote. Hence the love of friends and of country takes the lead in our affections and gives rise to that true patriotism, which fires the soul with the most generous flame, creates the best and most disinterested virtue, and inspires that public spirit and heroic ardor which enable us to support a good cause, and risk our lives in its defense.

This commendable virtue crowns the lover of his country with unfading laurels, gives luster to his actions, and consecrates his name in later ages. The warrior's glory may consist in murder, and the rude ravage of the desolating sword; but the blood of thousands will not stain the hands of his country's friend. His virtues are open, and of the noblest kind. Conscious integrity supports him against the arm of power; and should he bleed by tyrant hands, he gloriously dies a martyr in the cause of liberty, and leaves to posterity an everlasting monument of the greatness of his soul.

Though friendship appears divine when employed in preserving the liberties of our country, it shines with equal splendor in more tranquil scenes. Before it rises into the noble flame of patriotism, aiming destruction at the heads of tyrants, thundering for liberty, and courting danger in defense of rights; we behold it calm and moderate, burning with an even glow, improving the soft hours of peace, and heightening the relish for virtue. In those happy moments contracts are formed, societies are instituted, and vacant hours of life are employed in the cultivation of social and polished manners.

On this ground plan the universality of our system is established. Were friendship confined to the spot of our nativity, its operation would be partial, and imply a kind of enmity to other nations. Where the interests of one country interfere with those of another, nature dictates an adherence to the welfare of our own immediate connections; but such interference apart, the true mason is a citizen of the world, and his philanthropy extends to the entire human race. Uninfluenced by local prejudices, he knows no preference in virtue but according to its degree, from whatever clime it may spring.

Origin of Masonry, and its general advantages

rom the commencement of the world, we may trace the foundation of Masonry. Ever since symmetry began, and harmony displayed her charms, our Order has had a being. During many ages, and in many different countries, it has flourished. No art, no science preceded it. In the dark periods of antiquity, when literature was in a low state, and the rude manners of our forefathers withheld from them that knowledge we now so amply share, Masonry diffused its influence. This science unveiled, arts arose, civilization took place, and the progress of knowledge and philosophy gradually dispelled the gloom of ignorance and barbarism. Government being settled, authority was given to laws, and the assemblies of the fraternity acquired the patronage of the great and the good, while the tenets of the profession diffused unbounded utility.

Abstracting from the pure pleasures which arise from friendship so widely constituted as that which subsists among masons, and which is scarcely possible that any circumstance or occurrence can erase, masonry is a science confined to no particular country but extends over the whole terrestrial globe. Wherever arts flourish, there it flourishes too. Add to this, that by secret and inviolable signs, carefully preserved among the fraternity, it becomes an universal language. Hence many advantages are gained. The distant Chinese, the wild Arab, the American savage, will embrace a brother Briton; and will know that beside the common ties of humanity, there is still a stronger obligation to induce him to kind and friendly offices. The spirit of the fulminating priest will be tamed; and a moral brother, though of a different persuasion, engage his esteem; for mutual toleration in religious opinions is one of the most distinguishing and most valuable characteristics of the Craft. As all religions teach morality, if a brother be found to act the part of a truly honest man, his private speculative opinions are left to God and himself. Thus, through the influence of Masonry, which is reconcilable to the best policy, all those disputes which embitter life, and sour the tempers of men are avoided; while the common good, the general object, is zealously pursed.

From this view of our system, its utility is sufficiently obvious. The universal principles of the art unite, in one indissoluble bond of affection, men of the most opposite tenets, of the most distant countries, and of the most contradictory opinions; hence in every nation a Mason may find a friend, and in every climate a home.

Such is the nature of the institution, that in a Lodge, union is cemented by sincere attachment, and pleasure reciprocally communicated in the cheerful observances of every obliging office. Virtue, the grand object in view, luminous as the meridian sun, shines resurgent on the mind, enlivens the heart, and heightens cool approbation into warm sympathy and cordial attention.

Masonry considered under two denominations

asonry passes under two denominations, operative and speculative. By the former, we allude to a proper application of the useful rules of architecture, whence a structure derives figure, strength, and beauty, and whence result a due proportion and a just correspondence in all its parts. By the latter we learn to subdue patterns, act upon the square, keep a tongue of good report, maintain secrecy, and practice charity.

Speculative Masonry is so far interwoven with religion, as to lay us under the strongest obligations to pay that rational homage to the Deity, which at once constitutes our duty and our happiness. It leads the contemplative to view with reverence and admiration the glorious works of creation, and inspires them with the most exalted ideas of the perfection of the divine Creator, Operative Masonry furnishes us with dwellings, and convenient shelters from the in clemencies of seasons; and while it displays the effects of human wisdom, as well in the choice as in the arrangement of the materials of which an edifice is composed, it demonstrates what a fund of science and industry is implanted inn man for the best, most salutary, and beneficent purposes.

The lapse of time, the ruthless hand of ignorance, and the devastations of war, have laid waste and destroyed many valuable monuments of antiquity, on which the utmost exertions of human genius have been employed. Even the temple of Solomon, so spacious and magnificent, and constructed by so many celebrated artists, escaped not the unsparing ravages of barbarous forces force. Freemasonry, notwithstanding, has still survived. The attentive ear receives the sound of the instructive tongue, and the sacred mysteries are safely lodged in the repository of faithful breasts. Tools and implements of architecture, (symbols the most expressive!) are selected by the fraternity, to imprint on the memory serious truths; and thus the excellent tenets of the institution are transmitted unimpaired, under circumstances precarious and adverse, through the succession of ages.

The Government of the Fraternity

he mode of government observed by the fraternity will give the best idea of the nature and design of the Masonic system. Three classes are established among Masons, under different appellations. The privileges of each class are distinct, and particular means adopted to preserve those privileges to the just and meritorious. Honor and probity are recommendations to the first class; in which the practice of virtue is enforced, and the duties of morality are inculcated, while the mind is prepared for a regular progress in the principles of knowledge and philosophy, Diligence, assiduity, and application, are qualifications for the second class; in which is given an accurate elucidation of science, both in theory and practice. Here human reason is cultivated by a due exertion of the intellectual powers and faculties; nice and difficult theories are explained; new discoveries are produced, and those already known are beautifully embellished. The third class is restricted to a selected few, whom truth and fidelity have distinguished, whom years and experience have improved, and whom merit and abilities have entitled to preferment. With them the ancient landmarks of the Order are preserved, and from them we learn the necessary and instructive lessons, which dignify the art, and qualify its professors to illustrate its excellence and utility.

This is the established plan of the Masonic system. By this judicious arrangement, true friendship is cultivated among different ranks of men, hospitality promoted, industry rewarded and ingenuity encouraged.

Reasons why the secrets of Masonry ought not to be publicly exposed; and the importance of those secrets demonstrated.

f the secrets of Masonry are replete with such advantage to mankind, it may be asked, why are they not divulged for the general good of society? To this may be answered; were the privileges of Masonry to be indiscriminately dispensed, the institution would be subverted; and being familiar, like other important matters, would lose their value, and sink into disregard.

Is a weakness in human nature, that men are generally more charmed with novelty, than with the intrinsic value of things. Innumerable testimonies might be adduced to confirm this truth. The most wonderful operations of the Divine Artificer, however, beautiful, magnificent and useful, are overlooked, because common and familiar. The sun rises and sets, the sea flows and reflows, rivers glide along their channels, trees and plants vegetate, men and beasts act, yet this is unnoticed. The most astonishing productions of Nature on the same account escape observation, and excite no emotion, either in admiration of the great cause, or of gratitude for the blessing conferred. Even Virtue herself is not exempted from this unhappy bias in the human frame. Novelty influences all our actions and determinations. What is new, or difficult in the acquisition, however, trifling or insignificant, readily captures the imagination, and ensures a temporary admiration; while what is familiar, or easily attained, however, noble or eminent, is sure to be disregarded by the giddy and the unthinking.

Did the essence of masonry consist in the knowledge of particular secrets or peculiar forms, it might be alleged that our amusements were trifling and superficial. But this is not the case. These are the keys to our treasure and having their use are preserved, while from the recollection of the lessons they inculcate, the well informed Mason derives instruction; he draws them to a near inspection; he views them through a proper medium; he adverts to the circumference which gave them rise; and he dwells upon the tenets they convey. Finding them replete with useful information, he prizes them as sacred; and convinced of their propriety, he estimates their value from their utility.

Many persons are deluded by the vague supposition that our mysteries are merely nominal; that the practices established among us are frivolous; and that our ceremonies may be adopted, or waved, at pleasure. On this false foundation, we find them hurrying through all the degrees of the Order, without adverting to the propriety of one step they pursue, or possessing a single qualification requisite for advancement. Passing through the usual formalities, they consider themselves entitled to rank as master of the art, solicit and accept offices, and assume the government of lodges, equally and assume the government of lodges, equally unacquainted with the rules of the institution they pretend to support, or the nature of the trust reposed in them. The consequences are obvious; anarchy and confusion ensue, and the substance is left in shadow. Hence men eminent for ability, rank, and fortune, are often led to view the honors of Masonry with such indifference, that when their patronage is solicited, they accept offices with reluctance, or reject them with disdain.

Masonry has long labored under these disadvantages, and every zealous friend to the Order must earnestly wish for a correction of the abuse. Of late years it must be acknowledged, that Lodges are in general better regulated, and the good effects of such government are sufficiently displayed in the proper observance of the general regulations.

Were brethren who preside over Lodges, properly instructed previous to their appointment, and regularly apprised of the importance of their respective offices, a general reformation would speedily take place. This would establish the propriety of our government, and lead men to acknowledge; that our hours were deservedly conferred. Till prudent actions shall distinguish our title to the honors of Masonry, and our regular deportment display the influence and utility of our rules, the world in general will not be led to reconcile our proceedings with the tenets of the profession.

Few Societies exempted from censure. Irregularities of Masons no argument against the Institution

mong the various societies of men, few, if any, are wholly exempted from censure. Friendship, however valuable in itself, however universal in its pretensions, has seldom operated so powerfully in general associations, as to promote that sincere attachment to the welfare and prosperity of each other, which is necessary to constitute true happiness. This may be ascribed to sundry causes, but none with more propriety, than to the reprehensible motives which too frequently lead men to a participation of social entertainment. If to pass an idle hour, to oblige a friend, or probably to gratify an irregular indulgence, be our only inducement to mix in company, is it surprising that the important duties of society should be neglected, and that, in the quick circulation of the cheerful glass, our noble faculties should be sometimes buried in the cup of ebriety (*The condition of being drunk.*). It is an obvious truth that the privileges of Masonry have long been prostituted for unworthy considerations, and hence their good effects have not been so conspicuous. Many have enrolled their names in our records for the mere purposes of conviviality, without inquiring into the nature of the particular engagements to which they are subjected by becoming

Masons. Several have been prompted by motives of interest, and many introduced to gratify an idle curiosity, or to please as jolly companions. A general odium, or at least a careless indifference, has been the result of such conduct. But the evil stops not here. Persons of the description, ignorant of the true nature of the institution, probably without any real defect in the own morals, are induced to recommend others of the same cast, to join the society for the same purpose. Hence the true knowledge of the art decreases with the increase of its members, the most valuable part of Masonry is turned into ridicule; while the dissipation of luxury and intemperance bury in oblivion principles which might have dignified the most exalted characters.

When we consider the variety of members of which the society of Masons is composed, and the small number who are really conversant with the tenets of the institution, we cannot wonder that so few should be distinguished for exemplary lives. From persons who are precipitately introduced into the mysteries of the art without the requisite qualifications, it cannot be expected that much regard will be paid to the observance of duties which they perceive to be openly violated by the own institution; and it is an incontrovertible truth; that such is the unhappy bias in the disposition of some men, though the fairest and best ideas were imprinted on the mind, they are so careless of their own reputation as to disregard the most instructive of lessons. We have reason to regret, that even persons distinguished for knowledge in the art, are too frequently induced to violate the rules to which a pretended conformity has gained them applause. The hypocrisy is soon unveiled: no sooner are they liberated from the trammels *(A hindrance or impediment to free action; restraint.)*, as they conceive, of a regular and virtuous conduct in the government of the Lodge, than, by improperly abusing the innocent and cheerful repast, they become slaves to vice and intemperance, and not only disgrace themselves, but reflect dishonor on the fraternity. By such indiscretion, the best of the institution is brought into contempt, and the more deserving part of the community justly conceives a prejudice against the society, of which it is ever afterwards difficult to wipe off the impression.

But if some do transgress, no wise man will thence argue against the whole fraternity for the errors of a few individuals. Were the wicked lives of men admitted as an argument against the religion which they profess, the wisest, the wisest and most judicious establishment, might be exposed to censure. It may be averred in favor of Masonry, that whatever imperfections may be found among its professors, the institution countenances no deviation from the rules of right reason.

Those who violate the laws, or infringe on good order, are kindly admonished by secret monitors; and when these have not the intended effect, public reprehension becomes necessary; at last, when every mild endeavor to effect a reformation is of no avail, they are expelled the Lodge, as unfit members of the society.

Vain, therefore, is each idle surmise against the plan of our government; while our laws are properly supported, they will be proof against every attack of our most inveterate enemies. Men are not aware, that by decrying any laudable system, they derogate from the dignity of human nature itself, and from that good order and wise disposition of things, which the almighty Author of the world has framed for the government of mankind, and established as the basis of the moral system. Friendship and social delights can never be the object of reproach; nor can that wisdom which hoary *(Gray or white with or as if with age; extremely old.)* Time has sanctified, be subject to ridicule. Whoever attempts to censure what he does not comprehend degrades himself; and the generous heart will always be led to pity the mistakes of such ignorant presumptions.

Charity the distinguishing characteristic of Masons

harity is the chief of every social virtue, and the distinguishing characteristic of the Order. This virtue includes a supreme degree of live to the great Creator and Governor of the universe, and an unlimited affection to the beings of his creation, of all characters and of every denomination. This last duty is forcibly inculcated by the example of the Deity himself, who liberally dispenses his beneficence to unnumbered worlds.

It is not particularly our province to enter into disquisition of every branch of the amiable virtue; we shall only briefly state the happy effects of a benevolent disposition toward mankind, and shew that charity, exerted on proper objects, is the greatest pleasure man can possibly enjoy.

The bounds of the greatest nation, or the most extensive empire, cannot circumscribe the generosity of a liberal mind. Men, in whatever situation they are placed, are still, in a great measure, the same. They are exposed to similar dangers and misfortunes. They have not wisdom to foresee, or power to prevent, the evils incident to human nature. They hang as it were, in perpetual suspense between hope and fear, sickness and health, plenty and want. A mutual chain of dependence subsists throughout the animal creation. The whole human species are therefore proper objects for the exercise of charity.

Beings, who partake of one common nature, ought to be actuated by the same motives and interests. Hence, to soothe the unhappy, by sympathizing with their misfortunes, and to restore peace and tranquility to agitated spirits, constitute the general and great ends of the Masonic institution. This humane, this generous disposition fires the breath with manly feelings, and enlivens that spirit of compassion, which is the glory of the human frame, and not only rivals, but outshines, every other pleasure the mind is capable of enjoying.

All human passions, when directed by the superior principle of reason, promote some useful purpose; but compassion towards proper objects is the most beneficial of all the affections, as it extends to greater numbers, and tends to alleviate the infirmities and evils which are incident to human existence.

Possessed of this amiable, this godlike disposition, Masons are shocked at misery under every form and appearance. When we behold an object pining under the miseries of a distressed body or mind, the healing accents which flow from the tongue, mitigate the pain of the unhappy sufferer, and make even adversity, in its dismal state, look gay. When our pity is excited, we assuage grief, and cheerfully relieve distress. If a brother be in want, eerie heart is moved; when he is hungry, we feed him; when he is naked, we clothe him; when he is in trouble, we fly to his relief. Thus we confirm the propriety of the title we bear, and convince the world at large, that BROTHER among Masons is something more than a name.

The discernment displayed by Masons in the choice of objects of charity

he most inveterate enemies of Masonry must acknowledge, that no society is more remarkable for the practice of charity, or any association of men more famed for disinterested liberality. It cannot be said that Masons indulge in convivial *(Fond of feasting, eating, and good company.)* mirth, while the poor and needy pine for relief. Our quarterly contributions, exclusive of private subscriptions to relieve distress, prove that we are ever ready with cheerfulness, in proportion to our circumstances, to contribute to alleviate the misfortunes of our fellow-creatures. Considering, however, the variety of object, whose distress the dictates of Nature as well as the ties of Masonry incline us to relieve, we find it necessary sometimes to inquire into the cause of misfortunes; lest a misconceived tenderness of disposition, or an impolitic generosity of heart, might prevent us from making a proper distinction in the choice of objects.

Though our ears are always open to the distresses of the deserving poor, yet our charity is not to be dispensed with a profuse liberality on impostors. The parents of a numerous offspring, who, through age, sickness, infirmity, or any unforeseen accident in life, are reduced to want, particularly claim our attention, and seldom fail to experience the happy effects of our friendly association. To such objects, whose situation is more easy to be conceived than expressed, we are induced liberally to extend our bounty. Hence we give convincing proofs of wisdom and discernment; for though our benevolence, like our laws, be unlimited, yet our hearts glow principally with affection toward the deserving part of mankind.

From this view of the advantages which result from the practice and profession of Masonry, every candid and impartial mind must acknowledge its utility and importance to the state; and surely, if the picture here drawn be just, it must be no trifling acquisition to any government, to have under its jurisdiction, a society of men, who are not only true patriots and loyal subject, but the patrons of science and the friends of mankind.

Friendly admonitions

aving explained the principles of the Order, and endeavored to demonstrate the excellence and utility of the institution, I shall conclude my observations with a few friendly admonitions to my brethren.

As useful knowledge is the great object of our desire, let us steadily adhere to the principles it inculcates, check our progress, or damp our zeal; but let us recollect, that the ways of wisdom are beautiful, and lead to pleasure. Knowledge is attained by degrees, and cannot everywhere be found. Wisdom seeks the secret shade, the lonely cell designed for contemplation. There enthroned she sits, delivering her sacred oracles. There let us seek her, and pursue the real bliss. Though the passage be difficult, the farther we trace it, the easier it will become.

Union and harmony constitute the essence of Freemasonry: while we enlist under that banner, the society must flourish, and privet animosities give place to peace and good fellowship. Uniting in one design let it be our aim to be happy ourselves, and contribute to the happiness of others. Let us make our superiority and distinction among men, by the sincerity of our profession as Masons; let us cultivate the moral virtues, and improve in all that is good and amiable; let the Genius of Masonry preside over our conduct, and under her sway let us perform our part with becoming dignity. Let us preserve an elevation of understanding, with a politeness of manner, and an evenness of temper. Let our recreations be innocent, and pursued with moderation; and never let irregular indulgences lead to the subversion of our system, by impairing our faculties, and exposing our character to derision. But, in conformity to our precepts, as patterns worthy of imitation, let the respectability of our lives be supported by the regularity of our conduct, and the uniformity of our deportment. Thus, as citizens of the world, as friends to every clime, we shall be living examples of virtue and benevolence, equally zealous to merit as to obtain universal approbation.

EULOGIUM

asonry comprehends within its circle every branch of useful knowledge and learning, and stamps an indelible mark of preeminence on its genuine professors, which neither chance, power, nor fortune can bestow. When its rules are strictly observed, it is a sure foundation of tranquility amidst the various disappointments of life; a friend that will not deceive, but will comfort and assist, in prosperity and adversity; a blessing that will remain with all times. Circumstances, and places, and to which recourse may be had, when earthly comforts sink into disregard.

Masonry gives real and intrinsic excellency to man, and renders him fit for the duties of society. It strengthens the mind against the storms of life, paves the way to peace, and promotes domestic happiness. It meliorates the temper, and improves the understanding; it is company in fortitude, and gives vivacity, variety, and energy to social conversation. In youth, it governs the passions, and employs usefully our most active faculties; and in age, when sickness, imbecility, and disease have benumbed the corporal frame, and rendered the union of soul and body almost intolerable, it yields a fund of comfort and satisfaction.

These are its general advantages; to enumerate them separately, would be an endless labor: it may be sufficient to observe, that he who cultivates this science, and acts agreeably to the character of a Mason, has within himself the spring and support of every social virtue; a subject of contemplation, that enlarges the mind, and expands all its powers; a theme that is inexhaustible, ever new, and always interesting.

General Remarks

asonry is an art useful and extensive. In every art there is a mystery, which requires a progress of study and application to arrive at any degree of perfection. Without much instruction, and more exercise, no man can be skillful in any art; in like manner, without an assiduous application to the carious subjects treated in the different lectures of masonry, no person can be sufficiently acquainted with its true value.

From this remark it must not be inferred, that person who labor under the disadvantage of a confined education, or whose sphere of life requires assiduous attention to business or useful employment, are to be discouraged in the endeavors to gain a knowledge of masonry. To qualify an individual to enjoy the benefits of the society at large, or to partake of its privileges, it is not absolutely necessary that he should be acquainted with all the intricate parts of the science. These are only intended for persons who may have leisure and opportunity to indulge such pursuits.

Some men may be more able than others, some more eminent, some more useful, but all, in their different spheres, may prove advantageous to the community; and our necessities, as well as our consciences, bind us to love one another. To those, however, whose early years have been dedicated to literary pursuits, or whose circumstances and situation in life render them independent, the offices of a Lodge ought to be principally restricted. The industrious tradesman proves himself a valuable member of society, and worthy of every honor that we can confer; but the nature of every man's profession will not admit of that leisure which is necessary to qualify him to become an expert Mason, so as to discharge the official duties of a lodge with propriety. And it must be admitted that those who accept offices and exercise authority in a Lodge, ought to be men of superior prudence and genteel address, with all the advantages of a tranquil, well cultivated mind, and retentive memory. All men are not blessed with the same powers, nor have all men the same talents; all men, therefore, are not equally qualified to govern. But he who wishes to teach, must submit to learn; and no one is qualified to support the higher offices of a Lodge, until he has previously discharged the duties of those which are subordinate, which require time and experience. All men may rise by graduation, and merit and industry are the first steps to preferment. Masonry is widely calculated to suit different ranks and degrees, as every one, according to his station and ability, may be employed, and class with his equal in every station. Founded upon the most, generous principles, no disquietude appears among professor of the art; each class is happy in its particular association, and when the whole meet in general convention, arrogance and presumption appear not on the one hand, or diffidence and inability on the other; but all unite in the same plan, to promote that endearing happiness which constitutes the essence of civil society.

The Ceremony of Opening and Closing A Lodge

n regular assemblies of men, convened for wise and useful purposes, the commencement and conclusion of business are accompanied with some form. In every country of the world the practice prevails, and is deemed essential. From the most remote periods of antiquity it is traced, and the refined improvements of modern items have not abolished it.

Ceremonies, simply considered, are little more than visionary delusions; but their effects are sometimes important. When they impress awe and reverence on the mind, and engage attention, by external attraction, to solemn rites, they are interesting objects. There purposes are affected when judicious ceremonies are regularly conducted and properly arranged. On this ground they have received the sanction of the wisest of men in all ages, and consequently could not escape the notice of Masons. To begin well, is the most likely means to end well: and it is justly remarked, that when order and method are neglected at the beginning, they will be seldom found to take place at the end.

The ceremony of opening and closing a Lodge with solemnity and decorum is there universally adopted among masons; and though the mode in some lodges may vary, still an uniformity in the general practice prevails in every lodge; and the variation is solely occasioned by a want of method, which a little application might easily remove.

To conduct this ceremony with propriety, ought to be the peculiar study of every Mason; especially of those who have the honor to rule in our assemblies. To persons thus dignified, every eye is directed for propriety of conduct and behavior; and from them, other brethren, less informed, will naturally expect to derive example worthy of imitation.

From a share in this ceremony no mason is exempted. It is a general concern, in which all must assist. This is the first request of the Master, and the prelude to business. No sooner has it been signified, than every officer repairs to his station, and the brethren rank according to their degrees. The intent of the meeting becomes the object of attention, and the mind is insensibly drawn from those indiscriminate subjects of conversation which are apt to intrude on our less serious moments.

Our care is first directed to the external avenues of the lodge, and the proper officers whose province it is to discharge that duty, execute the trust with fidelity. By certain mystic forms, of no recent date, they intimate that we may safely proceed. To detect impostors among ourselves, an adherence to order in the character of masons ensues, and the lodge is opened or closed in solemn form.

At opening the lodge two purposes are affected; the Master is reminded of the dignity of his character, the brethren of the homage and veneration due from them in the sundry stations. These are not the only advantages resulting from due observance of the ceremony; a reverential awe for the Deity is inculcated, and the eye fixed on that object from whose radiant beams light only can be derived. Hence in this ceremony we are taught to adore God of Heaven, and to supplicate his protection on our well-meant endeavors. Thus the Master assumes his government in due form, and under him his Wardens; who accept their trust, after the customary salutations, as disciples of one general patron. After which the brethren, with one accord, unite in duty and respect, and the ceremony concludes.

At closing the lodge, a similar form takes place. Here the less important duties of masonry are not passed over unobserved. The necessary degree of subordination, which takes place in the government of a lodge, is peculiarly marked, while the proper tribute of gratitude is offered up to the beneficent Author of life and his blessing invoked, and extended to the whole fraternity. Each brother faithfully locks up the treasure which he has acquired in his own repository, and pleased with his reward, retires, to enjoy, and disseminate, among the private circle of his friends, the fruits of his labor and industry in the lodge.

There are faint outlines of a ceremony which universally prevails among masons in every county, and distinguishes all their meetings. Hence it is arranged as a general section in every degree, and takes the lead in all our illustrations.

A Prayer used at opening the Lodge

May the favor of Heaven be upon this meeting and as it is happily begun, may it be conducted with order, and closed with harmony.

Amen

A Prayer used at closing the Lodge

May the blessing of Heaven rest upon us, and all regular masons! May brotherly love prevail, and every moral and social virtue cement us!

Amen

Charges and Regulations for the conduct and behavior of Masons

A rehearsal of the Ancient Charges properly succeed the opining and precede the closing of a lodge. This was the constant practice of our ancient brethren and ought never to be neglected in our regular assemblies. A recapitulation of our duty cannot be disagreeable to those who are aquatinted with it; and to those to whom it is not known, should any such be, it must be highly proper to recommend it.

Ancient Charges

On the Management of the Craft in working

asons employ themselves diligently in their sundry vocations, live creditably, and conform with cheerfulness to the government of the county in which they reside.

The most expert craftsman is chosen or appointed Master of the work, and is duly honored in that character by those over whom he presides.

The Master, knowing himself qualified, undertakes the government of the lodge, and truly dispenses his rewards, according to merit.

A craftsman who is appointed Warden of the work under the Master, is true to the Master and fellows, carefully oversees the work, and the brethren obey him.

The Master, Wardens and brethren are just and faithful, and carefully finish the work they begin, whether it be in the first or second degree; but never put that work to the first, which has been appropriated to the second degree.

Neither envy nor censure is discovered among masons. No brother is supplanted, or put out of his work, if he is capable to finish it; for he who is not perfectly skilled in the original design, can never with equal advantage to the Master finish the work begun by another.

All employed in Masonry meekly receive their reward, and use no disnobling name. Brother or Fellow are the appellations they bestow on each other. They behave courteously within and without the lodge, and never desert the Master till the work is finished.

Laws for the Government of the Lodge

You are to salute one another in a courteous manner, agreeably to the forms established among masons; you are freely to give such mutual instructions as shall be thought, necessary or expedient, not being over keen or overhead, without encroaching upon each other, derogating from that respect which is due to a gentleman were he not a mason; for thought as mason we rank as brethren on a level, yet masonry deprives no man of the honor due to his rank or character, but rather adds to his honor, especially if he has deserved well of the fraternity, who always render honor to whom it is due, and avoid ill-manners.

No private committees are to be allowed, or separate conversations encouraged; the Master or Wardens are not to be interrupted, or any brother who is speaking to the Master; but a due respect pair to the Master, and presiding officers.

These laws are to be strictly enforced, that harmony may be preserved, and the business of the lodge carried on with order and regularity.

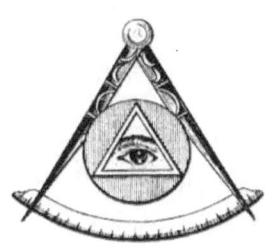

Charge on the Behavior of Masons

hen the Lodge is closed, you are to enjoy yourselves with innocent mirth and carefully to avoid excess. You are not to compel any brother to act contrary to his inclination, or to give offence by word or deed, but enjoy a free and easy conversation. You are to avoid immoral and obscene discourse, and at all time support with propriety the dignity of you character.

You are to be cautious in your words and carriage that the most penetrating stranger may not discover, or find, what is not proper to be intimated; and if necessary, you are to wave a discourse, and manage it prudently, for the honor of the fraternity.

At home and in your several neighborhoods, you are to behave as wise and moral men. You are never to communicate to your families, friends or acquaintances, the private transactions of our different assemblies; but upon every occasion to consult your honor, and the reputation of the fraternity at large.

You are to study the preservation of health, by avoiding irregularity and intemperance, that your families may not be neglected and injured your selves disabled from attending to you necessary employments in life.

If a stranger apply in the character of a Mason, you are cautiously to examine him in such a method as prudence may direct, and agreeably to the forms established among masons; that you may not be imposed upon by an ignorant false pretender, whom you are to reject with contempt, and beware of giving him any secret hints of knowledge. But if you discover him to be a true and genuine brother, you are to respect him; if he be in want, you are without prejudice to relieve him, or direct him how he may be relieved; you are to employ him, or recommend him to employment: however, you are never charged to do beyond your ability only to prefer a poor mason, who is a good man and true, before any other person in the same circumstances.

Finally; These rules you are always to observe and enforce, and also the duties which have been communicated in the lecture; cultivating brotherly love, the foundation and capstone, the cement and glory of this ancient fraternity; avoiding, upon every occasion, wrangling and quarrelling, slandering and backbiting; not permitting others to slander honest brethren, but defending their characters, and doing them good offices, as far as any be consistent with your honor and safety, but no farther. Hence all may see the benign influence of masonry, as all true masons have done from the beginning of the world, and will do to the end of time.

Remarks on the First Lecture

aving illustrated the ceremony of opening and closing a Lodge, and inserted the Charges and Prayers usually rehearsed in our regular assemblies on those occasions, we shall now enter on a disquisition of the different Sections of the Lectures appropriated to the three Degrees of Masonry, giving a brief summary of the whole, and annexing to every Remark the particulars to which the Section alludes. By these means the industrious mason will be better instructed in the regular arrangement of the Sections in each Lecture, and be enabled with more cease to acquire a knowledge of the Art.

The First Lecture is divided into Sections and each Section into Clauses. In this Lecture virtue is painted in the most beautiful colors, and the duties of morality are strictly enforced. In it we are taught such useful lessons as prepare the mind for a regular advancement in the principles of knowledge and philosophy, and these are imprinted on the memory by lively and sensible images, to influence our conduct in the proper discharge of the duties of social life.

The First Section

The First Section of the Lecture is suited to all capacities, and ought to be known by every person who wishes to rank as a mason. It consists of general heads, which, though short and simple carry weight with them. They not only serve as marks of distinction, but communicate useful and interesting knowledge when they are duly investigated. They qualify us to try and examine the rights of others to our privileges, while they prove ourselves; and as they induce us to inquire more minutely into other particulars of greater importance, they serve as an introduction to subjects which are more amply explained in the following Sections.

As we can annex to these remark no other explanation consistent with the rules of masonry. We must refer the more inquisitive to our regular assembles for further instruction.

The Second Section

The Second Section makes us acquainted with the peculiar forms and ceremonies at the initiation of candidates into masonry; and convinces us, beyond the power of contradiction, of the propriety of our rites; while it demonstrates to the most skeptical and hesitating mind, their excellence and utility.

The following particulars relative to that ceremony may be introduced here with propriety.

A Declaration to be assented to by every Candidate in an adjoining apartment, previous to Initiation

"Do you seriously declare, upon your honor, before these gentlemen, that, unbiased by friends against your own inclination, and uninfluenced by mercenary motives, you freely and voluntarily offer yourself a candidate for the mysteries of Masonry?" - I do.

"Do you seriously declare, upon your honor, before these gentlemen, that you are solely prompted to solicit the privileges of Masonry, by a favorable opinion conceived of the institution, a **desire** of knowledge, and a sincere wish of being serviceable to your fellow-creatures?" - I do.

"Do you seriously declare, upon your honor, before these gentlemen, that you will cheerfully conform to all the ancient established usages and customs of the fraternity?" - I do.

The Candidate is then proposed in open lodge, as follows:

"R. W. Master, and Brethren,

"At the request of Mr. A. B. I propose him in form as a proper candidate for the mysteries of Masonry; I recommend him, as worthy to partake the privileges of the fraternity; and, in consequence of a Declaration of his intentions, voluntarily made and properly attested, I believe he will cheerfully conform to the rules of the Order."

The Candidate is ordered to be prepared for Initiation.

A Prayer used at Initiation

"Vouchsafe thine aid, Almighty Father of the Universe, to this our present convention; and grant that this Candidate for Masonry may dedicate and devote his life to thy service, and become a true and faithful Brother among us! Endue him with a competence of thy divine wisdom, that, by the secrets of this Art, he may be better enabled to display the beauties of godliness, to the honor of thy holy Name! Amen."

The Third Section

The Third Section, by the reciprocal communication of our marks of distinction, proves us to be regular members of the Order; and inculcates those necessary and instructive duties which at once dignify our characters in the double capacity of men and masons.

We cannot better illustrate this Section, than by inserting the following

Charge at Initiation into the first Degree

Brother,

As you are now introduced into the first principles of our Order, it is my duty to congratulate you on being accepted a member of an ancient and honorable Society: ancient, as having subsisted from time immemorial; and honorable, as tending, in every particular, so to render all men, who will be conformable to its precepts. No institution was ever raised on a better principle, or more solid foundation; nor were ever more excellent rules and useful maxims laid down, than are inculcated on all persons at their initiation into our mysteries. Monarchs, in every age, have been encouragers and promoters of our Art, and have never deemed it derogatory from their dignities, to level themselves with the fraternities, to extend their privileges, and to patronize their assemblies.

As a mason you are to study the moral law, as contained in the sacred code; to consider it as the unerring standard of truth and justice and to regulate your life and actions by its divine precepts.

The three great moral duties, to God, your neighbor, and yourself, you are strictly to observe: To God, by never mentioning his name, but with that awe and reverence which is due from a creature to his creator; to implore his aid in your laudable undertakings; and to esteem him as the chief good: To your neighbor, by acting upon the square, and, considering him equally entitled with yourself to share the blessings of Providence, rendering unto him those favors, which in a similar situation you would expect to receive from him: - And to *yourself, by avoiding irregularity and intemperance, which might impair your faculties, and debase the dignity of your profession.*

In the state, you are to be quiet and peaceable subject, true to your sovereign, and just to your country; you are not to countenance disloyalty or rebellion, but patiently submit to legal authority, and conform with cheerfulness to the government under which you live, yielding obedience to the laws which afford you protection, and never forgetting the attachment you owe to the spot where you first drew breath.

In your outward demeanor, you are to avoid censure or reproach; and beware of all who may artfully endeavor to insinuate themselves into your esteem, with a view to betray your virtuous resolutions, or make you swerve from the principles of the institution. Let not interest, favor, or prejudice, bias your integrity, or influence you to be guilty of a dishonorable action; but let your conduct and behavior be regular and uniform, and your deportment suitable to the dignity of the profession.

Above all, practice benevolence and charity; for by these virtues, masons have been distinguished in every age and country. The inconceivable pleasure of contributing toward the relief of our fellow-creatures is truly experienced by persons of a humane disposition; who are naturally excited, by sympathy, to extend their aid in alleviation of the miseries of others. This encourages the generous mason to distribute his bounty with cheerfulness. Supposing himself in the situation of an unhappy sufferer, he listens to the tale of woe with attention, bewails misfortune, and speedily relieves distress.

The Constitutions of the Order ought next to engage your attentions. These contain the history of masonry from the earliest periods, with an account of illustrious characters who have enriched the Art in various countries; and the laws and charges, by which the brethren have been long governed.

A punctual attendance on our assemblies I am earnestly to enjoin, especially on the duties of the lodge in which you are enrolled a member. Here, and in all other regular meetings of the fraternity, you are to behave with order and decorum, that harmony may be preserved, and the business of masonry properly conducted. The rules of good manners you are not to violate; you are to use no unbecoming language, in derogation of the name of God, or toward the corruption of good manners: you are not to introduce or maintain any dispute about religion or politics; or behave irreverently while the lodge is engaged in what is serious and important; but you are to pay a proper deference and respect to the Master and presiding officers, and diligently apply to the practice of the Art, that you may sooner become a proficient therein, as well for your own credit, as the honor of the lodge in which you have been received.

But although your frequent appearance at our regular meetings is earnestly solicited, masonry is not intended to interfere with your necessary vocations in life, as these on no account are to be neglected: neither are you to suffer your zeal for the institution, however laudable, to lead you into argument with those who may ridicule it; but rather extend your pity toward all, who through ignorance contemn, what they never had an opportunity to comprehend. At leisure hours, study the liberal arts and sciences; and improve in Masonic disquisitions, by the conversation of well-informed brethren, who will be as ready to give, as you can be to receive instruction.

Finally; keep sacred and inviolable those mysteries of the Order which are to distinguish you from the rest of the community, and mark your consequence among the fraternity. If, in the circle of your acquaintance, you find a person desirous of being initiated into masonry, be particularly attentive not to recommend him unless you are convinced he will conform to our rules; that the honor, the glory, and the reputation of the institution may be firmly established, and the world at large convinced of its benign influence.

From the attention you have paid to the recital of this charge, we are led to hope that you will form a proper estimate of the value of freemasonry, and imprint on your mind the dictates of truth, honor, and justice.

This section usually closes with the EULOGIUM

The Fourth Section

The Fourth Section rationally accounts for the origin of hieroglyphical instruction, and points out the advantages which accompany a faithful observance of our duty; it illustrates, at the same time, certain particulars, of which our ignorance might lead us into error and which as masons, we are indispensably bound to know.

To make daily progress in the Art, is a constant duty, and expressly required by our general laws. What end can be more noble, than the pursuit of virtue? What motive more alluring, than the practice of justice? Or what instruction more beneficial, than an accurate elucidation of those symbols which tend to embellish and adorn the mind? Everything that strikes the eye, more immediately engages the attention, and imprints on the memory serious and solemn truths. Hence masons have universally adopted the plan of inculcating the tenets of their Order by typical figures and allegorical emblems, to prevent their mysteries from descending to the familiar reach of inattentive and unprepared novices, from whom they might not receive due veneration.

It is well known, that the usages and customs of masons have ever corresponded with those of the ancient Egyptians, to which they bear a near affinity. These philosophers, unwilling to expose their mysteries to vulgar eyes, concealed their particular tenets and principles of polity under hieroglyphical figures; and expressed their notions of government by signs and symbols, which they communicated to their Magi alone, who were bound by oath not to reveal them. Pythagoras seems to have established his system on a similar plan, and many orders of a more recent date have copied the example. Masonry, however, is not only the most ancient, but the most moral institution that ever subsisted; every character, figure, and emblem, depicted in a Lodge, has a moral tendency, and tends to inculcate the practice of virtue.

This section closes with a definition of Charity.

The Fifth Section

he Fifth Section explains the nature and principles of our constitution, and teaches us to discharge the duties of the different departments which we are top sustain in the government of a lodge. Here, too, our ornaments are displayed, our jewels and furniture specified, and proper attention is paid to our ancient and venerable patrons.

To explain the subject of this Section, and to assist the industrious mason to acquire it, we recommend a punctual attendance on the duties of a Lodge, and a diligent application to the truths there demonstrated.

The Sixth Section

he Sixth Section, though the last in rank, is not the least considerable in importance. It strengthens those which precede, and enforces in the most engaging manner, a due regard to character and behavior, in public as well as in private life, in the lodge as well as in the general commerce of society.

This Section forcibly inculcates the most instructive lessons. Brotherly Love, Relief and Truth are themes on which we expatiate; while the Cardinal Virtues claim our attention. By the exercise of Brotherly Love, we are taught to regard the whole human species as one family, the high and low, the rich and poor; who, as children of one Almighty Parent and inhabitants of the same planet, are to aid , support and protect each other. On this principle masonry unites men of every country, sect and opinion, and conciliates true friendship among those who might otherwise have remained at a perpetual distance. Relief is the next tenet of the profession. To relieve the distressed, is a duty incumbent on all men; particularly on masons, who are linked together by an indissoluble chain of sincere affection. To soothe calamity, to alleviate misfortune, to compassionate misery, and to restore peace to the troubled mind, is the grand aim of the true mason. On this basis, he establishes his friendship, and forms his connections. Truth is a divine attribute, and the foundation of every virtue. To be good and true is the first lesson we are taught. On this theme we contemplate, and by its dictates endeavor to regulate our conduct: influenced by this principle, hypocrisy and deceit are unknown, sincerity and plain-dealing distinguish us, while the heart and tongue join in promoting each other's welfare, and rejoicing in each other's prosperity.

To this illustration succeeds an explanation of Temperance, Fortitude, Prudence, and Justice. By Temperance, we are instructed to govern the passions and check unruly desires. The health of the body, and the dignity of the species, are equally concerned in a faithful observance of it. By Fortitude, we are taught to resist temptation, and encounter danger with spirit and resolution. This virtue is equally distant from rashness and cowardice; and he who possesses it, is seldom shaken, and never overthrown, by the storms that surround him. By Prudence, we are instructed to regulate our conduct by the dictates of reason, and to judge and determine with propriety in the execution of very than that can tend to promote either present or future well-being. In this virtue all other depend; it is therefore the chief jewel that can adorn the human frame. Justice, the boundary of right, constitutes the cement of civil society. Without the exercise of this virtue, universal confusion must ensue; lawless force would overcome the principles of equity, and social intercourse no longer exists. Justice in a great measure constitutes real goodness, and therefore it is represented to be the perpetual study of the accomplished mason.

The explanation of these virtues is accompanied with some general observations on the Equality observed among masons. In a Lodge no estrangement of behavior is discovered. Influenced by ones principles, a uniformity of opinion, useful in exigencies, and pleasing in familiar life, universally prevails, strengthens all the ties of friendship, and equally promotes love and esteem. Masons are brethren by a double tie, and among brothers no <u>invidious</u> *(Tending to cause discontent, animosity, or envy; envious.)* distinctions should still exist. Merit is always respected and honor rendered to whom it is due. A king is reminded that although a crown may adorn the head, or a scepter the hand, the blood in the veins is derived from the common parent of mankind. And is no better than that of the meanest subject. The senator and the artist are alike taught that, equally with other, they are by nature exposed to infirmity and disease; and an unforeseen misfortune , or a disordered frame, may impair their faculties, and level them with the most ignorance of the species. This checks pride, and incites courtesy or behavior. Men of inferior talents, or not placed by fortune on such exalted stations, are instructed to regard their superiors with peculiar esteem, when, divested of pride, vanity, and external grandeur, they condescend, in the badge of friendship, to trace wisdom, and follow virtue, asserted by those who are of a rank beneath them. Virtue is true nobility, and wisdom is the channel by which Virtue is directed and conveyed; Wisdom and Virtues only mark distinction among masons.

Such is the arrangement of the Sections in the Fifth Lecture of Masonry, which including the forms adopted at opening and closing a lodge, comprehends the whole of the First Degree. This plan has not only the advantage of regularity to recommend it, but the support of precedent and authority, and the sanction and respect which flow from antiquity, The whole is a regular system of morality, conceived in s strain of interesting allegory, which readily unfolds its beauties to the candid and industrious inquirer.

Remarks on the Second Lecture

 asonry is a progressive science, and divided into different classes or degrees, for a more regular advancement in the knowledge of its mysteries. According to the progress we make, we limit or extend our inquiries; and, in proportion to our capacity, we attain to a less or greater degree or perfection.

Masonry includes almost every branch of polite learning. Under the veil of its mysteries, is comprehended a regular system of science. Many of its illustrations may appear unimportant to the confined genius; but the man of more enlarged faculties will consider them in the highest degree useful and interesting. To please the accomplished scholar and ingenious artist, it is wisely planned; and in the investigation of its latent doctrines, the philosopher and mathematician may experience satisfaction and delight.

To exhaust the various subjects of which masonry treats, would transcend the powers of the brightest genius; still, however, nearer approaches to perfection may be made, and the man of wisdom will not check the progress of his abilities, though the task he attempts may at first seem insurmountable. Perseverance and application will remove each difficulty as it occurs; every step he advances, new pleasures will open to his view, and instruction of the noblest kind attends his researches. In the diligent pursuit of knowledge, great discoveries are made, and the intellectual faculties are employed in promoting the glory of God, and the good of man.

Such is the tendency of every illustration in masonry. Reverence for the Deity, and gratitude for the blessings of heaven, are inculcated in every degree. This is the plan of our system, and the result of all our inquiries.

The First Degree is intended to enforce the duties of morality, and imprint on the memory the noblest principles which can adorn the human mind. The Second Degree extends the fame plan, and comprehends a more diffusive system of knowledge. Practice and theory qualify the industrious mason to share the pleasures which advancement in the Art necessarily affords. Listening with attention to the wise opinions of experienced craftsmen on important subjects, his mind is gradually familiarized to useful instruction, and he is soon enabled to investigate truths of the utmost concern in the general transactions of life.

From this system proceeds a rational amusement; the mental powers are fully employed, and the judgement is properly exercised. A spirit of emulation prevails; and every one vies, who shall most excel in promoting the valuable rules of institution.

The First Section

he First Section of the Second Degree elucidates the mode of introduction into this class; and instructs the diligent craftsman how to proceed in the proper arrangement of the ceremonies, which enables him to judge of their importance, and convinces him of the necessity of adhering to the established usages of the Order. Here he is entrusted with particular tests, to prove his title to the privileges of this degree, and satisfactory reasons are given for their origin. Many duties which cement in the firmest union will-informed brethren are illustrated; and an opportunity is given to make such advances in masonry as must always distinguish the abilities of able craftsmen.

This Section recapitulates the ceremony of initiation, and contains many important particulars with which no officer of a lodge should be unacquainted.

Charge at Initiation into the Second Degree

Brother,

Being advanced to the Second Degree we congratulate you on your preferment. The internal, and not the external, qualifications of a man, are what masonry regards. As you increase in knowledge, you will improve in social intercourse.

It is unnecessary to recapitulate the duties which, as a mason, you are bound to discharge; or enlarge on the necessity of a strict adherence to them, as your own experience must have established their value. It may be sufficient to observe, that You're past behavior and regular deportment have merited the honor which we have conferred; and in your new character, it is expected that you will conform to the principles of the Order, and steadily persevere in the practice of every commendable virtue.

The study of the liberal arts that valuable branch of education, which tends so effectually to polish and adorn the mind, is earnestly recommended to your consideration; especially the science of geometry, which is established as the basis of our Art. Geometry, or Masonry, originally synonymous terms, being divine and moral nature, is enriched with the most useful knowledge; while it proves the wonderful properties of nature, it demonstrates the more important truths of morality.

As the solemnity of our ceremonies requires a serious deportment, you are to be particularly attentive to your behavior in our regular assemblies; you are to preserve our ancient usages and customs sacred and inviolable; and you are to induce others, by your example, to hold them in veneration.

The laws and regulations of the Order you are strenuously to support and maintain. You are not to palliate, or aggravate, the offences of your brethren; but, in the decision of every trespass against our rules, judge with candor, admonish with friendship, and reprehend with justice.

As a craftsman, in our private assemblies you may offer your sentiments and opinions on such subjects as are regularly introduced in the Lecture. By this privilege you may improve your intellectual powers; qualify yourself to become a useful member of society; and, like a skillful brother, strive to excel in everything that is good and great.

All regular signs and summonses, given and received, you are duly to honor, and punctually to obey; inasmuch as they consist with our professed principles. You are to supply the wants, and relieve the *necessities, of your brethren, to the utmost of your power and ability: and you are on no account to wrong them, or see them wronged; but apprise them of approaching danger, and view their interest as inseparable from your own.*

Such is the nature of your engagements as a craftsman; and to these duties you are bound by the most sacred ties.

The Second Section

The Second Section of this Degree presents an ample field for the man of genius to perambulate. It cursorily specifies the particular classes of the Order, and explains the requisite qualifications for preferment in each. In the explanation of our usages, many remarks are introduced, equally useful to the experienced artist and the sage moralist. The various operations of the mind are demonstrated, as far as they will admit of elucidation, and a fund of extensive science is explored throughout. Here we find employment for leisure hours, trace science from its original source, and, drawing the attention to the sum of perfection, contemplate with admiration on the wonderful works of the Creator. Geometry is displayed, with all its powers and properties; and, in the disquisition of this science, the mind is filled with pleasure and delight. Such is the latitude of this Section, that the most judicious may fail in an attempt to explain it, as the rational powers are exerted to their utmost stretch, in illustration the beauties of nature, and demonstrating the more important truths of morality.

As the orders of architecture come under consideration in this Section, a brief description of them may not be improper

y order in architecture, is meant a system of all the members, proportions, and ornaments of columns and pilasters; or, it is a regular arrangement of the projecting parts of a building, which, united with those of a column, form a beautiful, perfect, and complete whole. Order in architecture may be traced from the first formation of society. When the rigor of seasons obliged men to contrive shelter from the inclemency of the weather, we learn that they first planted trees on end, and then laid others across, to support a covering. The bands which connected those trees at top and bottom are said to have suggested the idea of the base and capital of pillars; and from this simple hint originally preceded the more improved art of architecture.

The five orders are thus classed: the Tuscan, Doric, Ionic, Corinthian, and Composite

he <u>Tuscan</u> *(It is basically a simplified Roman Doric, with unfluted columns and with no decoration other than moldings)* is the most simple and solid of the five orders. It was invented in Tuscany, whence it derives its name. Its column is seven diameters high; and its capital, base, and entablature have but few moldings. The simplicity of construction of this column renders it eligible where solidity is the chief object, and where ornament would be <u>superfluous</u> *(Being more than is sufficient or required; excessive)*.

The <u>Doric order</u> *(The order encompasses the entire building system columns and entablature, while individual columns have characteristics belonging to one of the orders. In ancient Greece, Doric columns were stouter than those of the Ionic or Corinthian orders. Their smooth, round capitals are simple and plain compared to the other two Greek orders.)*, which is plain and natural, is the most ancient, and was invented by the Greeks. Its column is eight diameters high, and has seldom any ornaments on base or capital, except moldings; though the frieze *(Is the wide central section part of an entablature and may be plain in the Ionic or Doric order, or decorated with bas-reliefs.)* is distinguished by triglyphs *(Is an architectural term for the vertically channeled tablets of the Doric frieze in classical architecture, so called because of the angular channels in them. The rectangular recessed spaces between the triglyphs on a Doric frieze are called metopes.)* and metopes *(A square space between triglyphs in a Doric frieze.)*, and the triglyphs compose the ornaments of the frieze. The solid composition of this order gives it a preference, in structures where strength and a noble simplicity are chiefly required.

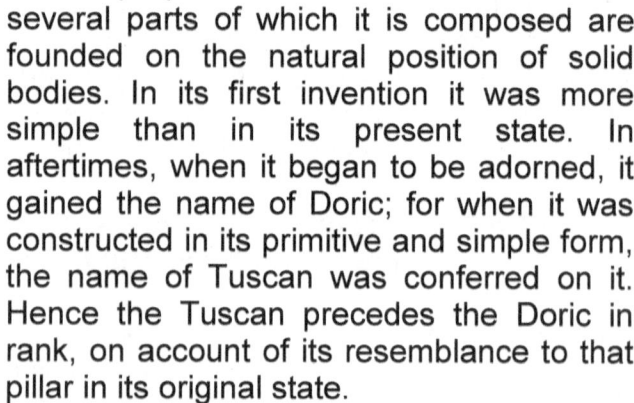
(Diana)

The Doric is the best proportioned of all the orders. The several parts of which it is composed are founded on the natural position of solid bodies. In its first invention it was more simple than in its present state. In aftertimes, when it began to be adorned, it gained the name of Doric; for when it was constructed in its primitive and simple form, the name of Tuscan was conferred on it. Hence the Tuscan precedes the Doric in rank, on account of its resemblance to that pillar in its original state.

The Ionic bears a kind of mean proportion between the more solid and delicate orders. Its column is nine diameters high; its capital is adorned with volutes *(Architecture. a spiral ornament, found especially in the capitals of the Ionic, Corinthian, and Composite orders.)* and its cornice has denticles *(A small tooth or tooth like projection.)*. There is both delicacy and ingenuity displayed in this pillar; the invention of which is attributed to the Ionians *(A member of one of the four main divisions of the prehistoric Greeks who invaded the Greek mainland and, after the Dorian invasions, emigrated to the Aegean islands and the coast of Asia Minor.)*, as the famous temple of Diana at Ephefus *(A deity of Asiatic origin, the mother goddess of the earth, whose seat of worship was the temple in Ephesus.)* was of this order. It is said to have been formed after the model of an agreeable young woman, of an elegant shape, dressed in her hair; as a contrast to the Doric order, which was formed after that of a strong robust man.

The Corinthian *(Is the most elegant of the five orders. Its distinguishing characteristic is the striking capital, which is carved with two staggered rows of stylized acanthus leaves and four scrolls. The shaft has 24 sharp-edged flutes, while the column is 10 diameters high.)*, the richest of the five orders, is deemed a master-piece of art, and was invented at Corinth by Callimachus. Its column is ten diameters high, and its capital is adorned with two rows of leaves, and eight volutes, which sustain the abacus. The frieze is ornamented with curious devices, the cornice with denticles and modillions *(A projecting bracket under the corona of a cornice in the Corinthian and other orders.)*. This order is used in stately and superb structures.

Callimachus *(Greek poet and scholar, the most representative poet of the erudite and sophisticated Alexandrian school.)* is said to have taken the hint of the capital of this pillar from the following remarkable circumstance. Accidentally passing by the tomb of a young lady, he perceived a basket of toys, covered with a tile placed over a can, but root, having been left there by her nurse. As the branches grew up, they encompassed the basket, till, arriving at the tile, they met with an obstruction, and bent downwards. Callimachus, struck with the object, set about imitating the figure; the vase of the capital he made to represent the basket; the abacus, the tile; and the volute, the bending leaves.

The Composite is compounded of the other orders, and was contrived by the Romans. Its capital has the two rows of leaves of the Corinthian, and the volutes of the Ionic. Its column has the quarter-round as the Tuscan and Doric orders, is ten diameters high, and its cornice has denticles or simple modillions. This pillar is generally found in buildings where strength, elegance, and beauty are united.

The original orders of architecture, revered by masons, are no more than three, the Doric, Ionic, and Corinthian. To these the Romans have added two, the Tuscan, which they made plainer than the Doric; and the Composite, which was more ornamental, if not more beautiful, than the Corinthian. The first three orders alone, however, shew invention and particular character, and essentially differ from each other: the two others have nothing but what is borrowed, and differ only accidentally; the Tuscan is the Doric in its earliest state; and the Composite is the Corinthian enriched with the Ionic. To the Greeks, and not the Romans, we are indebted for what is great, judicious, and distinct in architecture.

These observations are intended to induce the industrious craftsman to pursue his researches into the rise and progress of architecture, by consulting the works of learned writers professedly upon the subject.

An analysis of the human faculties is also given in this Section, in which the five external senses particularly claim attention.

When these topics are proposed in our assemblies, we are not confined to any peculiar mode of explanation; but every brother is at liberty to offer his sentiments under proper restrictions. The following thoughts on this important branch of learning may, however, be useful.

The senses we are to consider as the gifts of Nature and the primary regulators of our active powers; as by them alone we are conscious of the distance, nature, and properties of external objects. Reason, properly employed, confirms the documents of Nature, which are always true and wholesome: she distinguishes the good from the bad; rejects the last with modesty, adheres to the first with reverence.

The objects of human knowledge are innumerable; the channels by which this knowledge are innumerable; the channels by which this knowledge is conveyed, are few. Among these, the perception of external things by the senses, and the information we receive from human testimony, are not the least considerable; the analogy between them is obvious. In the testimony of Nature given by the senses, as well as in human testimony given by information, things are signified y signs. In one as well as the other, the mind, either by original principles or by custom, passes from the sign to the conception and belief of the thing signified. The signs in the natural language, as well as the signs in our original perceptions, have the same signification in all climates and nations, and the skill of interpreting them is not acquired, but innate.

Having made these observations, we shall proceed to give a brief description of the five senses.

Hearing is that sense by which we distinguish sounds, and are capable of enjoying all the agreeable charms of music. By it we are enabled to enjoy the pleasures of society, and reciprocally to communicate to each other, our thoughts and intentions, our purposes and desires; while our reason is capable of exerting its utmost power and energy.

The wise and beneficent Author of Nature intended, by the formation of this sense, that we should be social creatures, and receive the greatest and most important part of our knowledge by the information of others. For these purposes we are endowed with Hearing, that by a proper exertion of our rational powers, our happiness may be complete.

Seeing is that sense by which we distinguish objects, and in an instant of time, without change of place or situation, view armies in battle array, figures of the most stately structures, and all the agreeable variety displayed in the landscape of nature. By this sense we find our way in the pathless ocean, traverse the globe of earth, determine its figure and dimensions, and delineate any region or quarter of it. By it we measure the planetary orbs, and make new discoveries in the sphere of the fixed stars. Nay more; by it we perceive the tempers and dispositions, the passions and affections, of our fellow-creatures, when they wish most to conceal them, so that though the tongue might be taught to lie and dissemble, the countenance would display the hypocrisy to the discerning eye. In fine, the rays of light, which administer to this sense, are the most astonishing parts of the inanimate creation, and render the eye a peculiar object of admiration.

Of all the faculties, sight is the noblest. The structure of the eye, and its appurtenances, evince the admirable contrivance of Nature for performing all its various external and internal motions; while the variety displayed in the eyes of different animals, suited to their several ways of life, clearly demonstrates this organ to be the master-piece of Natures work.

Feeling is that sense by which we distinguish the different qualities of bodies; such as heat and cold, hardness and softness, roughness and smoothness, figure, solidity, motion, and extension; which, by means of certain corresponding sensations of touch, are presented to the mind as real external qualities, and the conception or belief of them is invariably connected with those corresponding sensations, by an original principle of human nature, which far transcends our inquiry.

All knowledge beyond our original perceptions is got by experience. The constancy of Nature's laws connects the sign with the thing signified, and we rely on the continuance of that connection which experience hath discovered. These three senses, hearing, seeing, and feeling, are deemed peculiarly essential among masons.

Smelling is that sense by which we distinguish odors, which convey different impressions to the mind. Animal and vegetable bodies, and indeed most other bodies, continually send forth effluvia of vast subtlety, as well in the state of life and growth, as in the state of fermentation and putrefaction. The volatile particles probably repel each other, and scatter themselves in the air, till they meet with other bodies to which they bear a chemical affinity, with which they unite, and form new concretes. These effluvia being drawn into the nostrils along with the air are the means by which all bodies are smelled. Hence it is evident, there is a manifest appearance of design in the great Creator's having planted the organ of smell in the inside of that canal, through which the air continually passes in respiration.

Tasting enables us to make a proper distinction in the choice of our food. The organ of this sense guards the entrance of the alimentary canal, as that of smell guards the entrance of the canal for respiration. From the situation of these organs, it is plain that they were intended by Nature to distinguish wholesome food from that which is nauseous. Everything that enters into the stomach must undergo the scrutiny of Tasting, and by it we are capable of discerning the changes which the same body undergoes in the different compositions of art, cookery, chemistry, pharmacy, etc.

Smelling and Tasting are inseparably connected, and it is by the unnatural kind of life men commonly lead in society, that these senses are rendered less fit to perform their natural offices.

Through the medium of the senses we are enabled to form just and accurate notions of the operations of Nature; and when we reflect on the means by which the senses are gratified, we become conscious of the existence of bodies, and attend to them, till they are rendered familiar objects of thought.

To understand and analyze the operations of the mind is an attempt in which the most judicious may fail. All we know is that the senses are the channels of communication to the mind, which is ultimately affected by their operation; and when the mind is diseased, every sense loses its virtue. The fabric of the mind, as well as that of the body, is curious and wonderful; the faculties of the one are adapted to their several ends with equal wisdom, and no less propriety, than the organs of the other. The inconceivable wisdom of an Almighty Being is displayed in the structure of the mind, which extends its power over every branch of science; and is therefore a theme peculiarly worthy of attention. In the arts and sciences which have least connection with the mind, its faculties are still the engines which we must employ; the better we understand their nature and use, their defects and disorders, we shall apply them with the greater success. In the noblest arts, the mind is the subject upon which we operate.

Wise men agree that there is but one way to the knowledge of Nature's works the way of observation and experiment. By our constitution we have a strong propensity to trace particular facts and observations to general rules, and to apply those rules to account for other effects, or to direct us in the production of them. This procedure of the understanding is familiar in the common affairs of life, and is the means by which every real discovery in philosophy is made.

On the mind all our knowledge must depend; it therefore constitutes a proper subject for the investigation of masons.

Although by anatomical dissection and observation we may become acquainted with the body, it is by the anatomy of the mind alone we can discover its powers and principles.

To sum up the whole of this transcendent measure of God's bounty to man, we may add, that memory, imagination, taste, reasoning, moral perception, and all the active powers of the soul, present such a vast and boundless field for philosophical disquisition, as far exceeds human inquiry, and are peculiar mysteries, known only to Nature, and to Nature's God, to whom all are indebted for creation, preservation, and every blessing they enjoy.

From this theme we proceed to illustrate the moral advantages of Geometry

eometry is the first and noblest of sciences, and the basis on which the superstructure of free-masonry is erected. The contemplation of this science in a moral and comprehensive view fills the mind with rapture. To the true Geometrician, the regions of matter with which he is surrounded, afford ample scope for his admiration, while they open a sublime field for his inquiry and disquisition.

Every particle of matter on which he treads, every blade of grass which covers the field, every flower which blows, and every insect which wings its way in the bounds of expanded space, proves the existence of a first cause, and yields pleasure to the intelligent mind.

The symmetry, beauty, and order displayed in the various parts of animate and inanimate creation, is a pleasing and delightful theme, and naturally leads to the source whence the whole is derived. When we bring within the focus of the eye the variegated carpet of the terrestrial creation, and survey the progress of the vegetative system, our admiration is justly excited. Every plant which grows, every flower that displays its beauties or breathes its sweets, affords instruction and delight. When we extend our lives to the animal creation, and contemplate the varied clothing of every species, we are equally struck with astonishment! And when we trace the lines of geometry drawn by the divine pencil in the beautiful plumage of the feathered tribe, how exalted is our conception of the heavenly work! The admirable structure of plants and animals, and the infinite number of fibers and vessels which runs through the whole, with the apt disposition of one part to another, is a perpetual subject of study to the Geometrician, who, while he adverts to the changes which all undergo in their progress to maturity, is lost in rapture and veneration of the great cause which governs the system.

When he descends into the bowels of the earth, and explores the kingdom of ores, minerals, and fossils, he finds the same instances of divine wisdom and goodness displayed in their formation and structure; every gem and pebble proclaims the handiwork of an Almighty Creator.

When he surveys the watery element, and directs his attention to the wonders of the deep, with all the inhabitants of the mighty ocean, he perceives emblems of the fame supreme intelligence. The scales of the largest whale, as well as the penciled shell of the meanest fry, equally yield a theme for this contemplation, on which he fondly dwells, while the symmetry of their formation, and the delicacy of the tints, evince the wisdom of the Divine Artist.

When he exalts his view to the more noble and elevated parts of Nature, and surveys the celestial orbs, how much greater is his astonishment! If, on the principles of geometry and true philosophy, he contemplates the sun, the moon, the stars, the whole concave of heaven, his pride will be humbled while he is lost in awful admiration. The immense magnitude of those bodies, the regularity and rapidity of their motions, and the inconceivable extent of space through which they move, are equally inconceivable; and as far as they exceed human comprehension, baffle his most daring ambition, while, lost in the immensity of the theme, he sinks into his primitive insignificance.

By geometry, therefore, we may curiously trace Nature, through her various windings, to her most concealed recesses. By it, we may discover the power, the wisdom, and the goodness of the grand Artificer of the universe, and view with delight the proportions which connect this vast machine. By it, we may discover how the planets move in their different orbits, and demonstrate their various revolutions. By it, we may account for the return of seasons and the variety of scenes which each season displays to the discerning eye. Numberless worlds are around us, all framed by the same Divine Artist, which roll through the vast expanse, and are all conducted by the same unerring laws of Nature.

A survey of Nature, and the observation of her beautiful proportions, first determined man to imitate the divine plan, and study symmetry and order. This gave rise to societies, and birth to every useful art. The architect began to design, and the plans which he laid down, improved by experience and time, produced works which have been the admiration of every age.

The Third Section

The Third Section of this degree has recourse to the origin of the institution, and views masonry under two denominations, operative and speculative. These are separately considered, and the principles on which both are founded, particularly explained. Their affinity is pointed out, by allegorical figures, and typical representations. Here the rise of our government, or division into classes, is examined; the disposition of our rulers, supreme and subordinate, is traced; and reasons are assigned for the establishment of several of our present practices. The progress made in architecture, particularly in the reign of Solomon, is remarked; the number of artists employed in building the temple of Jerusalem, and the privileges which they enjoyed, are specified; the period stipulated for regarding merit is fixed, and the inimitable moral to which that circumstance alludes, explained; the creation of the world is described, and many particulars recited, all of which have been carefully preserved among masons, and transmitted from one age to another by oral tradition. In short, this Section contains a store of valuable knowledge, founded

on reason and sacred record, both entertaining and instructive. The whole operates powerfully in enforcing the veneration due to antiquity.

We can afford little assistance by writing to the industrious mason in this section, as it can only be acquired by oral communication.

As many of the particulars in this Section have a reference to the temple of Jerusalem, we shall here insert the Invocation of Solomon at the Dedication of that edifice:

Invocation

And Solomon stood before the altar of the Lord, in the presence of all the congregation of Israel, and spread forth his hands; saying:

O Lord God, there is no god like unto thee, in heaven above, or in the earth beneath; who keepest covenant, and shewest mercy, unto thy servants; who walk before thee with all their hearts.

Let thy Word be verified, which thou hast spoken unto David, my father.

Let all the people of the earth know, that the Lord is God; and that there is none else.

Let all the people of the earth know thy Name; and fear thee.

Let all the people of the earth know, that I have built this house, and consecrated it to thy Name.

But, will God indeed dwell upon the earth? Behold - the heaven, and heaven of heavens, cannot contain thee; how much less this house, which I have built:

Yet, I have respect unto my prayer, and to my supplication, and hearken unto my cry:

May thine eyes be open, toward this house, by day and by night; even toward the place, of which thou hast said, My Name shall be there!

And when thy servant, and thy people Israel, shall pray toward this house, hearken to their supplication; hear thou them in heaven, thy dwelling-place; and when thou hearest, forgive!

And the Lord answered, and said, I have hollowed the house which thou hast built, to put my Name there forever; and mine eyes and mine heart shall be there perpetually.

And all the people, answered, and said - The Lord is gracious, and his mercy endureth forever.

The Fourth Section

he Fourth and last Section of this Degree is no less replete with useful instruction. Circumstances of great importance to the fraternity are here particularized, and many traditional tenets and customs confirmed by sacred and profane record. The celestial and terrestrial gloves are considered with a minute accuracy; and here the accomplished gentleman may display his talents to advantage, in the elucidation of the sciences, which are classed in a regular arrangement. The stimulus to preferment, and the mode of rewarding merit, are pointed out; the marks of distinction which were conferred on tour ancient brethren as the reward of excellence, explained; and the duties, as well as privileges, of the first branch of their male offspring, defined. This Section also contains many curious observations on the validity of our forms, and concludes with the most powerful incentives to the practice of piety and virtue.

As the seven liberal arts and sciences are illustrated in this Section, it may not be improper to give a short explanation of them.

Grammar teaches the proper arrangement of words, according to the idiom or dialect of any particular people; and that excellency of pronunciation, which enables us to speak or write a language with accuracy, agreeably to reason, an correct usage.

Rhetoric teaches us to speak copiously and fluently on any subject, not merely with propriety, but with all the advantages of force and elegance; wisely contriving to captivate the hearer by strength of argument and beauty of expression, whether it be to entreat or exhort, to admonish or applaud.

Logic teaches us to guide our reason discretionally in the general knowledge of things, and direct our inquiries after truth. It consists of a regular train of argument, whence we infer, deduce, and conclude, according to certain premises laid down, admitted, or granted; and in it are employed, the faculties of conceiving, judging, reasoning, and disposing; which are naturally led on from one gradation to another, till the point in question is finally determined.

Arithmetic teaches the powers and properties of numbers, which is variously effected, by letters, tables, figures, and instruments. By this art, reasons and demonstrations are given, for finding out any certain number, whole relation or affinity to others is already known.

Geometry treats of the powers and properties of magnitudes in general, where length, breadth, and thickness are considered. By this science, the architect is enabled to construct his plans; the general to arrange his soldiers; the engineer to mark out ground for encampments; the geographer to give us the dimensions of the world; to delineate the extent of seas, and specify the divisions of empires, kingdoms, and provinces; and by it the astronomer is enabled to make his observations, and fix the duration of times and seasons, years and cycles. In fine, geometry is the foundation of architecture, and the root of the mathematics.

Music teaches the art of forming concords, so as to compose delightful harmony, by a proportional arrangement of acute, grave, and mixed sounds. This art, by a series of experiments, is reduced to a science, with respect to tones, and the intervals of sound only. It inquires into the nature of concords and discords, and enables us to find out the proportion between them by numbers.

Astronomy is that art, by which we are taught to read the wonderful works of the almighty Creator in those sacred pages the celestial hemisphere. Assisted by astronomy, we can observe the motions, measure the distances, comprehend the magnitudes, and calculate the periods and eclipses, of the heavenly bodies. By it, we learn the use of the globes, the system of the world, and the primary law of nature. While we are employed in the study of this science, we must perceive unparalleled instances of wisdom and goodness, and, through the whole of creation, trace the glorious Author by his works.

Thus ends the different Sections of the Second Lecture, which, with the ceremony used at the opening and closing the Lodge, comprehend the whole of the Second Degree of Masonry. Beside a complete theory of philosophy and physics, this Lecture contains a regular system of science, demonstrated on the clearest principles, and established on the firmest foundation.

Remarks on the Third Lecture

n treating with propriety on any subject, it is necessary to observe a regular course. In the former Degrees of Masonry, we have recapitulated the contents of the several Sections, and should willingly have pursued the same plan in this Degree, did not the variety of particulars of which it is composed, render it impossible to give an abstract, without violating the laws of the Order. It may be sufficient to remark, that, in twelve Sections, of which the lecture consists, every circumstance that respects government and system, <u>antient</u> *(Obsolete spelling of ancient.)* lore and deep research, curious invention and ingenious discovery, is accurately traced, while the mode of proceeding on public as well as on private occasions is satisfactorily explained. Among the brethren of this degree, the land-marks of the Order are preserved; and from them is derived that fund of information, which expert and ingenious craftsmen only can afford, whole judgement has been matured by years and experience. To a complete knowledge of this lecture, few attain; but it is an infallible truth, that he who acquires by merit the mark of pre-eminence which this degree affords, receives a reward which amply compensates all his past diligence and assiduity.

From this class, the rulers of the Craft are selected; as it is only from those who are capable of giving instruction that we can properly expect to receive it.

The First Section

The ceremony of initiation into the third degree, is particularly specified in this branch of the lecture, and many useful instructions are given.

Such is the importance of this Section that we may safely declare, that the person who is unacquainted with it, is ill qualified to act as a ruler or governor of the work of Masonry.

Prayer at Initiation into the Third Degree

O Lord, direct us to know and serve thee aright! Prosper our laudable undertakings and grant, that, as we increase in knowledge, we may improve in virtue, and still farther promote thy honor and glory! Amen

Charge at Initiation into the Third Degree

Brother,
Your zeal for our institution, the progress you have made in our art, and your conformity to our regulations, have pointed you out as a proper object of favor and esteem.

In the character of a Master mason, you are henceforth to correct the errors and irregularities of uninformed brethren, and guard them against a breach of fidelity. To improve the morals and manners of men in society, must be your constant care; and with this view, you are to recommend to your inferiors, obedience and submission; to your equals, courtesy and affability; to your superiors, kindness and condescension. Universal benevolence you are to inculcate; and, by the regularity of your behavior, afford the best examples for the conduct of others. The ancient landmarks of our Order, now instructed to your care, you are to preserve sacred and inviolable; and never suffer an infringement of our rites, or countenance a deviation from our established usages and customs.

Duty, honor, and gratitude, now bind you to be faithful to every truth; to support with becoming dignity your new character; and to enforce, by example and precept, the tenets of our system. Let no motive, therefore, make you swerve from your duty, violate your vows, or betray your trust; but be true and faithful, and imitate the example of that celebrated artist whom you have once represented. Thus your exemplary conduct must convince the world that merit is the title to our privileges, and that on you our favors have not been undeservedly bestowed.

The Second Section

The Second Section is an introduction to the proceedings of a Chapter of Master-masons, and illustrates several points well known to experienced craftsmen. It investigates, in the ceremony of opening a chapter, the most important circumstances in the two preceding degrees.

The Third Section

The Third Section commences the historical traditions of the Order, which are chiefly collected from sacred record, and other authentic documents.

The Fourth Section

The Fourth Section farther illustrates the historical traditions of the Order, and presents to view a finished picture, of the utmost consequence to the fraternity.

The Fifth Section

The Fifth Section continues the explanation of the historical traditions of the Order.

The Sixth Section

The Sixth Section concludes the historical traditions of the Order.

The Seventh Section

The Seventh Section illustrates the hieroglyphical emblems restricted to the Third Degree, and inculcates many useful lessons, in order to extend knowledge, and promote virtue.

This Section is indispensably necessary to be understood by every Master of a lodge.

The Eighth Section

The Eighth Section treats of the government of the society, and the disposition of the rulers in different degrees. It is therefore generally rehearsed at installations.

The Ninth Section

The Ninth Section recites the qualifications of the rulers, and illustrates the ceremony of installation, in the grand lodge, as well as in private lodges.

The Tenth Section

The Tenth Section comprehends the ceremonies of constitution and consecration, with a variety of particulars explanatory of those ceremonies.

The Eleventh Section

The Eleventh Section illustrates the ceremonies used at laying the foundation stones of churches, chapels, palaces, hospitals, &c. also the ceremonies observed at the Dedication of Lodges, and at the Interment of Master Masons.

The Twelfth Section

The Twelfth Section contains a recapitulation of the most essential points of the lectures in all the degrees, and corroborates the whole by infallible testimony.

Having thus given a general summary of the lectures restricted to the different degrees of masonry, and made such remarks on each degree, as may tend to illustrate the subjects treated, little farther will be wanted to encourage the zealous mason to persevere in his researches. He who has traced the Art in a regular progress, from the commencement of the First to the conclusion of the Third Degree, according to the plan here laid down, will have amassed an ample store of useful learning; he will reflect with pleasure on the good effects of his past diligence and attention, and by applying the whole to the general advantage of society, will secure to himself the veneration of masons, and the approbation of all good men.

Of the Ancient Ceremonies of the Order

We shall now proceed to illustrate the Ancient Ceremonies of the Order, particularly those observed at the Constitution and Consecration of a Lodge, and the Installation of Officers, with the usual Charges delivered on those occasions. We shall likewise annex an explanation of the Ceremonies used at laying the Foundation Stones of Public Structures, at the Dedication of Public Halls, and at Funerals; and close this part of the treatise with the Funeral Services.

The Manner of constituting a Lodge, including the Ceremony of Consecration Etc.

Any number of Master-masons, not under seven, resolved to form a New Lodge, must apply, by petition, to the Grand Master; setting forth that they are regular masons, and are at present, or have been, members of regular lodges: That having the prosperity of the fraternity at heart, they are willing to exert their best endeavors to promote and diffuse the genuine principles of masonry: That, for the convenience of their respective dwellings, and other good reasons, they have agreed to form a New Lodge, to be named.

In consequence of this dispensation, a lodge is held at the place specified; and the transactions of that lodge being properly recorded, are valid for the time being, provided they are afterwards approved by the brethren convened at the time of Constitution.

When the Grand Lodge has signified his approbation of the New Lodge, and the Grand Master is thoroughly satisfied of the truth of the allegations set forth in the petition, he appoints a day and an hour for constituting and consecrating the New Lodge; and for installing its Master, Wardens, and Officers.

If the Grand Master in person attend the ceremony, the lodge is said to be constituted in ample form; if the Deputy Grand Master acts a Grand Master, it is said to be constituted in due form; and if the power of performing the ceremony is vested in the Master of a private lodge, it is said to be constituted in form.

Ceremony of Constitution

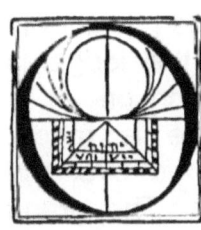

On the day and hour appointed, the Grand Master and this Officers, or the Master and Officers of any private Lodge authorized by the Grand Master for that purpose, meet in a convenient room; and when properly clothed, walk in procession to the lodge room, where the usual ceremonies being observed, the lodge is opened by the Grand Master, or the Master in the Chair, in all the degrees of Masonry. After a short prayer, an ode in honor of masonry is sung. The Grand Master, or Master in the Chair, is then informed by the Grand Secretary, or his locum tenens. That the brethren then present, being duly instructed in the mysteries of the Art, naming them, desire to be formed into a New Lodge, under the Grand Master's patronage; that a dispensation has been granted to them for that purpose, and by virtue of that authority, they had assembled as regular masons, and had duly recorded their transactions. The petition is read, as is also the dispensation, and the warrant or charter of constitution, granted in consequence of it. The minutes of the New Lodge while under dispensation, are read, and being approved, are declared to be regular, valid and constitutional. The Grand Master, or Master in the Chair, then takes the warrant in his hand and requests the brethren of the New Lodge, publicly to signify their approbation or disapprobation of the Officers nominated in the warrant to preside over them. This being signified accordingly, an anthem is sung, and an oration on the nature and design of masonry delivered.

Ceremony of Consecration

he Grand Master and his Officers, accompanied by some distinguished Clergyman, having taken their stations, and the lodge which is placed in the center, being covered with white satin, the ceremony of Consecration commences. All devoutly kneel, and the preparatory prayer is rehearsed. The chaplain, or orator, produces his authority, and being properly assisted proceeds to consecrate. Solemn music is introduced, while the necessary preparations are making. At length the lodge is uncovered, and the first clause of the consecration prayer is rehearsed, all devoutly kneeling. The response is made, GLORY TO GOD ON HIGH. Incense is scattered over the lodge, and the grand honors of masonry given. The grand

Invocation is then pronounced, with the honors; after which the consecration prayer is concluded, and the response repeated as before, together with the honors. The lodge is again covered, and all rising up, solemn music is resumed, after which a blessing is given, and the response made as before, accompanied by honors. An anthem is then sung and the brethren of the New Lodge advance according to rank, and offer homage to the Grand Master, when the consecration ends.

The above ceremony being finished, the Grand Master then advances to the Pedestal, and constitutes the New Lodge in the following manner:

In the elevated character to which the suffrages of my brethren have raised me, I invoke the NAME of the MOST HIGH, to whom be glory and honor! May he be with you at your beginning, may he strengthen you in the principles of our royal Art, may he prosper you with all success, and may your zealous pursuits rebound to the good of the Craft! By the divine aid, I constitute and form you, my good brethren, into a Lodge of Free and Accepted Masons; and from henceforth empower you to act as a regular lodge, constituted in conformity to the rites of our venerable Order, and charges of our ancient fraternity. May God be with you! Amen.

Flourish with drums and trumpets.

The grand honors are given, and the ceremony of Installation succeeds.

Ceremony of Installation

he Grand Master asks his Deputy, whether he has examined the Master nominated in the warrant, and finds him well skilled in the noble science and the royal Art. The Deputy answering in the affirmative, by the Grandmaster's order takes the candidate from among his fellows, and presents him at the pedestal, saying,

Most worshipful Grand Master, or right worshipful, as it happens I present to you my worthy brother, A.B. to be installed Master of this New Lodge. I find him to be of good morals, and of great skill, true and trusty; and as his is a lover of the whole fraternity, where forever dispersed over the face of the earth, I doubt not he will discharge his duty with fidelity.

The Grand Master orders a summary of the ancient charges to be read by the Grand Secretary or acting Secretary to the Master elect.

    I. **You agree to be good man and true and strictly obey the moral law.**

    II. **You agree to be a peaceable subject and cheerfully conform to the laws of the country in which you reside.**

    III. **You promise, not to be concerned in plots or conspiracies against government, but patiently to submit to the decision of the supreme legislature.**

    IV. **You agree to pay a proper respect to the civil magistrate, to work diligently, live creditably, and act honorably by all men.**

    V. **You agree to hold in veneration the original rulers and patrons of the Order of Masonry, and their regular successors, supreme and subordinate, according to their stations; and to submit to the awards and resolutions of your brethren in general chapter convened, in every case consistent with the constitutions of the Order.**

    VI. **You agree to avoid private piques and quarrels, and to guard against intemperance and excess.**

    VII. **You agree to be cautious in carriage and behavior, courteous to our brethren, and faithful to our lodge.**

    VIII. **You promise to respect genuine brethren, and to discountenance impostors, and all dissenters from the original plan of Masonry.**

IX. You agree to promote the general good of society, to cultivate the social virtues, and to propagate the knowledge of the Art.

On the Master Elect signifying his assent to these Charges, the Secretary proceeds to read the following regulations

I. You admit that it is not in the power of any man, or body of men, to make innovation in the body of masonry.

II. You promise to pay homage to the Grand Master for the time being, and to his Officers, when duly installed, and strictly to conform to every edict of the Grand Lodge, or General Assembly of Masons, that is not subversive of the principles and groundwork of Masonry.

III. You promise a regular attendance on the committees and communications of the Grand Lodge, on receiving proper notice; and to pay attention to all the duties of masonry, on convenient occasions.

IV. You admit that no new lodge shall be formed without permission of the Grand Master or is Deputy; and that no countenance be given to any irregular lodge, or to any person clandestinely initiated therein, being contrary to the ancient charges of the Order.

V. You admit that no person can be regularly made a mason in, or admitted member of, a regular lodge, without previous notice, and due inquiry into his character.

VI. You agree that no visitors shall be received into your lodge without due examination, and producing proper vouchers of their regular initiation.

These are the regulations of the Grand Lodge of Free and Accepted Masons.

The Grand Master then addresses the Master Elect in the following manner:

Do you submit to those Charges, and promise to support those Regulations, as Masters have done in all ages before you?

The New Master having signified his cordial submission, is regularly installed, bound to his trust and invested with the badge of office by the Grand Master, who thus salutes him:

Brother A. B., in consequence of your cheerful conformity to the Charges and Regulations of the Order, I appoint you Master of this New Lodge, not doubting of your care, skill, and capacity.

The warrant of constitution is then delivered over to the Master; after which the Holy Writings, the rule and line, the square and compasses, the constitutions, the minute book, the mallet, the trowel, the chisel, the movable jewels, and all the insignia of the different Officers, are separately presented to him, and charges suitable for each delivered. The New Master is then conducted by the Grand Stewards, amidst the acclamations of the brethren, to the Grand Master's left hand, where he returns his becoming acknowledgements; first, to the Grand Master; and next, to all the Officers in order; after which he is saluted by the Brethren in a grand chorus suitable for the occasion. The members of the New Lodge advance in procession, pay due homage to the Grand Master, and signify their promise of subjection and obedience by the usual congratulations in the different degrees of masonry.

This ceremony being concluded, the Grand Master orders the New Master to enter immediately upon the exercise of his office; by appointing his Wardens. They are conducted to the pedestal, presented to the Grand Master, and installed by the Grand Wardens; after which the New Master proceeds to invest them with the badges of their offices in the following manner:

Brother C.D. I appoint you Senior Warden of this lodge; and invest you with the ensign of your office. Your regular attendance on our stated meetings is essentially necessary; as in my absence you are to govern this lodge, and in my presence to assist me in the government of it. I firmly rely on your knowledge of the Art, and attachment to the lodge, for the faithful discharge of the duties of this important trust.

Brother E.F. I appoint you Junior Warden of this lodge; and invest you with the badge of your office. To you I entrust the examination of visitors, and the introduction of candidates. You're regular and punctual attendance is particularly requested; and I have no doubt that you will faithfully execute the duty which you owe to your present appointment.

The New Master then addresses his Wardens together:

Brother Wardens, you are too expert in the principles of masonry, to require more information in the duties of your respective offices; suffice it to mention, that I expect that what you have seen praiseworthy in others, you will carefully imitate; and what in them may have appeared defective, you will in yourselves amend. Good order and regularity you must endeavor to promote; and, by due regard to the laws in your own conduct, enforce obedience to them from the other members.

The Wardens retire to their seats, and the Treasurer is invested. The Secretary is then called to the pedestal, and invested with the jewel of his office; upon which the New Master addresses him:

I appoint you, Brother G.H., Secretary of this lodge. It is your province to record the minutes, settle the accounts, and issue out the summons for our regular meetings. Your good inclinations to masonry and the lodge, I hope, will induce you to discharge your office with fidelity, and by so doing, you will merit the esteem and applause of your brethren.

The Deacons are then named, and invested, upon which the New Master addresses them as follows:

Brothers I.K. and L.M. I appoint you Deacons of this lodge. It is your province to attend on the Master, and to assist the Wardens in the active duties of the lodge; such as in the reception of candidates into the different degrees of masonry, and in the immediate practice of our rites. Those columns, as badges of your office, I entrust to your care, not doubting your vigilance and attention.

The Stewards are next called up, and invested, upon which the following charge is delivered to them by the New Master:

Brothers N.O. and P.Q. I appoint you Stewards of this lodge, the duties of your office are, introduce visitors, and see that they are properly accommodated, to collect subscriptions and other fees, and keep an exact account of the lodge expenses. Your regular and early attendance will afford the best proof of your zeal and attachment.

The Master then appoints the Tyler, and delivers over to him the instrument of his office, with a short charge on the occasion, after which he addresses the members of the lodge at large, as follows:

BRETHREN. Such is the nature of our constitution that as some must of necessity rule and teach, so others must of course learn to submit and obey. Humility in both is an essential duty. The brethren, whom I have appointed to assist me in the government of this lodge, are too well acquainted with the principles of masonry, and the rules of good manners, to extend the power with which they are entrusted; and you are too sensible of the propriety of their appointment, and of too generous dispositions to envy their preferment. From the knowledge I have of both officers and members, I trust we shall have but one aim, to please each other, and unite in the grand design of communicating happiness.

The Grand Master then gives the Brethren joy of their Officers, recommends harmony, and expresses a wish that the only contention in lodge may be, a generous emulation to vie in cultivating the royal Art, and the moral virtues. The New Lodge joins in the general salute, and the new-installed Master returns thanks for the honor of the constitution.

The Grand Secretary then proclaims the New Lodge three ties, with the honors of Masonry; flourish with horns each time; after which the Grand Master orders the lodge to be registered in the Grand Lodge books, and the Grand Secretary to notify the same to the regular lodges.

A song with a chorus, accompanied by the music, concludes the ceremony of constitution, when the lodge is closed with the usual solemnities in the different degrees, by the Grand Master and his Officers; after which the procession is resumed to the apartment whence it set out.

This is the usual ceremony at the Constitution of a New Lodge, which the Grand Master may abridge or extend at pleasure; but the material points are on no account to be omitted.

The Ceremony observed at the laying of the Foundation Stones of Public Structures

his ceremony is conducted by the Grand Master and his Officers, assisted by the Members of the Grand Lodge. No private member, or inferior officer of any private lodge, is admitted to join in the ceremony. Provincial Grand Masters are authorized to execute this trust in their several provinces, accompanied by their Officers, and the Masters and Wardens of regular lodges under their jurisdiction. The Chief Magistrate, and other civil officers of the place where the building is to be erected, generally attends on the occasion. The ceremony is thus conducted:

At the time appointed, the Grand Lodge is convened at some convenient place approved by the Grand Master. A band of martial music is provided, and the brethren appear in the insignia of the Order, elegantly dressed, with white gloves and aprons. The lodge is opened by the Grand Master, and the rules regulating the procession to and from the place where the ceremony is to be performed, are read by the Grand Secretary. The necessary cautions are then given from the chair, and the lodge is adjourned; The Brethren, being in their proper clothing and jewels and wearing their white gloves, the procession moves in the following order, viz.,

Two Tylers, with drawn swords

Music

Members of the Grand Lodge, two and two;

A Tyler in his uniform;

Past Grand Stewards;

Grand Tyler;

Present Grand Stewards, with white rods;

Secretary of the Stewards' Lodge;

Wardens of the Stewards' Lodge;

Master of the Stewards' Lodge'

Choristers;

Architect;

Sword bearer, with the sword of state;

Grand Secretary, with his bag;

Grand Treasurer, with his staff;

The Bible, Square and Compasses, on a crimson velvet cushion, carried by the Master

of a lodge, supported by two

Stewards with white rods;

Grand Chaplain;

Provincial Grand Masters;

Past Grand Wardens;

Past Deputy Grand Masters;

Past Grand Masters;

Chief Magistrate of the place;

Grand Wardens;

Deputy Grand Master;

The Constitution carried by the Master of the oldest Lodge;

GRAND MASTER.

Two Stewards close the procession.

A triumphal arch is usually erected at the place where the ceremony is to be performed, with proper, scaffolding for the reception of private brethren. The procession passes through the arch, and the brethren repairing to their stands, the Grand Master and his Officers take their places on a temporary platform, covered with carpet. An ode on masonry is sung. The Grand Master commands silence and the necessary preparations are made for laying the Stone, on which are engraved the year of our Lord and of Masonry, the name of the reigning Sovereign and the name, titles, Etc. of the Grand Master. The Stone is raised up, by an engine erected for that purpose, and the Grand Chaplain or Orator repeats a short prayer. The Grand Treasurer then, by the Grand Master's command, places under the Stone various sorts of coins and medals of the present reign. Solemn music is introduced, an anthem sung, and the Stone let down into its place and properly fixed; upon which the Grand Master descends to the Stone, and gives three knocks with his mallet, amidst the acclamations of the spectators. The Grand Master then delivers over to the Architect the various implements of architecture, entrusting him with the superintendence and direction of the work; after which he re-ascends the platform, and an oration suitable to the occasion is delivered. A voluntary subscription is made for the workmen, and the sum collected is placed upon the Stone by the Grand Treasurer. A song in honor of masonry concludes the ceremony, after which the procession returns to the place whence it set, and the lodge is closed by the Grand Wardens.

The Ceremony observed at the Dedication of Mason's Halls

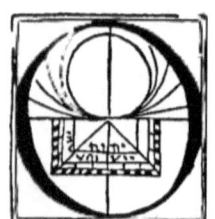

On the day appointed for the celebration of the ceremony of Dedication, the Grand Master and his Officers, accompanied by all the Brethren who are Members of the Grand Lodge, meet in a convenient room adjoining to the place where the ceremony is to be performed, and the Grand Lodge is opened in ample form in all the degrees of masonry. The order of procession is read by the Grand Secretary, and a general charge respecting propriety of behavior given by the Deputy Grand Master. The lodge is then adjourned and the procession formed as follows;

Two Tylers with drawn swords;

Music;

Members of the Grand Lodge, two by two;

A Tyler in his uniform;

Past Grand Stewards;

Grand Tyler;

Present Grand Stewards, with white rods;

Secretary of the Stewards' Lodge;

Wardens of the Stewards' Lodge;

Master of the Stewards' Lodge'

Choristers;

One Brother carrying a gold Pitcher; containing corn;

Two Brothers, with a silver Pitcher, containing wind and oil;

Four Tylers, carrying the Lodge, covered with white satin;

Architect;

Grand Sword bearer, with the sword of state;

Grand Secretary, with his bag;

Grand Treasurer, with his staff;

The Bible, Square and Compasses, on a crimson velvet cushion, carried by the Master of a Lodge, supported by two Stewards;

Grand Chaplain;

Provincial Grand Masters;

Past Grand Wardens;

Past Deputy Grand Masters;

Past Grand Masters;

Chief Magistrate of the place;

Two large lights;

Grand Wardens;

One large light;

Deputy Grand Master;

The Constitution carried by the Master of the oldest Lodge;

GRAND MASTER.

Two Stewards close the procession.

    The Ladies who attend are introduced, and the musicians repair to their station. On the procession reaching the Grand Master's chair, the Grand Officers are separately proclaimed according to rank; as they arrive at that station; and on the Grand Master's being proclaimed, the music strikes up, and continues during the procession three times round the Hall.

    The Lodge is then placed in the center, on a crimson velvet couch; and the Grand Master having taken the chair, under a canopy of state, the Grand Officers, and the Masters and Wardens of the Lodges, repair to the places which have been previously prepared for their reception: The three lights, and the gold and silver pitchers, with the corn, wine and oil, are placed on the Lodge, at the head of which stands the pedestal, on which is placed a crimson, velvet cushion, with the Bible open, the Square and Compasses being laid thereon, and the Constitution roll. An anthem is then sung, and an <u>exordium</u> *(The beginning of anything.)* on masonry given; after which the Architect addresses the Grand Master in an elegant speech, returns thanks for the honor conferred on him, and surrenders up the implements which had been entrusted to his care at the laying of the Foundation Stone. The Grand Master expresses his approbation of the Architect's conduct, an ode in honor of masonry is sung, accompanied by the band, and the ladies retire, with such of the musicians as are not masons.

The lodge is then tiled, and the business of masonry resumed. The Grand Secretary informs the Grand Master, that it is the design of the fraternity to have the Hall dedicated to Masonry; upon which he orders the Grand Officers to assist in the ceremony, during which the organ continues playing solemn music, excepting only at the intervals of Dedication. the Lodge being uncovered, the first procession is made round it, and the Grand Master having reached the East, the organ is silent, and he proclaims the *Hall duly dedicated to Masonry, In The Name Of The Great Jehovah, To Whom Be All Glory And Honor;* upon which the Chaplain strews corn over the Lodge. The organ plays, and the second procession is made round the Lodge, when, on the Grand Master's arrival at the East, the organ is silent, and he declares the Hall dedicated as before, to Virtue; on which the Chaplain sprinkles wine on the Lodge. The organ plays, and the third procession is made round the Lodge, when, the Grand Master having reached the East, the music is silent, and he declares the Hall dedicated to universal benevolence; upon which the Chaplain dips his fingers in the oil, and sprinkles it over the Lodge; and at each dedication the Grand honors are given. A solemn invocation is made to Heaven, and an anthem sung; after which the Lodge being covered, the Grand Master retires to his chair, and the business of masonry is again adjourned.

The ladies are then introduced; an ode for the occasion is performed; and an oration delivered by the Grand Chaplain, which is succeeded by an anthem. Donations for the charity are collected, and the grand procession is reformed. After marching three times round the Hall, preceded by the Tylers carrying the Lodge as at entrance, during which the music continues to play a grand piece, the brethren return to the place whence they set out, where the laws of the Order being rehearsed, the Grand Lodge is closed in ample form in all the degrees.

The Ceremony observed at Funerals, according to ancient Custom: with the Service used on that occasion

No mason can be interred with formalities of the Order, unless it be by his own special request, communicated to the Master of the lodge of which he died a member, foreigners and sojourners excepted; nor unless he has been advanced to the third degree of masonry, and form this restriction there can be no exception. Fellow-crafts, or apprentices, are not entitled to the funeral obsequies *(A funeral rite or ceremony.)*.

The Master of a lodge having received notice of a Master-mason's death, and of his request to be interred with the ceremonies of the Order, fixes the day and hour for the funeral, and issues his command to summon the lodge; if more lodges are expected to attend, he must make application by the Grand Secretary to the Grand Master or his Deputy, to reside over such brethren from other lodges as may assist in forming the procession, who are to be under his direction for the time; and all the brethren present must be properly clothed.

The dispensation being obtained, the Master may invite as many lodges as he thinks proper, and the members of those lodges may accompany their officers in from; but the whole ceremony must be under the direction of the Master of the lodge to which the deceased belonged, for which purpose on the dispensation is granted; and he and his officers must be duly honored, and cheerfully obeyed, on the occasion.

All the brethren who walk in procession, should observe, as much as possible, a uniformity in their dress. Decent mourning, with white stockings, gloves and aprons, is most suitable. No person should be distinguished with a jewel, unless he is an officer of one of the lodges invited to attend in form, and the officers of such lodges should be ornamented with sashes and hatbands; as also the officers of the lodge to whom the dispensation is granted, who are, moreover, to be distinguished with white rods.

A Letter from the learned Mr. John Locke, to the Right Hon. Thomas Earl of Pembroke, with an old Manuscript on the subject of Free-Masonry

(Damaris Masham (1658-1708) was one of the Earliest English woman philosophers. The main sources for her philosophy are two published books, A Discourse Concerning the Love of God (1696) and Occasional Thoughts in Reference to a Virtuous and Christian Life (1705), and her correspondence with Locke and with Leibniz. It was her good fortune to make Locke's acquaintance, since he certainly encouraged her interest in philosophy.)

6th May, 1696

My Lord,

I have at length, by the help of Mr. Collins, procured a copy of that MS. in the Bodleian library, which you were so curious to see: and, in obedience to your Lordship's commands, I herewith send it to you. Most of the notes annexed to it, are what I made yesterday for the reading of my Damaris Masham, who is become so fond of masonry, as to say, that she now more than ever wishes herself a man, that she might be capable of admission into the fraternity.

The MS of which this is a copy, appears to be about 160 years old; yet (as your Lordship will observe by the title) it is itself a copy of one yet more ancient by about 100 years: for the original is said to be the hand-writing of K. Henry VI. Where that prince had it, is at present an uncertainty; but it seems to me to be an examination (taken perhaps before the king) of some one of the brotherhood of masons; among whom he entered himself, as it is said, when he came out of his minority, and thenceforth put a stop to a persecution that had been raised against them: But I must not detain your Lordship longer by my preface from the thing itself.

I know not what effect the sight of this old paper may have upon your Lordship; but for my own part I cannot deny, that it has so much raised my curiosity, as to induce me to enter myself into the fraternity, which I am determined to do (if I may be admitted) the next time I go to London, and that will be shortly.

I am,

My Lord and most humble servant,

John Locke

Certayn Questyons, with Answeres to the same, concerning the Mystery of Maçonrye; writtene by the hande of kynge Henrye, the sixthe of the name, and faithfullye copyed by me Johan Leylande, Antiquarius, by the commande of his Highnesse

Quest. What mote ytt be?

Answ. Ytt beeth the skylle of nature, the understondynge of the myghte that ys hereynne, and its sondrye werckynges; sonderlyche, the skylle of rectenyngs, of waightes and metynges, and the true manere of façonnynge al thynges for nannes use; headlye, dwellinges, and buyldynges of alle kindes, and all odher thynges that make gudde to manne.

Quest. Where dyd it begynne?

Answ. Ytt dyd begynne with the fyrste menne in the este, whych were before the ffyrste manne of the weste, and comynge westlye, ytt hathe broughte herwyth alle comfortes to the wylde and comfortlesse.

Quest. Who dyd brynge ytt westlye?

Answ. The Venetians, whoo beynge grate merchaundes, comed ffyrste ffromme the este ynn Venetia, for the commodytye of marchaundysynge beithe este and weste bey the redde and myddlelonde fees.

Quest. Howe comede ytt yn Engelonde?

Answ. Peter Gower a Grecian, journeyedde ffor kunnyng yn Egypte, and in Syria, and yn everyche londe whereas the Venetians hadde plauntedde maçonrye, and wynnynge entraunce yn al lodges of maçonnes, he lerned muche, and retournedde, and woned yn Grecia Magna, wacksynge, and becommynge a myghtye wyseacre, and gratelyche renowned, and her he framed a grate lodge at Groton, and maked manye maçonnes, some whereoffe dyde journeye yn Fraunce, and maked manye maçonnes, wherefromme, yn processe of tyme, the arte passed yn Engelonde.

Quest. Dothe maçonnes descouer here artes unto odhers?

Answ. Peter Gower, whenne he journeyede to lernne, was ffyrste made, and anonne techedde; evenne soe shulde all odhers beyn recht. Natheless maçonnes hauethe alweys, yn everyche tyme, from tyme to tyme, communycatedde to mannkynde soche of her secrettes as generallyche myghte be usefulle; they haueth keped backe soche allein as shulde be harmfulle yff they comed yn euylle haundes, oder soche as ne myghte be holpynge wythouten the techynges to be joynedde herwythe in the lodge, oder soche as do bynde the freres more stronglyche togeder, bey the proffytte and commodytye commynge to the confrerie herfromme.

Quest. Qhatte artes haueth the maçonnes techedde mankynde?

Answ. The artes agricultura, architectura, astronomia, geometria, numeres, musica, poesie, kymistrye, governmente, and relygyonne.

Quest. Howe commethe maçonnes more teachers than odher monne?

Answ. The hemselfe haueth allein in arte of ffyndynge neue artes, whyche arte the ffyrste maçonnes receaued from Godde; by the whyche they fyndethe what artes hem plesethe, and the treu way of techynge the same, whatt odher menne doethe ffynde out, ys onelyche bey chaunce, and herfore but lytel I tro.

Quest. What dothe the maçonnes concele and hyde?

Answ. Thay concelethe the arte of ffyndynge neue artes, and thatt ys for her own proffytte, and preise: Thay concelethe the arte of kepynge secrettes, thatt soe the worlde mayeth nothinge concele from them. Thay concelethe the arte of wunderwerckynge, and of foresayinge thynges to comme, that so thay same artes may not be usedde of the wyckedde to an euyell ende. Thay also concelethe the arte of chaunges, the wey of wynnynge the facultye of Abrac, the skylle of becommynge gude and parfyghte wythouten the holpynges of fere and hope; and the universelle longage of maçonnes.

Quest. Wylle he teche me thay same artes?

Answ. Ye shalle be techedde yff ye be werthye, and able to lerne.
Quest. Dothe all maçonnes kunne more then odher menne?

Answ. Not so. Thay onlyche haueth recht and occasyonne more than odher menne to kunne, butt manye doeth fale yn capacity, and manye more doth want industrye, that ys pernecessarye for the gaynynge all kunnynge.

Quest. Are maçonnes gudder men then odhers?
Answ. Some maçonnes are not so virtuous as some odher menne; but, yn the moste parte, thay be more gude then thay woulde be yf thay war not maçonnes.

Quest. Doth maçonnes love eidher odher myghtylye as beeth fayde?

Answ. Yea verylyche, and yt may not odherwife be: for gude menne and treu, kennynge eidher odher to be soche, doeth always love the more as thay be more gude.

Here endethe the questyonnes, and awnsweres.

Remarks on the preceding Manuscript, and on the Annotations of Mr. Locke.

Remarks on the preceding manuscript, and the annotations of Mr. Locke

This dialogue possesses a double claim to our regard; first, for its antiquity, and next for the notes added to it by Mr. Locke, who, though not at that time enrolled in the order of masons, offers just conjectures on their history and traditions.

(John Locke)

Every reader must feel a secret satisfaction in the perusal of this ancient manuscript, especially the true mason, whom it more nearly concerns. The recommendation of a philosopher of as great merit and penetration as this nation ever produced, added to the real value of the piece itself, must give it a sanction, and render it deserving a serious examination.

The conjecture of the learned <u>annotator</u> *(A commentator who writes notes to a text.)* concerning its being an examination taken before King Henry of one of the fraternity of masons is just. The severe edict passed at that time against the society, and the discouragement given to the masons by the bishop of Winchester and his party, induced that prince, in his riper years, to make a strict scrutiny into the nature of the masonic institution; which was attended with the happy circumstance of gaining his favor, and his patronage. Had not the civil commotions in the kingdom during his reign, attracted the notice of government, this act would probably have been repealed, through the intercession of the Duke of Gloucester, whose attachment to the fraternity was conspicuous.

What mote ytt be? Mr. Locke observes, in his annotation on this question, that the answer imports, that masonry consists of natural, mathematical, and mechanical knowledge; some part of which, he says, the masons pretend to have taught mankind, and some part they still conceal. The arts which they have communicated to the world are particularly specified in an answer to one of the following questions; as are also those which they have restricted to themselves for wise purposes. Morality, however, ought to have been included in this answer, as it constitutes a principal part of the masonic system.

Where dyd ytt begynne? In the annotation to the answer on this question, Mr. Locke seems to suggest, that masons believed there were men in the east before Adam, which is indeed a mere conjecture. This opinion may be countenanced by many learned authors, but masons comprehend the true meaning of masonry taking rise in the east and spreading to the west, without having recourse to præadamites *(Before Adam)*. East and west are terms peculiar to their society, and when masonically adopted, are very intelligible to the fraternity, as they refer to certain forms and established customs among themselves. From the east, it is well known, learning extended to the western world, and gradually advanced into Europe.

Who dyd brynge ytt westlye? The judicious correction of an illiterate clerk, in the answer to this question as well as the next, reflects credit on the ingenious annotator. The explanation is just, and the elucidation accurate.

Howe comede ytt yn Engelonde? The records of the fraternity inform us, that Pythagoras was regularly initiated into masonry; and being properly instructed in the mysteries of the Art, propagated the principles of the Order in other countries into which he travelled.

Pythagoras lived at Samos, in the reign of Tarquin, the last king of the Romans, in the year of Rome 220; or, according to Livy, in the reign of Servius Tullius, in the year of the world 3472. He was the son of a sculptor, and was educated under one of the greatest men of his time, Therecydes of Syrus, who first taught the immortality of the soul. Upon the death of his patron, he determined to trace science to its source, and supply himself with fresh stores in every part of the world where these could be obtained. Animated by this desire of knowledge, he travelled into Egypt, and submitted to the tedious and discouraging course of preparatory discipline which was necessary to obtain the benefit of Egyptian initiation. When he had made himself a thorough master of all the sciences which were cultivated in the sacerdotal colleges of Thebes and Memphis, he pursued his travels through the east, conversing with the Magi and Indian Brachman's *(An ancient Indian sect that wore very little clothing and was given to asceticism and contemplation.)* and mixing their doctrines with those he had learnt in Egypt. He afterwards studied the laws of Minos at Crete, and those of Lycurgus at Sparta. Having spent the earlier part of his life in this useful manner, he returned to Samos well acquainted with everything curious either in nature or art in foreign countries, improved with all the advantages proceeding from a regular and laborious course of learned education, and adorned with that knowledge of mankind which was necessary to gain the ascendant over them.

Accustomed to freedom, he dislike the arbitrary of Samos, and retired to Crotona in Italy, where he opened a school of philosophy; and by the gravity and sanctity of his manners, the importance of his tenets, and the peculiarity of his institutions, soon spread his fame and influence over Italy and Greece. Among other projects which he used to create respect and gain credit to his assertion, he concealed himself in a cave, and caused it to be reported that he was dead. After some time he came abroad, and pretended that the intelligence which his friends gave him in his retreat, of the transactions of Crotona, was collected during his stay in the other world among the shades of the departed. He formed his disciples, who came from all parts to put themselves under his direction, into a kind of republic, where none were admitted till a severe probation had sufficiently exercised their patience and docility. He afterwards divided them into the esoteric and exoteric classes: to the former he entrusted the more sublime and secret doctrines, to the latter the more simple and popular. This great man found himself able to unite the character of the legislator to that of the philosopher, and to rival Lycurgus and Orpheus in the one, Pherecydes and Thales in the other; following, in this particular, the patterns set him by the Egyptian priests, his instructors, who are not less celebrated for settling the civil than the religious economy of their nation. In imitation of them, Pythagoras gave laws to the republic of Crotona, and brought the inhabitants from a state of luxury and dissoluteness, to be eminent for order and sobriety. While he lived, he was frequently consulted by the neighboring republics, as the composer of their differences, and the reformer of their manners; and since his death (Which happened about the fourth year of the 70th Olympiad, in a tumult raised against him by one Cylon) the administration of their affairs has been generally entrusted to some of his disciples, among whom, to produce the authority of their master for any assertion, was sufficient to establish the truth of it without further inquiry.

The most celebrated of the philosophical notions of Pythagoras are those concerning the nature of the Deity, the transmigration of souls into different bodies (which he borrowed from the Brachmans), and the system of the world. He was the first who took the name of philosopher; that is, a lover of wisdom. His system of morality was admirable. He made unity the principle of all things, and believed that between God and man there were various orders of spiritual beings, who administered to the divine will. He believed in the doctrine of the metempsychosis, or transmigration of souls; and held that God was diffused through all parts of the universe, like a kind of universal soul, pervading every particle of matter, and animating every living creature, from the most contemptible reptile to mankind themselves, who shared a larger portion of the divine spirit. The metempsychosis was founded on this maxim, that as the soul was of celestial origin, it could not be annihilated, and therefore, upon abandoning one body, necessarily removed into another, and frequently did penance for its former vicious inclinations, in the shape of a beast or an insect, before it appeared again in that of a human creature. He asserted, that he had a particular faculty given him by the gods, of remembering the various bodies his own soul had passed through, and confounded cavilers by referring them to his own experience. In his system of the world, the third doctrine which distinguishes his sect was a supposition, that the fun was at rest in the center, and that the earth, the moon, and the other planets moved round it in different orbits. He pretended to have great skill in the mysterious properties of numbers, and held that some particular ones contained a peculiar force and significance. He was a great geometrician, and admitted only those to the knowledge of his system, who had first undergone a probation of five years silence. To his discovery is attributed the <u>47th proposition</u> *(In right-angled triangles the square on the side opposite the right angle equals the sum of the squares on the sides.)* of the first book of Euclid, which, in geometrical solutions and demonstrations of quantities, is of excellent use; and for which as Mr. Locke observes, in the joy of his heart, he is said to have sacrificed a <u>hecatomb</u> *(In ancient Greece and Rome a public sacrifice of 100 oxen to the gods.).* His extraordinary desire of knowledge, and the pains he took to propagate his system, have justly transmitted his fame to posterity.

The pupils, who were initiated by him in the sciences and study of nature at the <u>Crotonian</u> *(A literary society.)* school, brought all their goods into a common stock, contemned the pleasures of sense, abstaining from swearing, and eat nothing that had life. Steady to the tenets and principles which they had imbibed, they dispersed abroad, and taught the doctrines of their preceptor, in all the countries through which they travelled.

Dothe maçonnes descouer here artes unto odhers? Masons, in all ages, have studied the general good of mankind. Every art, which is necessary for the support of authority and good government, or which can promote science, they have cheerfully communicated to the world. Points of no public utility, as their peculiar tenets, mystic forms, and solemn rites, they have carefully concealed. Thus masons have been distinguished in various countries, and the privileges of their Order kept sacred and inviolable.

Whatte artes haueth the maçonnes techedde mankynde? The arts which the masons have publicly taught are here specified. It appears to have surprised the learned annotator, that religion should be ranked among the arts taught by the fraternity; but it may be observed, that religion is the only tie which can bind men; and that where there is no religion, there can be no masonry. Among masons, however, it is an art, calculated to unite for a time opposite systems, without perverting or destroying those systems. By the influence of this art, the purposes of the institution are effectually answered, and all religious animosities happily terminated.

Masons have always paid due obedience to the moral law, and inculcated its precepts with powerful energy on their disciples. Hence the doctrine of God, the creator and preserver of the universe, has been their firm belief in every age; and under the influence of that doctrine, their conduct has been regulated through a succession of year. The progress of knowledge and philosophy, aided by divine revelation, having enlightened the minds of men with the knowledge of the true God, and the sacred tenets of the Christian faith, masons have readily acquiesced in a religion so wisely calculated to make men happy. But in those countries where the gospel has not reached, nor Christianity displayed her beauties, they have pursued the universal religion, or the religion of nature; that is, to be good men and true, by whatever denomination or persuasion they may be distinguished; and by this universal system, the be conduct of the fraternity still continues to be regulated. A cheerful compliance with the established religion of the country, in which they live, is earnestly recommended in their assemblies; and this universal conformity, notwithstanding private sentiment and opinion, is the art they practice, and affects the laudable purpose of conciliating true friendship among men of every persuasion, while it proves the cement of general union.

It may not be improper to state, that this universal system teaches men not to deviate from the line of instruction in which they have been educated, or to disregard the principles of religion they have been originally taught. Though they are to suit themselves to circumstances and situation, in the character of masons they are advised never to forget the wise maxims of their parents, or desert the faith in which they have been nurtured, unless from conviction they are justified in making a change; and in effecting that change, masonry has no share. The tenets of the institution interfere with no particular faith, but are alike reconcilable to all. Hence religious and political disputes never engage the attention of masons in their private seminaries; those points are left to the discussion and determination of other associations for whom the theme is better calculated: and it is a certain truth, that the wisest systems are more frequently injured than benefited by religious cavil. *(Make petty or unnecessary objections.)*

Notwithstanding the happiest events have arisen in many periods of the history of the world from the efforts of a wife, pious, learned, and moderate clergy, seconded by the influence and authority of religious princes, whose counsels and examples have always had a commanding power, which has enabled them to do good, with a facility peculiar to themselves; it must have been observed with a generous concern, that those efforts have not been sufficient to extinguish the unhappy spirit of fanaticism, of whose deplorable effects almost every age has exhibited a striking picture. Enthusiastical sects have been perpetually inventing new forms of religion, by working on the passions of ignorant and unwary; deriving their rules of faith and manners from the fallacious suggestions of a warm imagination, rather than from the clear and infallible dictates of the word of God. One set of men has covered religion with a tawdry habit of type and allegory; while another has converted it into an instrument of dissension and discord. The discerning mind may easily trace the unhappy consequences of departing from the divine simplicity of the gospel, and loading its pure and heavenly doctrines with the inventions and commandments of men. The tendency of true religion is to strengthen the springs of government, by purifying the motives and animating the zeal of those who govern, to promote the virtues which exalt a nation, by rendering its inhabitants good subjects and true patriots, and by confirming all the essential bonds and obligations of civil society. The enemies of religion are the enemies of mankind; and it is the natural tendency of infidelity and licentiousness to dissolve the most sacred obligations, to remove the most powerful motives to virtue, and, by corrupting the principles of individuals, to poison, the sources of public order and public prosperity.

Such are the mischiefs incident from zeal and enthusiasm, however laudably excited, when carried to excess. But if the principles of masonry are understood and practiced, they will be found the best correctors of misguided zeal and unrestrained licentiousness, and prove the ablest support of every well-regulated government.

Howe commethe maçonnes more teachers than odher menne? The answer implies that masons, from the nature and government of their association, have greater opportunities than other men, to improve their talents, and therefore are allowed to be better qualified to instruct others.

Mr. Locke's observation on masons having the art of finding new arts is judicious, and his explanation just. The fraternity has always made the study of arts, a principal part of their private amusement: in their assemblies, nice and difficult theories have been canvassed and explained; new discoveries produced, and those already known, illustrated. The different classes established, the gradual progression of knowledge communicated, and the regularity observed throughout the whole system of their government, are evident proofs, that those who are initiated into the mysteries of the masonic Art, may discover new arts; and this knowledge is acquired by instruction from, and familiar intercourse with, men of genius and ability, on almost every important branch of science.

What do the maçonnes concele and hyde? The answer imports, the art of finding new arts, for their profit and praise; and then particularizes the different arts they carefully conceal. Mr. Locke's remark, 'That this shews too much regard for their own society, and too little for the rest of mankind,' is rather severe, when he has before admitted the propriety of concealing from the world what is of no real public utility, left, by being converted to bad uses, the consequences
might be prejudicial to society. By the word praise, is here meant, that honor and respect to which masons are entitled, as the friends of science and learning, and which is absolutely necessary to give a sanction to the wife doctrines they propagate, while their fidelity gives them a claim to esteem, and the rectitude of their manners demand veneration.

Of all the arts which the masons profess, the art of secrecy particularly distinguishes them. Taciturnity *(The state or quality of being reserved or reticent in conversation.)* is a proof of wisdom, and is allowed to be of the utmost importance in the different transactions of life. The best writers have declared it is agreeable to the Deity himself, may be easily conceived, from the glorious example which he gives, in concealing from mankind the secrets of his providence. The wisest of men cannot pry into the arena of heaven; nor can they divine to-day, what to-morrow may bring forth.

Many instances might be adduced from history, to shew the high veneration which was paid to the art of secrecy by the ancients. Pliny informs us, that Anaxarchus *(A Greek philosopher of the school of Democritus.)*, being imprisoned with a view to extort from him some secrets with which he had been entrusted, and dreading that exquisite torture would induce him to betray his trust, bit his tongue in the middle, and threw it in the face of Nicocreon *(King of Salamis in Cyprus, at the time of Alexander the Great's (336–323 BC) expedition against Persia.)*, the tyrant of Cyprus. No torments could make the servants of Plancus *(a Roman senator.)* betray the secrets of their master; they encountered every pain with fortitude, and strenuously supported their fidelity, amidst the most severe tortures, till death put a period to their sufferings. The Athenians bowed to a statue of brass, which was represented without a tongue, to denote secrecy. The Egyptians worshipped Harpocrates *(Was the god of silence, secrets and confidentiality in the Hellenistic religion developed in Ptolemaic Alexandria.)*, the god of silence, who was always represented holding his finger at his mouth. The Romans had their goddess of silence, named *Angerona* *(Was an old Roman goddess.)*, to whom they offered worship. Lycurgus, the celebrated law-giver, as well as Pythagoras, the great scholar, particularly recommended this virtue; especially the last, who, as we have before observed, kept his disciples silent during five years, that they might learn the valuable secrets he had to communicate unto them. This evinces that he deemed secrecy the rarest, as well as the noblest art.

Mr. Locke has made several judicious observations on the answer which is given to the question here proposed. His being in the dark concerning the meaning of the faculty of Abrac, I am no ways surprised at, nor can I conceive how he could otherwise be. ABRAC is an abbreviation of the word ABRACADABRA. In the days of ignorance and superstition, that word had a magical signification; but the explanation of it is now lost.

Our celebrated annotator has taken no notice of the masons having the art of working miracles, and fore saying things to come. But this was certainly not the least important of their doctrines. Hence astrology was admitted as one of the arts which they taught, and the study of it warmly recommended.

The ancient philosophers applied with unwearied diligence to discover the aspects, magnitude, distances, motions, and revolutions of the heavenly bodies; and, according to the discoveries they made, pretended to foretell future events, and to determine concerning the secrets of Providence. This study became, in a course of time, a regular science.

That astrology, however vain and delusive in itself, has proved extremely useful to mankind, by promoting the excellent science of astronomy, cannot be denied. The vain hope of reading the fates of men, and the success of their designs, has been one of the strongest motives to induce them, in all countries, to an attentive observation of the celestial bodies; whence they have been taught to measure time, to mark the duration of seasons, and to regulate the operations of agriculture.

The science of astrology, which is nothing more than the study of nature, and the knowledge of the secret virtues of the heavens, is founded on scripture, and confirmed by reason and experience. Moses tells us, that the sun, moon, and stars, were placed in the firmament, to be for signs, as well as for seasons. We find the Deity thus addressing Job, "Canst thou bind the sweet influences of the Pleiades, or loose the bonds of Orion?" We are instructed in the Book of Judges, that "they fought from heaven; the stars in their courses fought against Sisera *(Sisera was commander of the Canaanite army of King Jabin of Hazor, who is mentioned in Judges 4-5 of the Hebrew Bible.)*." The ancient philosophers were unanimous in the same opinion; and among the moderns, we may cite Lord Bacon *(Francis Bacon)* and several others as giving it a sanction. Milton *(John Milton was an English poet, polemicist, man of letters, and civil servant for the Commonwealth of England under Oliver Cromwell.)* thus expresses himself on the subject:

> Of planetary motions and aspects
> In Sextile, Square, and trine, and opposite,
> Of noxious efficacy, and when to join
> In synod unbenign, and taught the fixed
> Their influence malignant when to shower, etc.

It is well known that inferior animals, and even birds and reptiles, have a foreknowledge of futurity; and surely Nature never intended to with-hold from man those favors, which she has so liberally bestowed on the raven, the cat, and the sow?

No, the aches in our limbs, and the shootings of our corns, before a tempest or a shower, evince the contrary. Man, who is a microcosm, or world in miniature, unites in himself all the powers and qualities which are scattered throughout nature, and discerns from certain signs the future contingencies of his being; finding his way through the palpable obscure to the visible diurnal and nocturnal sphere, he marks the presages and predictions of his happiness or misery. The mysterious and recondite doctrine of sympathies in Nature is admirably illustrated from the sympathy between the moon and the sea, by which the waters of the ocean are, in a certain though inconceivable manner, drawn after that luminary. In these celestial and terrestrial sympathies, there is no doubt that the vegetative soul of the world transfers a specific virtue from the heavens to the elements, to animals, and to man. If the moon alone rules the world of waters, what effects must the combination of solar, stellar, and lunar influences have upon the land? In short, it is universally confessed, that astrology is the mother of astronomy; and though the daughter has rebelled against the mother, it has long been predicted and expected that the venerable authority of the parent would prevail in the end.

Wylle he teche me thay same artes? By the answer to this question, we learn the necessary qualifications which are required in a candidate for masonry - a good character, and an able capacity.

Dothe all maçonnes kunne more than odher menne ? The answer only implies, that masons have a better opportunity than the rest of mankind, to improve in useful knowledge; but a want of capacity in some, and of application in others, obstructs the progress of many.

Are maçonnes gudder menne then odhers? Masons are not understood to be collectively more virtuous in their lives and actions, than other men; but it is an undoubted fact, that a strict conformity to the rules of the profession, may make them better than they otherwise would be.

Dothe maçonnes love eidher odher myghtylye as beeth sayde? The answer to this question is truly great, and is judiciously remarked upon by the learned annotator.

By the answers to the three last questions, the objections of caviller's *(To raise irritating and trivial objections; find fault with unnecessarily.)* against masonry are amply refuted; the excellency of the institution is displayed; and every censure, on account of the transgressions of its professors, entirely removed. A bad man, whose character is known, can never be enrolled in our records; and should we unwarily be led to receive an improper object, then our endeavors are exerted to reform him: so that, by being a mason, it is probable he may become a better subject to his sovereign, and a more valuable member to the state, than he would have done had he not been in the way of those advantages.

To conclude, Mr. Locke's observations on this curious manuscript deserve a serious and careful examination; and though he was not at the time one of the brotherhood, he seems pretty clearly to have comprehended the value and importance of the system it was intended to illustrate. We may therefore fairly conjecture, that the favorable opinion he conceived of the society of masons before his admission, was afterwards sufficiently confirmed.

Masonry Early introduced into England, - Account of the Druids. - Progress of Masonry in England under the Romans. - Masons highly favored by St. Alban

he history of Britain, previous to the invasion of the Romans, is so mixed with fable, as not to afford any satisfactory account, either of the original inhabitants of the island, or of the arts practiced by them. It appears, however, from the writings of the best historians, that they were not destitute of genius or taste. There are yet in being the remains of some stupendous works, executed by them much Earlier than the time of the Romans; and those vestiges of antiquity, though defaced by time, display no small share of ingenuity, and are convincing proofs that the science of masonry was not unknown even in those rude ages.

The Druids, we are informed, retained among them many usages similar to those of masons; but of what they consisted, at this remote period we cannot with certainty discover. In conformity to the antient practices of the fraternity, we learn that they held their assemblies in woods and groves, and observed the most impenetrable secrecy in their principles and opinions; a circumstance we have reason to regret, as these, being known only to themselves, must have perished with them.

They were the priests of the Britons, Gauls, and other Celtic nations, and were divided into three classes: the bards, who were poets and musicians, formed the first class; the vates, who were priests and physiologists, composed the second class; and the third class consisted of the Druids, who added moral philosophy to the study of physiology.

As study and speculation were the favorite pursuits of those philosophers, it has been suggested that they chiefly derived their system of government from Pythagoras. Many of his tenets and doctrines seem to have been adopted by them. In their private retreats, they entered into a disquisition of the origin, laws, and properties of matter, the form and magnitude of the universe, and even ventured to explore the most sublime and hidden secrets of Nature. On these subjects they formed a variety of hypotheses, which they delivered to their disciples in verse, in order that they might be more easily retained in memory; and administered an oath not to commit them to writing.

In this manner the Druids communicated in their particular tenets, and concealed under the veil of mystery every branch of useful knowledge, which tended to secure to their order universal admiration and respect, while the religious instructions propagated by them were everywhere received with reverence and submission. They were entrusted with the education of youth; and from their seminaries alone issued curious and valuable productions. As judges of law, they determined all causes, ecclesiastical and civil; as tutors, they taught philosophy, astrology, politics, rites, and ceremonies; and as bards, in their songs they recommended the heroic deeds of great men to the imitation of posterity.

To enlarge on the usages that prevailed among those ancient philosophers, on which we can offer at best but probable conjectures, would be a needless waste of time; we shall therefore leave the experienced mason to make his own reflections on the affinity of their practices to the rites established among the fraternity, and proceed to a disquisition of other particulars and occurrences better authenticated, and of more importance.

On the arrival of the Romans in Britain, arts and sciences began to flourish. According to the progress of civilization, masonry rose into esteem; hence we find that Cæsar, and several of the Roman generals who succeeded him in the government of this island, ranked as patrons and protectors of the Craft. Although at this period the fraternity was employed in erecting walls, forts, bridges, cities, temples, palaces, courts of justice, and other stately works, history is silent respecting their mode of government, and affords no information in regard to the usages and customs prevalent among them. Their lodges and conventions were regularly held, but being open only to the initiated fellows, the legal restraints they were under, prevented the public communication of their private transactions.

(Carausius)

The wars which afterwards broke out between the conquerors and conquered, considerable obstructed the progress of masonry in Britain, so that it continued in a very low state till the time of the emperor Carausius, *(Marcus Aurelius Mausaeus Valerius Carausius was a military commander of the Roman Empire in the 3rd century.)* by whom it was revived under his own immediate auspices. Having shaken off the Roman yoke, he contrived the most effectual means to render his person and government acceptable to the people, and assuming in the character of a mason, he acquired the love and esteem of the most enlightened part of his subjects. He possessed real merit, encouraged learning and learned men, improved the country in the civil arts, and, in order to establish an empire in Britain, he collected into this dominions the best workmen and artificers from all parts, all of whom, under his auspices, enjoyed peace and tranquility. Among the first class of his favorites, came the masons; for their tenets he professed the highest veneration, and appointed Albanus, his steward, the principal superintendent of their assemblies. Under his patronage, lodges, and conventions of the fraternity, were regularly formed, and the rites of masonry practiced. To enable the masons to hold a general council to establish their own government, and correct errors among themselves, he granted to them a charter, and commanded Albanus to preside over them in person as Grand Master. This worthy knight proved a zealous friend to the Craft, and afterwards assisted at the initiation of many persons into the mysteries of the Order. To this council, the name of Assembly was afterwards given.

Some particulars of a man so truly exemplary among masons will certainly merit attention

lbanus was born at Verulam, (now St. Alban's, in Hertfordshire,) of a noble family. In his youth he travelled to Rome, where he served seven years under the Emperor Diocletian. On his return home, by the example and persuasion of Amphibalus of Caer-leon, (now Chester,) who had accompanied him in his travels, he was converted to the Christian faith, and, in the tenth and last persecution of the Christians, was beheaded, A. D. 303.t. Alban was the first who suffered martyrdom for the Christian religion in Britain, of which the venerable Bede gives the following account. The Roman governor having been informed that St. Alban harbored a Christian in his house, sent a party of soldiers to apprehend Amphibalus *(Is a venerated Early Christian priest said to have converted Saint Alban to Christianity)*. St. Alban immediately put on the habit of his guest, and presented himself to the officers. Being carried before a magistrate, he behaved with such a manly freedom, and so powerfully supported the cause of his friend, that he not only incurred the displeasure of the judge, but brought upon himself the punishment above specified.

(St. Albanus)

The old constitutions affirm, that St. Alban was employed by Carausius to environ the city of Verulam with a wall, and to build for him a splendid palace; and that, to reward his diligence in executing those works, the emperor appointed him steward of his household, and chief ruler of the realm. However this may be, from the corroborating testimonies of ancient historians, we are assured that this knight was a celebrated architect, and a real encourager of able workmen; it cannot therefore be supposed, that free-masonry would be neglected under so eminent a patron.

History of Masonry in England under St. Austin, King Alfred, and Athelstane; and also under the Knights Templars

fter the departure of the Romans from Britain, masonry made but a slow progress, and in a little time was almost totally neglected, on account of the irruptions of the Picts *(Picts were a tribal confederation of peoples who lived in what is today eastern and northern Scotland during the Late Iron Age and Early Medieval periods. They are thought to have been ethnolinguistically Celtic.)* and Scots, which obliged the southern inhabitants of the island to solicit the assistance of the Saxons, to repel these invaders. As the Saxons increased, the native Britons sunk into obscurity, and ere long yielded the superiority to their protectors, who acknowledged their sovereignty and jurisdiction. These rough and ignorant heathens, despising everything but war, soon put a finishing stroke to all the remains of ancient learning which had escaped the fury of the Picts and Scots. They continued their depredations with unrestrained rigor, till the arrival of some pious teachers from Wales and Scotland, when many of these savages being reconciled to Christianity, masonry got into repute, and lodges were again formed; but these being under the direction of foreigners, were seldom convened, and never attained to any degree of consideration or importance.

Masonry continued in a declining state till the year 557, when Austin *(Austin was a Catholic Benedictine monk who became the first Archbishop of Canterbury in the year 597. He is considered the "Apostle to the English" and a founder of the Catholic Church in England.)*, with forty more monks, among whom the sciences had been preserved, came into England. Austin was commissioned by Pope Gregory, to baptize Ethelbert King of Kent, who appointed him the first archbishop of Canterbury. This monk, and his associates, propagated the

(King Ethebert)

principles of Christianity among the inhabitants of Britain, and by their influence, in little more than sixty years, all the kings of the heptarchy *(Is a collective name applied to seven Anglo-Saxon kingdoms.)* were converted. Masonry flourished under the patronage of Austin, and many foreigners came at this time into England, who introduced the Gothic style of building. Austin seems to have been a zealous encourager of architecture, for he appeared at the head of the fraternity in founding the old cathedra of Canterbury in 600, and the cathedral of Rochester in 602; St. Paul's, London, in 604; St. Peter's, Westminster, in 605; and many others. Several palaces and castles were built under his auspices, as well as other fortifications on the borders of the kingdom, by which means the number of masons in England was considerably increased.

Some expert brethren arrived from France in 680, and formed themselves into a lodge, under the direction of Bennet,

Abbot of Wirral, who was soon after appointed by Kenred, King of Mercia, inspector of the lodges, and general superintendent of the masons.

During the heptarchy, masonry continued in a low state; but in the year 856, it revived under the patronage of St. Swithin, who was employed by Ethelwolph, the Saxon King, to repair some pious houses; and from that time it gradually improved till the reign of Alfred, A. D. 872, when, in the person of that prince, it found a zealous protector.

Masonry has generally kept pace with the progress of learning; the patrons and encouragers of the latter having been most remarkable for cultivating and promoting the former. No prince studied more to polish and improve the understandings of his subjects than Alfred, and no one ever proved a better friend to masonry. By his indefatigable assiduity in the pursuit of knowledge, his example had powerful influence, and he speedily reformed the dissolute and barbarous manners of his people. Mr. Hume, in his History of England, relates the following particulars of this celebrated prince:

"Alfred usually divided his time into three equal portions: one was employed in sleep, and the refection of his body by diet and exercise; another in the dispatch of business; and a third, in study and devotion. That he might more exactly measure the hours, he made use of burning tapers of equal lengths, which he fixed in lanthorns *(Lanthorns were first recorded in 1580-90; alteration by folk etymology (lanterns formerly had reflectors made of translucent sheets of horn)*; and expedient suited to that rude age, when the art of describing sun-dials, and the mechanism of clocks and watches, were totally unknown. By this regular distribution of time, though he often labored under great bodily infirmities, this martial hero, who fought in person fifty-six battles by sea and land, was able, during a life of no extraordinary length, to acquire more knowledge, and even to compose more books, than most studious men, blest with greater leisure and application, have done in more fortunate ages."

As this prince was not negligent in encouraging the mechanical arts, masonry claimed a great part of his attention. He invited from all quarters industrious foreigners to re-people his country, which had been desolated by the ravages of the Danes. He introduced and encouraged manufactures of all kinds among them: no inventor or improver of any ingenious art did he suffer to go unrewarded; and he appropriated a seventh part of his revenue for maintaining a number of workmen, whom he constantly employed in rebuilding his ruined cities, castles, palaces, and monasteries. The University of Oxford was founded by him.

On the death of Alfred in 900, Edward succeeded to the throne, during whose reign the masons continued to hold their lodges, under the sanction of Ethered, his sister's husband, and Ethelward, his brother, to whom the care of the fraternity was entrusted. Ethelward was a prince of great learning, and an able architect; he founded the University of Cambridge.

Edward died in 924, and was succeeded by Athelstane his son, who appointed his brother Edwin, patron of the masons, this prince procured a charter from Athelstane, empowering them to meet annually in communication at York, where the first Grand Lodge of England was formed in 926, at which Edwin presided as Grand Master. Here many old writings were produced, in Greek, Latin, and other languages, from which the constitutions of the English lodges are originally derived.

(Ethelred)

Athelstane kept his court for some time at York, where he received several embassies from foreign princes, with rich presents of various kinds. He was loved, honored, and admired by all the princes of Europe, who sought his friendship and courted his alliance. He was a mild sovereign, a kind brother, and a true friend. The only blemish which historians find in the whole reign of Athelstane, is the supposed murderer of his brother Edwin. This youth, who was distinguished for his virtues, having died two years before his brother, a false report was spread, of his being wrongfully put to death by him. But this is so improbable in itself, so inconsistent with the character of Athelstane, and indeed so slenderly attested, as to be undeserving a place in history.

(William the Conqueror)

The activity and princely conduct of Edwin qualified him, in every respect, to preside over so celebrated a body of men as the masons, who were employed under him in repairing and building many churches and superb edifices, which had been destroyed by the ravages of the Danes and other invaders, not only in the city of York, but at Beverley, and other places.

On the death of Edwin, Athelstane undertook in person the direction of the lodges, and the art of masonry was propagated in peace and security under his sanction.

When Athelstane died, the masons dispersed, and the lodges continued in an unsettled state till the reign of Edgar in 960, when the fraternity was again collected by St. Dunstan *(Abbot of Glastonbury Abbey, Bishop of Worcester, Bishop of London, and Archbishop of Canterbury.)*, under whole auspices they were employed on some pious structures, but met with no permanent encouragement.

After Edgar's death, masonry remained in a low condition upwards of fifty years. In 1041, it revived under the patronage of Edward the Confessor, who superintended the execution of several great works. He rebuilt Westminster Abbey, assisted by Leofrick, Earl of Coventry, whom he appointed to superintend the masons. The Abbey of Coventry, and many other structures, was finished by this accomplished architect.

Having acquired the crown of England in 1066, he appointed Gundulph Bishop of Rochester, and Roger de

Montgomery Earl of Shrewsbury, joint patrons of the masons, who at this time excelled both in civil and military architecture. Under their auspices the fraternity was employed in building the Tower of London, which was completed in the reign of William Rufus, who rebuilt London-bridge with wood, and first constructed the palace and hall of Westminster in 1087.

On the accession of Henry I. the lodges continued to assemble. From this prince, the first Magna Charta, or charter of liberties, was obtained by the Normans. Stephen succeeded Henry in 1135, and employed the fraternity in building a chapel at Westminster, now the House of Commons, and several other works. These were finished under the direction of Gilbert de Clare marquis of Pembroke, who at this time presided over the lodges.

During the reign of Henry II. the Grand Master of the Knights Templars superintended the masons, and employed them in building their Temple in Fleet-street, A. D. 1155. Masonry continued under the patronage of this Order till the year 1199, when John succeeded his brother Richard in the crown of England. Peter de Colechurch was then appointed Grand Master. He began to rebuild London-bridge with stone, which was afterwards finished by William Alcmain in 1209. Peter de Rupibus succeeded Peter de Colechurch in the office of Grand Master, and Geoffrey Fitz-Peter, chief surveyor of the king's works, acted as his deputy. Under the auspices of these two artists, masonry flourished during the remainder of this and the following reign.

History of Masonry in England, during the Reigns of Edward I. Edward II. Edward III. Richard II. Henry V. and Henry VI.

n the accession of Edward I. A. D. 1272, the care of the masons was entrusted to Walter Giffard, Archbishop of York; Gibert de Clare, Earl of Gloucester; and Ralph, Lord of Mount Hermer, the progenitor of the family of the Mantagues. These architects superintended the finishing of Westminster Abbey, which had been begun in 1220, during the minority of Henry III. In the reign of Edward II the fraternity were employed in building Exeter and Oriel colleges, Oxford; Clare-hall, Cambridge; and many other structures; under the auspices of Walter Stapleton, bishop of Exeter, who had been appointed Grand Master in 1307.

Masonry flourished in England during the reign of Edward III who became the patron of science, and the encourager of learning. He applied with indefatigable assiduity to the constitutions of the Order; revised and <u>meliorated</u> *(Past participle)* the ancient charges, and added several useful regulations to the original code of laws. He patronized the lodges, and appointed five deputies under him to inspect the proceedings of the fraternity; viz. I. <u>John de Spoulee</u> *(Master of then Cljibum)*, who rebuilt St. George's Chapel at Windsor, where the order of the garter was first instituted, A. D .1350; 2. William a Wykeham, afterwards Bishop of Winchester, who rebuilt the castle of Windsor at the head of 400 free-masons A. D. 1357; 3. Robert a Barnham, who finished St. George's hall at the head of 250 free-masons, with other works in the castle, A. D. 1375; 4. Henry Yeuele, (called in the old records, the King's free-mason,) who built the Charter-house in London; King's hall, Cambridge; Queensborough castle; and rebuilt St. Stephen's chapel, Westminster: and 5. Simon Langham, Abbot of Westminster, who rebuilt the body of that cathedral as it now stands. At this period, lodges were numerous, and communications of the fraternity held under the protection of the civil magistrate.

Richard II succeeded his grandfather Edward III in 1377, and William a Wykeham was continued Grand Master. He rebuilt Westminster-hall as it now stands; and employed the fraternity in building New College, Oxford, and Winchester college, both of which he founded at his own expense.

Henry, Duke of Lancaster, taking advantage of Richard's absence in Ireland, got the parliament to depose him, and next year caused him to be murdered.

Having supplanted his cousin, he mounted the throne by the name of Henry IV and appointed Thomas Fitz Allen, Earl of Surrey, Grand Master. After the famous victory of

(Henry Chicheley)

Shrewsbury, he founded Battle-abbey and Fotheringay; and in this reign the Guildhall of London was built. The king died in 1413, and Henry V. succeeded to the crown; when Henry Chicheley, archbishop of Canterbury, obtained the direction of the fraternity, under whose auspices lodges and communications were frequent.

Henry VI a minor, succeeding to the throne in 1422, the parliament endeavored to disturb the masons, by passing the following act to prohibit their chapters and conventions:
3 Hen. VI. cap. 1. A. D. 1425.

Masons shall not confederate in Chapters or Congregations

hereas, by the yearly congregations and confederacies made by the masons in their general assemblies, the good course and effect of the statutes of laborers be openly violated and broken, in subversion of the law, and to the great damage of all the commons; our sovereign Lord the King, willing in this case to provide a remedy, by the advice and consent aforesaid, and at the special request of the commons, hath ordained and established that such chapters and congregations shall not be hereafter holden; and if any such be made, they that cause such chapters and congregations to be assembled and holden, if they thereof be convict, shall be judged for felons: and that the other masons, that come to such chapters or congregations, be punished by imprisonment of their bodies, and make find and ransom at the king's will.'

This act was never put in force, nor the fraternity deterred from assembling, as usual, under Archbishop Chicheley, who still continued to preside over them. Notwithstanding this rigorous edict, the effect of prejudice and malevolence in an arbitrary set of men, lodges were formed in different parts of the kingdom; and tranquility and felicity reigned among the fraternity.

As the attempt of parliament to suppress the lodges and communications of masons renders the transactions of this period worthy attention, it may not be improper to state the circumstances which are supposed to have given rise to this harsh edict.

The Duke of Bedford, at that time regent of the kingdom, being in France, the regal power was vested in his brother Humphrey, Duke of Gloucester, who was styled protector and guardian of the kingdom. The care of the young king's person and education was entrusted to Henry Beaufort, bishop of Winchester, the capacity and experience, but of an intriguing and dangerous character. As he aspired to the sole government of affairs, he had continual disputes with his nephew the protector, and gained frequent advantages over the vehement and impolitic temper of that prince. Invested with power, he soon began to shew his pride and haughtiness, and wanted not followers and agents to augment his influence.

The animosity between the uncle and nephew daily increased, and the authority of parliament was obliged to interpose. On the last day of April 1425, the parliament met at Westminster. The servants and followers of the peers coming thither, armed with clubs and staves, occasioned its being named THE BATT PARLIAMENT. Several laws were made, and, among the rest, the act for abolishing the society of masons; at least, for preventing their assemblies and congregations. Their meetings being secret attracted the attention of the aspiring prelate *(A bishop or other high ecclesiastical dignitary.)*, who determined to suppress them.

The sovereign authority being vested in the Duke of Gloucester, as protector of the realm, the execution of the laws, and all that related to the civil magistrate, centered in him: a fortunate circumstance for the masons at this critical juncture. The Duke, knowing them to be innocent of the accusations which the Bishop of Winchester had laid against them, took them under his protection, and transferred the charge of rebellion, sedition, and treason, from them, to the bishop and his followers; who, he asserted, were the first violators of the public peace, and the most rigorous promoters of a civil discord.

The bishop, sensible that his conduct could not be justified by the laws of the land, prevailed on the king, through the intercession of the parliament, whose favor his riches had obtained, to grant letters of pardon for all offences committed by him, contrary to the statute of provisors, and other acts of præmunire *(The offense of asserting or maintaining papal jurisdiction in England. a writ charging a sheriff to summon a person accused of this offense.)*; and five years afterward, procured another pardon, under the great seal, for all crimes whatever from the creation of the world to the 26th of July 1437.

Notwithstanding these precautions of the cardinal, the Duke of Gloucester drew up, in 1442, fresh articles of impeachment against him, and presented them in person to the king; earnestly entreating that judgment might be passed upon him, according to his crimes. The king referred the matter to his council, at that time composed principally of ecclesiastics, who extended their favor to the cardinal, and made such a slow progress in the business, that the Duke, wearied out with their tedious delays and fraudulent evasions, dropt the prosecution, and the cardinal escaped.

Nothing could now remove the <u>inveteracy</u> *(The quality or state of being obstinate or persistent: tenacity.)* of the cardinal against the Duke; he resolved to destroy a man whose popularity might become dangerous, and whose resentment he had reason to dread. The Duke having always proved a strenuous friend to the public, and, by the authority of his birth and station, having hitherto prevented absolute power from being vested in the king's person, Winchester was enabled to gain many partisans, who were easily brought to concur in the ruin of the prince.

To accomplish this purpose, the bishop and his party concerted a plan to murder the Duke. A parliament was summoned to meet at St. Edmondsbury in 1447, where they expected he would lie entirely at their mercy. Having appeared on the second day of the session, he was accused of treason, and thrown into prison; where he was found, the next day, cruelly murdered. It was pretended that his death was natural; but though his body, which was exposed to public view, bore no marks of outward injury, there was little doubt of his having fallen a sacrifice to the vengeance of his enemies. After this dreadful catastrophe, five of his servants were tried for aiding him in his treasons, and condemned to be hanged, drawn, and quartered. They were hanged accordingly, cut down alive, stripped naked, and marked with a knife to be quartered; when the marquis of Suffolk, through a mean and pitiful affectation of popularity, produced their pardon, and saved their lives; the most barbarous kind of mercy that can possibly be imagined!

(Sir Richard Beauchamp)

The Duke of Gloucester's death was universally lamented throughout the kingdom. He had long obtained, and deserved, the surname of GOOD. He was a lover of his country, the friend of good men, the protector of masons, the patron of the learned, and the encourager of every useful art. His inveterate persecutor, the hypocritical bishop, stung with remorse, scarcely survived him two months; when, after a long life spent in falsehood and politics, he sunk into oblivion, and ended his days in misery.

After the death of the cardinal, the masons continued to hold their lodges without danger of interruption. Henry established various seats of erudition, which he enriched with ample endowments, and distinguished by peculiar immunities; thus inviting his subjects to rise above ignorance and barbarism, and reform their turbulent and licentious manners. In 1442, he was initiated into masonry, and, from that time, spared no pains to obtain a complete knowledge of the Art. He perused the ancient charges, revised the constitutions, and, with the consent of his council, honored them with his sanction.

Encouraged by the example of the sovereign, and allured by an ambition to excel, many Lords and gentlemen of the court were initiated into masonry, and pursued the Art with diligence

(William Waynflete (c. 1398 – 11 August 1486), born William Patten, was Provost of Eton ... Waynflete was born in Wainfleet in Lincolnshire (whence his surname) in about 1398. He was the eldest son of Richard Patten (alias Barbour). Waynflete's reputation for learning and piety was great. He is now, however, best remembered as the founder of Magdalene College, Oxford. Throughout the Wars of the Roses, he remained constant to his early patron, King Henry V).

and assiduity. The king in person presided over the lodges, and nominated William Wanefleet, Bishop of Winchester, Grand Master; who built at his own expense Magdalene College, Oxford, and several pious houses. Eton College, near Windsor, and King's college, Cambridge, were founded in this reign, and finished under the direction of Wanefleet. Henry also founded Christ's college, Cambridge' and his queen, Margaret of Anjou, Queen's college, in the same university. In short, during the life of this prince, the arts flourished, and many sagacious statesmen, consummate orators, and admired writers, were supported by royal munificence *(The quality or action of being lavishly generous; great generosity.)* .

History of Masonry in the South of England from 1471 to 1567

asonry continued to flourish in England till the peace of the kingdom was interrupted by the civil wars between the two royal houses of York and Lancaster; during which it fell into an almost total neglect, that continued till 1471, when it again revived under the auspices of Richard Beauchamp, Bishop of Sarum; who had been appointed Grand Master by Edward IV, and had been honored with the title of chancellor of the garter, for repairing the castle and chapel of Windsor.

During the short reigns of Edward V. and Richard III. masonry was on the decline; but on the accession of Henry VII. A. D. 1485, it rose again into esteem, under the patronage of the Master and fellows of the order of St. John at Rhodes, (now Malta,) who assembled their grand lodge in 1500, and chose Henry their protector. Under the royal auspices the fraternity once more revived their assemblies, and masonry resumed its pristine splendor.

(The eldest surviving son of King Edward IV and Queen Elizabeth (Woodville), Edward was born at Westminster Abbey while his father, momentarily deposed, was in exile in Holland. In June 1471, after Edward IV had crushed his foes and reclaimed his crown, young Edward was made Prince of Wales.)

On the 24th of June 1502, a lodge of masters was formed in the palace, at which the king presided in person as Grand Master; and having appointed John Islip, abbot of Westminster, and <u>Sir Reginald Bray</u> *(Sir Reginald Bray KG was the Chancellor of the Duchy of Lancaster under Henry VII, English courtier, and architect of the Henry VII Lady Chapel in Westminster Abbey.)*, Knight of the Garter, his wardens for the occasion, proceeded in ample form to the east end of Westminster Abbey, where he laid the foundation stone of that rich masterpiece of Gothic architecture, known by the name of Henry the seventh's chapel. This chapel is supported by fourteen Gothic buttresses, all beautifully ornamented, and projecting from the building in different angles; it is enlightened by a double range of windows, which throw the light into such a happy disposition, as at once to please the eye, and afford a kind of solemn gloom. These buttresses extend to the roof, and are made to strengthen it, by being crowned with Gothic arches. The entrance is from the east end of the abbey, by a flight of black marble steps, under a noble arch, leading to the body of the chapel. The gates are of brass. The stalls on each side are of oak, as are also the seats, and the pavement is black and white marble. The capstone of

(Magdalene College)

this building was celebrated in 1507.

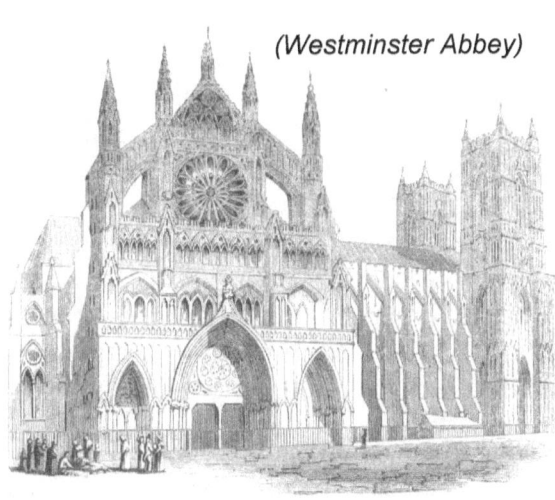
(Westminster Abbey)

Under the direction of Sir Reginald Bray, the palace of Richmond was afterwards built, and many other stately works. Brazen-nose College, Oxford, and Jesus and St. Jon's colleges, Cambridge, were all finished in this reign.

Henry VIII succeeded his father in 1509, and appointed Cardinal Wolsey, Grand Master. This prelate built Hampton court, Whitehall, Christ church college, Oxford, and several other noble edifices; all of which, upon his disgrace, were forfeited to the crown, A. D. 1530. Thomas Cromwell, Earl of Essex, succeeded the cardinal in the office of Grand Master; and employed the fraternity in building St. James's palace, Christ's hospital, and Greenwich castle. In 1534, the king and parliament threw off allegiance to the pope of Rome, and the King being declared supreme head of the church, no less than 926 pious houses were suppressed; many of which were afterwards converted into stately mansions for the nobility and gentry. Under the direction of John Touchet Lord Audley, who, on Cromwell's being beheaded in 1540, had succeeded to the office of Grand Master, the fraternity were employed in building Magdalene college, Cambridge, and several other structures.

(Sir Thomas Sackville)

Edward VI a minor, succeeded to the throne in 1547, and his

guardian and regent, Edward Seymour, Duke of Somerset, undertook the management of the masons, and built Somerset house in the Strand; which, on his being beheaded, was forfeited to the crown in 1552. John Poynet, Bishop of Winchester, then became the patron of the fraternity, and presided over the lodges till the death of the king in 1553.

The masons remained without any nominal patron till the reign of Elizabeth, when Sir Thomas Sackville accepted the office of Grand Master. Lodges were held, during this period, in different parts of England; but the General or Grand Lodge assembled in York, where the fraternity were numerous and respectable.

The following circumstance is recorded of Elizabeth:

Hearing that the masons were in possession of secrets which they would not reveal, and being jealous of all secret assemblies, she sent an armed force to York, with intent to break up their annual grand lodge. This design, however, was happily frustrated by the interposition of Sir Thomas Sackville; who took care to initiate some of the chief officers which she had sent on this duty. They joined in communication with

(Inigo Jones)

the masons, and made so favorable a report to the queen on their return, that she countermanded her orders, and never afterwards attempted to disturb the meetings of the fraternity.

Sir Thomas Sackville held the office of Grand Master till 1567, when he resigned in favor of Francis Russel, Earl of Bedford, and Sir Thomas Gresham, an eminent merchant, distinguished by his abilities, and great success in trade. To the former, the care of the brethren in the northern part of the kingdom was assigned, while the latter was appointed to superintended the meetings in the south, where the society had considerably increased, in consequence of the honorable report which had been made to the queen. Notwithstanding this new appointment of a Grand Master for the fourth, the General Assembly continued to meet in the city of York as heretofore, where all the records were kept; and to this assembly, appeals were made on every important occasion.

Progress of Masonry in the South of England from the Reign of Elizabeth to the Fire of London in 1666

he queen being assured that the fraternity was composed of skillful architects, and lovers of the Arts, and that state affairs were points in which they never interfered, was perfectly reconciled to their assemblies, and masonry made a great progress at this period. During her reign, lodges were held in different places of the kingdom, particularly in London, and its environs, where the brethren increased considerably, and several great works were carried on, under the auspices of Sir Thomas Gresham, from whom the fraternity received every encouragement.

Charles Howard, Earl of Essingham, succeeded Sir Thomas in the office of Grand Master, and continued to preside over the lodges in the fourth till the year 1588, when George Hastings, Earl of Huntingdon, was chosen, who remained in that office till the death of the queen in 1603.

(Cardinal Wolsey, Thomas was born in Ipswich, Suffolk, around 1475. His father, who is thought to have been a butcher, provided a good education and he went on to Magdalen College, Oxford. Wosley was ordained in around 1498. He became chaplain to the archbishop of Canterbury and later chaplain to Henry VII, who employed him on diplomatic missions.)

On the demise of Elizabeth, the crowns of England and Scotland were united in here successor James VI of Scotland, who was proclaimed king of England, Scotland, and Ireland, on the 25th of March 1603. At this period, masonry flourished in both kingdoms, and lodges were convened under the royal patronage. Several gentlemen of fine taste returned from their travels, full of laudable emulation to revive the old Roman and Grecian masonry. These ingenious travelers brought home fragments of old columns, curious drawings, and books of architecture. Among the number was the celebrated Inigo Jones, son of Inigo Jones, *(Jones, was the first significant English architect in the Early modern period, and the first to employ Vitruvian rules of proportion and symmetry in his buildings.)* a citizen of London, who was put apprentice to a joiner, and had a natural taste for the art of designing. He was first renowned for his skill in landscape painting, and was patronized by the learned William Herbert, afterward Earl of Pembroke. He made the tour of Italy at his Lordship's expense, and improved under some of the best disciples of the famous Andrea Palladio. On his return to England, having laid aside the pencil and confined his study to architecture, he became the Vitruvius of Britain, and the rival of Palladio.

(Andrea Palladio, original name Andrea di Pietro della Gondola (born Nov. 30, 1508, Padua, Republic of Venice [Italy]—died August 1580, Vicenza), Italian architect, regarded as the greatest architect of 16th-century northern Italy. His designs for palaces (palazzi) and villas, notably the Villa Rotonda (1550–51) near Vicenza, and his treatise I quattro libri dell'architettura (1570; The Four Books of Architecture) made him one of the most influential figures in Western architecture.)

(Sir Peter Paul Rubens)

This celebrated artist was appointed general surveyor to King James I. Under whose auspices the science of masonry flourished. He was nominated Grand Master of England, and was deputized by his sovereign to preside over the lodges. During his administration, several learned men were initiated into masonry, and the society considerably increased in reputation and consequence. Ingenious artists daily resorted to England, where they met with great encouragement. Lodges were constituted as seminaries of instruction in the sciences and polite arts, after the model of the Italian schools; the communications of the fraternity were established, and the annual festivals regularly observed.

Many curious and magnificent structures were finished under the direction of this accomplished architect; and, among the rest, he was employed, by command of the sovereign, to plan a new palace at Whitehall, worthy the residence of the kings of England, which he accordingly executed; but for want of a parliamentary fund, no more of the plan than the present Banqueting-house was ever finished. In 1607, the foundation stone of this elegant piece of true masonry was laid by King James, in presence of Grand Master Jones, and his wardens, William Herbert Earl of Pembroke, and <u>Nicholas Stone Esq.</u>, master-mason of England *(Nicholas Stone, was an English sculptor and architect. In 1619 he was appointed master-mason to James I, and in 1626 to Charles I.)*, who were attended by many brothers, clothed in form, and other eminent persons, invited on the occasion. The ceremony was conducted with the greatest pomp and splendor, and a purse of broad pieces of gold laid upon the stone, to enable the masons to

(Sir Charles Howard)

regale. This building is said to contain the finest single room of its extent since the days of Augustus, and was intended for the reception of ambassadors, and other audiences of state. The whole is a regular and stately building, of three stories; the lowest has a rustic wall, with small square windows, and by its strength happily serves as a basis for the orders. Upon this is raised the Ionic, with columns and pilasters; and between the columns, are well-proportioned windows, with arched and pointed pediments: over these, is placed the proper entablature: on which is raised a second series of the Corinthian order, consisting of columns and pilasters, like the other, column being placed over column, and pilaster over pilaster. From the capitals are carried festoons, which meet with masks, and other ornaments, in the middle. This series is also crowned with its proper <u>entablature</u> *(A horizontal, continuous lintel on a classical building supported by columns or a wall, comprising the architrave, frieze, and cornice.)*, on which is raised the <u>balustrade</u> *(A railing supported by balusters, especially an ornamental parapet on a balcony, bridge, or terrace.)*, with attic pedestals between, which crown the work. The whole is finely proportioned, and happily executed. The projection of the columns from the wall has a fine effect in the entablatures; which being brought forward in the same proportion, yields that happy diversity of light and shade so essential to true architecture. The internal decorations are also striking. The ceiling of the grand room, in particular, which is now used as a chapel, is richly painted by the celebrated Sir Peter Paul Rubens, who was ambassador in England in the time of Charles I. The subject is, the entrance, inauguration, and coronation of King James, represented by pagan emblems;
and it is justly esteemed one of the most capital performances of this eminent master. It has been pronounced one of the finest ceilings in the world.

Inigo Jones continued in the office of Grand Master till the year 1618, when he was succeeded by the Earl of Pembroke; under whose auspices many eminent, wealthy, and learned men were initiated, and the mysteries of the Order held in high estimation.

(Sir Henry Danvers)

On the death of King James in 1625, Charles ascended the throne. The Earl of Pembroke presided over the fraternity till 1630, when he resigned in favor of Henry Danvers, Earl of Danby; who was succeeded in 1633 by Thomas Howard, Earl of Arundel, the progenitor of the Norfolk family. In 1635, Francis Russel, Earl of Bedford, accepted the government of the society; but Inigo Jones having, with indefatigable assiduity, continued to patronize the lodges during his Lordship's administration, he was re-elected the following year and continued in office till his death in 1646.

The taste of this celebrated architect was displayed in many curious and elegant structures, both in London and the country; particularly in designing the magnificent row of Great Queen-street, and the west side of Lincoln's Inn Fields, with Lindsey-house in the center; the late Chirurgions's Hall and Theatre, now Barbers-Hall, in Monkwell-street; Shaftesbury-house, late the London lying-in hospital for married women, in Aldersgate-street; Bedford-House in Bloomsbury-Square; Berkley-House, Piccadilly, lately burnt, and rebuilt, now in the possession of the Duke of Devonshire; and York-stairs, at Thames, Etc. Beside these, he designed Gunnersbury-House near Brentford; Wilton-house in Wiltshire; Castle-Abbey in Northampton-shire; Stoke-park; part of the quadrangle at St. John's, Oxford; Charlton-house, and Cobham-hall, in Kent; Coleshill in Berkshire; and the Grange, in Hampshire.

(Sir Henry Jermyn)

The breaking out of the civil wars obstructed the progress of masonry in England for some time. After the Restoration, however, it began to revive under the patronage of Charles II who had been received into the Order during his exile.

On the 27th December 1663, a general assembly was held, at which Henry Jermyn, Earl of St. Alban's, was elected Grand Master;

(Sir Thomas Howard)

who appointed Sir John Denham Knt. his deputy, and Mr. (afterwards Sir) Christopher Wren, and John Webb his wardens. Several useful regulations were made at this assembly, for the better government of the lodges, and the greatest harmony prevailed among the whole fraternity.

Thomas Savage, Earl of Rivers, having succeeded the Earl of St. Alban's in the office of Grand Master in June 1666, Sir Christopher Wren was appointed Deputy under his Lordship, and distinguished himself more than any of his predecessors in office, in promoting the prosperity of the few lodges which occasionally met at this time; particularly the old lodge of St. Paul's, now the Lodge of Antiquity, which he patronized upwards of 18 years. The honors which this celebrated character afterwards received in the society, are evident proofs of the unfeigned attachment of the fraternity toward him.

The History of Masonry in England from the Fire of London, to the Accession of George I

The year 1666 afforded a singular and awful occasion for the utmost exertion of masonic abilities. The city of London, which had been visited in the preceding year by the plague, to whole ravages, it is computed, above 100,000 of its inhabitants fell a sacrifice, had scarcely recovered from the alarm of that dreadful contagion, when a general conflagration reduced the greatest part of the city within the walls to ashes, This dreadful

(Sir Thomas Savage)

fire broke out on the 2d of September, at the house of a baker in Pudding-lane, a wooden building, pitched on the outside, as were also all the rest of the houses in that narrow lane. The house being filled with faggots and brush-wood, soon added to the rapidity of the flames, which raged with such fury, as to spread four ways at once.

Jonas Moore and Ralph Gatrix, who were appointed surveyors on this occasion to examine the ruins, reported, that the fire over-ran 373 acres within the walls, and burnt 13,000 houses, 89 parish churches, besides chapels, leaving only 11 parishes standing. The Royal Exchange, Custom-House, Guildhall, Blackwell-hall, St. Paul's cathedral, Bridewell, the two compters, fifty-two city companies halls, and three city gates, were all demolished. The damage was computed at 10,000,000 sterling.

After so sudden and extensive a calamity, it became necessary to adopt some regulations to guard against any such catastrophe in future. It was therefore determined, that in all the new buildings to be erected, stone and brick should be substituted in the room of timber. The King and the Grand Master immediately ordered deputy Wren to draw up the plan of a new city, with broad and regular streets.

Dr. Christopher Wren was appointed surveyor general and principle architect for rebuilding the city, the cathedral of St. Paul, and all the parochial churches enacted by parliament, in lieu of those that were destroyed, with other public structures. This gentleman, conceiving the charge too important for a single person, selected Mr. Robert Hooke, professor of geometry in Gresham College, to assist him; who was immediately employed in measuring, adjusting, and setting out the grounds of the private streets to the several proprietors. Dr. Wren's model and plan were laid before the king and the house of commons, and the practicability of the whole scheme, without the infringement of property, clearly demonstrated: it unfortunately happened, however, that the greater part of the citizens were absolutely averse to alter their old possessions, and to recede from building their houses again on the old foundations . Many were unwilling to give up their properties into the hands of public trustees, till they should receive an equivalent of more advantage; while others expressed distrust.

Every means were tried to convince the citizens, that by removing all the church-yards, gardens Etc. to the out-skirts of the city, sufficient room would be given to augment the streets, and properly to dispose of the churches, halls, and other public buildings, to the perfect satisfaction of every proprietor; but the representation of all these improvements had no weight. The citizens chose to have their old city again, under all its disadvantages, rather than a new one, the principles of which they were unwilling to understand, and considered as innovations. Thus an opportunity was lost, of making the new city the most magnificent, as well as the most commodious for health and trade, of any in Europe. The architect, cramped in the execution of his plan, was obliged to abridge his scheme, and exert his utmost labor, skill, and ingenuity, to model the city in the manner in which it has since appeared.

On the 23d of October 1667, the king in person levelled in form the foundation stone of the new Royal Exchange, now allowed to be the finest in Europe; and on the 28th September 1669, it was opened by the Lord mayor and aldermen. Round the inside of the square, above the arcades, and between the windows, are the statues of the sovereigns of England. In the center of the square, is erected the king's statue to the life, in a Cæsarean habit of white marble, executed in a masterly manner by Mr. Gibbons, then grand warden of the society.

(Sir Robert Hooke)

In 1668, the Custom-house

(Sir Christopher Wren, (born October 20, 1632, East Knoyle, Wiltshire, England—died February 25, 1723, London), designer, astronomer, geometrician, and the greatest English architect of his time. Wren designed 53 London churches, including St. Paul's Cathedral, as well as many secular buildings of note. He was a founder of the Royal Society (president 1680–82), and his scientific work was highly regarded by Sir Isaac Newton and Blaise Pascal. He was knighted in 1673. Wren was the only surviving son of a rector, and from an early age he was delicate in health. Before Wren was three, his father was appointed dean of Windsor, and the Wren family moved into the precincts of the court. It was among the intellectuals around King Charles I that the boy first developed his mathematical interests. The life at Windsor was rudely disturbed by the outbreak of the English Civil Wars in 1642.)

for the port of London, situated on the south side of Thames-street, was built, adorned with an upper and lower order of architecture. In the latter, are stone columns, and <u>entablement</u> *(A platform supporting a statue, above the dado and base.)* of the Tuscan order: and in the former, are pilaster, entablature, and five pediments of the Ionic order. The wings are elevated on columns, forming piazzas; and the length of the building is 189 feet; its breadth in the middle, 27; and at the west end, 60 feet.

This year also, deputy Wren and his warden Webb finished the Theatrum Sheldonium at Oxford, designed and executed at the private expense of Gilbert Sheldon, archbishop of Canterbury, an excellent architect and able designer. On the 9th of July 1669, the capstone of this elegant building was celebrated with joy and festivity by the craftsmen, and an elegant oration delivered on the occasion by Dr. South. Deputy Wren, at the same time also, built, at the expense of the University, that other master-piece of architecture, the pretty museum near this theatre.

In 1671, Mr. Wren began to build that great fluted column called the Monument, in memory of the burning and re-building of the city of London. This stupendous pillar was finished in 1677. It is 24 feet higher than Trajan's pillar at Rome, and built of Portland stone, of the Doric order. Its altitude, from the ground, is 202 feet; the greatest diameter of the shaft or body of the column, 15 feet; the ground plinth, or bottom of the pedestal, 28 feet square; and the pedestal 40 feet high. Over the capital, is an iron balcony, encompassing a cone 32 feet high, supporting a blazing urn of gilt brass. Within is a large stair-case of black marble, containing 345 steps, each step ten inches

(Conversion of St. Paul)

and an half broad, and six inches thick.

The west side of the pedestal is adorned with curious emblems, by the masterly hand of Mr. Cibber, father to the late poet-laureate Colley Cibber; in which eleven principal figures are done in alto, and the rest in basso relieve *(Bas-relief- from the Italian basso rilievo)*. That to which the eye is particularly directed, is a female, representing the City of London, sitting in a languishing posture, on a heap of ruins. Behind her, is Time, gradually raising her up; and at her side, a woman, representing Providence, gently touching her with one hand, while, with a winged scepter in the other, she directs her to regard two goddesses in the clouds; one with a cornucopia, denoting Plenty; the other, with a palm branch, the emblem of Peace. At her feet is a bee-hive, to shew that, by industry and application, the greatest misfortunes may be overcome. Behind time, are the citizens, exulting at his endeavors to restore her; and beneath, in the midst of the ruins, is a dragon, the supporter of the city arms, who endeavors to preserve them with his paw. At the north end, is a view of the City in flames, the inhabitants in consternation, with their arms extended upward, crying for assistance. Opposite the City, on an elevated pavement, stands the King, in a Roman habit, with a laurel on his head, and a truncheon in his hand; who, on approaching her, commands three of his attendants to descend to her relief.

(Monument to London)

The first represents the Sciences, with a winged head, and circle of naked boys dancing thereon, and holding Nature in her hand, with her numerous breasts, ready to give assistance to all. The second is Architecture, with a plan in one hand, and a square and pair of compasses in the other. The third is Liberty, waving a hat in the air, and showing her joy at the pleasing prospect of the City's speedy recovery. Behind the King, stands his brother, the Duke of York, with a garland in one hand, to crown the rising city, and a sword in the other, for her defense. The two figures behind them, are Justice and Fortitude; the former with a coronet, and the latter with a reined lion; while, under the pavement, in a vault, appears Envy gnawing a heart. In the upper part of the back ground, the re-construction of the city is represented by scaffolds and unfinished houses, with builders at work on them. The north and south sides of the pedestal have each a Latin inscription, one describing the desolation of the city, the other its restoration. The east side of the pedestal has an inscription, expressing the time in which the pillar was begun, continued, and brought to perfection.

In one line continued round the base, are these words: "This pillar was set up in perpetual remembrance of the most dreadful burning of this Protestant city, begun and carried on by the treachery and malice of the Popish faction, *(The Popish Plot was a fictitious conspiracy concocted by Titus Oates that between 1678 and 1681 gripped the Kingdoms of England and Scotland in anti-Catholic hysteria. Oates alleged that there existed an extensive Catholic conspiracy to assassinate Charles II, accusations that led to the executions of at least 22 men and precipitated the Exclusion Bill Crisis. Eventually Oates' intricate web of accusations fell apart, leading to his arrest and conviction for perjury.)* in the beginning of September, in the year of our Lord 1666, in order to the carrying on their horrid plot for extirpating the Protestant religion, and old English liberty, and introducing popery and slavery." This inscription, upon the Duke of York's accession to the crown, was erased; but, soon after the Revolution, restored again.

The rebuilding of the city of London was vigorously prosecuted, and the restoration of St. Paul's cathedral claimed particular attention. Dr. Wren drew several designs, to discover what would be most acceptable to the general taste; and finding persons of all degrees declare for magnificence and grandeur, he formed a design according to the very best stile of Greek and Roman architecture, and caused a large model of it to be made in wood; but the bishops deciding that it was not

Cathedral Church of St. Paul, London.

sufficiently in the cathedral stile, the surveyor was ordered to amend it, and he then produced the scheme of the present structure, which was honored with the king's approbation. The original model, however, which was only of the Corinthian order, like St. Peter's at Rome, is still kept in an apartment of the cathedral, as a real curiosity.

In 1673, the foundation stone of this magnificent cathedral, designed by deputy Wren, was laid in solemn form by the King, attended by Grand Master Rivers, his architects and craftsmen, in the presence of the nobility and gentry, the Lord mayor and aldermen, the bishops and clergy, Etc. During the whole time this structure was building, Mr. Wren acted as master of the work and surveyor, and was ably assisted by his wardens, Mr. Edward Strong and is son.

St. Paul's cathedral is planned in the form of a long cross; the walls are wrought in rustic, and strengthened, as well as adorned, by two rows of coupled pilasters, one over the other; the lower Corinthian, and the upper Composite. The spaces between the arches of the windows, and the architecture of the lower order, as well as those above, are filled with a variety of enrichments. He west front is graced with a most magnificent portico, a noble pediment, and two stately turrets. There is a grand flight of steps of black marble that extend the whole length of the portico, which consists of twelve lofty Corinthian columns below, and eight of the Composite order above; these are all coupled and fluted. The upper series support a noble pediment, crowned with its <u>acroteria</u> *(Acroteria is an architectural ornament placed on a flat base called the acroter or plinth, and mounted at the apex of the pediment of a building in the classical style.)*; and in this pediment is an elegant representation in bas relief, of the conversion of St. Paul, executed by Mr. Bird, an artist whose name, on account of this piece alone, is worthy of being transmitted to posterity. The figures are well executed: the magnificent figure of St. Paul, on the apex of the pediment, with St. Peter on his right, and St. James on his left, produce a fine effect. The four Evangelists, with their proper emblems, on the front of the towers, are judiciously disposed, and skillfully finished; St. Matthew is distinguished by an angel; St. Mark, by a lion; St. Luke, by an ox; and St. John, by an eagle.

To the north portico, there is an ascent by twelve circular steps of black marble, and its dome is supported by six grand Corinthian columns. Upon the dome is a well-proportioned urn, finely ornamented with festoons; over the urn is a pediment, supported by pilasters in the wall, in the face of which are carved the royal arms, with the regalia, supported by angels. Statues of five of the apostles are placed on the top, at proper distances.

The south portico answers to the north, and, like that, is supported by six noble Corinthian columns; but as the ground is considerably lower on this side of the church than the other, the ascent is by a flight of twenty-five steps. This portico has also a pediment above, in which is a phoenix rising out of the flames, with the motto, RESURGAM *("Rise gain")*, underneath it; as an emblem of rebuilding the church. A curious accident is said to have given rise to this device, which was particularly observed by the architect as a favorable omen. When Dr. Wren was marking our dimensions of the building, and had fixed on the center of the great dome, a common laborer was ordered to bring him a flat stone from among the rubbish, to leave as a direction to the masons. The stone which the man brought happened to be a piece of a grave-stone, with nothing remaining of the inscription but this single word, in large capitals, RESURGAM; and this circumstance left an impression on Dr. Wrens' mind, that could never afterwards be erased. On this side of the building are likewise five statues, which correspond with those on the apex of the north pediment.

At the east end of the church is a sweep, or circular projection for the altar, finely ornamented with the orders, and with sculpture; particularly a noble piece in honor of king William III.

The dome, which rises in the center of the whole, is superlatively grand. Twenty feet above the roof of the church is a circular range of thirty-two columns, with niches placed exactly against others within. These are terminated by their entablature, which supports a handsome gallery, adorned with a balustrade. Above these columns is a range of pilasters, with windows between; and from the entablature of these, the diameter decreases very considerably; and two feet above that, it is again contracted. From this part the external sweep of the dome begins, and the arches meet at 52 feet above. On the summit of the dome, is an elegant balcony, and from its center rises the lantern, adorned with Corinthian columns. The whole is terminated by a ball, on which stands a cross, both of which are elegantly gilt.

This noble fabric is surrounded, at a proper distance, by a dwarf stone wall, on which is placed the most magnificent balustrade of cast iron perhaps in the universe, four feet six inches in height, exclusive of the wall. In this enclosure are seven beautiful iron gates, which, together with the balusters, in number about 2500, weigh 200 tons and 85 pounds.

In the center of the area of the grand west front, on a pedestal of excellent workmanship, stands a statue of Queen

Anne, formed of white marble, with proper decorations. The figures on the base represent Britannia, with her spear; Gallia, with the crown in her lap Hibernia, with her harp; and America, with her bow. These, are the colossal statues with which the church are adorned, were executed by the ingenious Mr. Hill.

A strict regard to the situation of this cathedral, due east and west, has given it an oblique appearance with respect to Ludgate-street in front; so that the great front gate in the surrounding iron rails, being made to regard the street in front, rather than the church to which it belongs, the statue of queen Anne, that is exactly in the middle of the west front, is thrown on one side the straight approach from the gate to the church, and gives an idea of the whole edifice being awry.

Under the grand portico, at the west end, are three doors, ornamented at the top with bas relief. The middle door, which is by far the largest, is cased with white marble, and over it is a fine piece of basso relievo, in which St. Paul is represented preaching to the Bereans. On entering the door, the mind is struck by the extends of the vista. An arcade, supported by lofty and massy pillars on each hand, divide the church into the body and two aisles; and the view is terminated by the altar at the extremity of the choir; subject, nevertheless, to the intervention of the organ standing across, which forms a heavy obstruction. The pillars are adorned with columns and pilasters of the Corinthian and Composite orders; and the arches of the roof and enriched with shields, festoons, chaplets, and other ornaments. In the aisle, on one hand, is the consistory; and opposite, on the other, the Morning Prayer Chapel. These have very beautiful screens of carved wainscot, which are much admired.

Over the center, where the great aisles cross each other, is the grand cupola, or dome, the vast concave of which inspires a pleasing awe. Under its center is fixed in the floor, a brass plate, round which the pavement is beautifully variegated; but the figures into which it is formed, can nowhere be so well seen as from the whispering-gallery above. Here the spectator has at once a full view of the organ, richly ornamented with carved work, and the entrance to the choir directly under it. The two aisles on the side of the choir, as well as the choir itself, are enclosed with very fine iron rails and gates.

The altar-piece is adorned with four noble fluted pilasters, painted and veined with gold, in imitation of lapis lazuli, and their capitals are double gilt. In the intercolumniations below, are nine marble panels, and above are six windows, in the two series. The floor of the whole church is paved with marble; and within the rails of the altar, with porphyry, polished, and laid in several geometrical figures.

In the great cupola, which is 108 feet in diameter, the architect seems to have imitated the Pantheon at Rome, excepting that the upper order is there only umbra tile, and distinguished by different colored marbles; while, in St. Paul's, it is extant out of the wall. The Pantheon is no higher within than its diameter; St. Peter's is two diameters; the former shews its concave too low, the latter too high: St. Paul's is proportioned between both, and therefore shews its concave every way, and is very lightsome by the windows of the upper order. These strike down the light through the great colonnade that encircles the dome without, and serves for the abutment, which is brick of the thickness of two bricks; but as it rises every way five feet high, it has a course of excellent brick of 18 inches long, banding through the whole thickness; and, to make it still more secure, it is surrounded with a vast chain of iron, strongly linked together at every ten feet. This chain is let into a channel, cut into the bandage of Portland stone, and defended from the weather by filling the groove with lead. The concave was turned upon a center, which was judged necessary to keep the work true; but the center was laid without any standards below for support. Every story of the scaffolding being circular, and the ends of all the ledgers meeting as so many rings, and truly wrought, it supported itself.

As the old church of St. Paul had a lofty spire, Dr. Wren was obliged to give his building an altitude that might secure it from suffering by the comparison. To do this, he made the dome without, much higher than within, by raising a strong brick cone over the internal cupola, so constructed as to support an elegant stone lantern on the apex. This brick cone is supported by a cupola formed of timber, and covered with lead: between which and the cone are easy stairs, up to the lantern. Here the spectator may view contrivances that are truly astonishing. The outward cupola is only ribbed, with the architect thought less Gothic than to stick it full of such little lights as are in the cupola of St. Peter's, that could not without difficulty be mended, and, if neglected, might soon damage the timbers. As the architect was sensible that paintings are liable to decay, he intended to have beautified the inside of the cupola with mosaic work; which, without the least fading of colors, would be as durable as the building itself: but in this he was over-ruled, though he had undertaken to procure four of the most eminent artists in that profession from Italy, for the purpose. This part, therefore, is now decorated by the pencil of Sir James Thornhill, who has represented the principal passages of St. Paul's life, in eight compartments. These paintings are all seen to advantage by means of a circular opening, through which the light is transmitted with admirable effect from the lantern above; but they are now cracked, and sadly decayed.

Divine service was performed in the choir of this cathedral for the first time on the thanksgiving day for the peace of Ryswick, Dec. 2, 1697; and the last stone on the top of the lantern laid by Mr. Christopher Wren, the son of the architect, in 1710. This noble fabric, lofty enough to be discerned at sea eastward, and at Windsor to the west, was begun and completed in the space of 35 years, by one architect, the great Sir Christopher Wren; one principal mason, Mr. Strong; and under one Bishop of London, Dr. Henry Compton: whereas St. Peter's at Rome was 155 years in building, under twelve successive architects, assisted by the police and interest of the Roman see, and attended by the best artists in sculpture, statuary, painting, and mosaic work.

The various parts of this superb edifice I have been thus particular in describing, as it reflects honor on the ingenious architect who built it, and as there is not an instance on record of any work of equal magnitude having ever been completed by one man.

hile the cathedral of St. Paul's was carrying on, as a national undertaking, the citizens did not neglect their own immediate concerns, but restored such of their halls and gates as had been destroyed. In April 1675, was laid the foundation stone of the present Bethlehem-hospital for lunatics, in Moorfields. This is a magnificent building, 540 feet long, and 40 broad, beside the two wings, which were not added until several years afterward. The middle and ends of the edifice project a little, and are adorned with pilasters, entablatures, foliage's, Etc. which, rising above the rest of the building, have each a flat roof, with a handsome balustrade of stone. In the center is an elegant turret, adorned with a cloak, gilt ball, and vane. The whole building is brick and stone, enclosed by a handsome wall, 680 feet long, of the same materials. In the center of the wall, is a large pair of iron gates; and on the piers on which these are hung, are two images, in a reclining posture, one representing raving, the other melancholy, madness. The expression of these figures is admirable; and they are the workmanship of Mr. Cibber, the father of the laureate before mentioned.

The college of Physicians also, about this time, discovered some taste in erecting their college in Warwick-lane, which, though little known, is esteemed by good judges a delicate

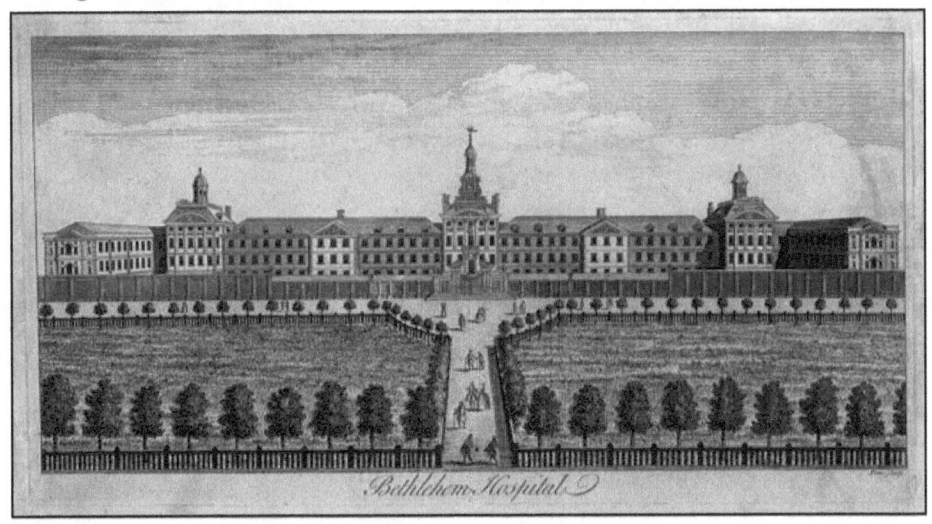

building. *(Bethlehem Hospital 1789)*

The fraternity was now fully employed; and by them the following parish churches, which had been consumed by the great fire, were gradually rebuilt, or repaired:

Allhallows, Bread-street, finished 1694; and the steeple completed 1697.
Allhallows the Great, Thames-street, 1683.
Allhallows, Lombard-street, 1694.
St. Alban, Wood-street, 1685.
St. Anne and Agnes, St. Annes's-lane, Aldersgate-street, 1680.
St. Andrew's Wardrobe, Puddledock-hill, 1692.
St. Andrew's, Holborn, 1687.
St. Anthony's, Watling-street, 1682.
St. Augustin's, Watling-street, 1683; and the steeple finished 1695.
St. Bartholomew's, Royal Exchange, 1679.
St. Benedict, Grace-church-street, 1685.
St. Benedict's, Threadneedle-street, 1673.
St. Bennet's, Paul's Wharf, Thames-street, 1683.
St. Bride's, Fleet-street, 1680; and farther adorned in 1699.
Christ-church, Newgate-street, 1687.
St. Christopher's, Threadneedle-street, (since taken down to make room for the Bank,) repaired in 1696.
St. Clement Danes, in the Strand, taken down 1680, and rebuilt by Sir Christopher Wren, 1682.
St. Clement's, East Cheap, St. Clement's-lane, 1686.
St. Dennis Back, Lime-street, 1674.
St Dunstan's in the East, Tower-street, repaired in 1698.
St. Edmond's the King, Lombard-street, rebuilt in 1674.
St. George, Botolph-lane, 1674.
St. James, Garlick-hill, 1683.
St. James, Westminster, 1675.
St. Lawrence Jewry, Cateaton-street, 1677.
St. Magnes, London-bridge, 1676; and the steeple in 1705.
St. Margaret, Lothbury, 1690.
St. Margaret Pattens, Little Tower-street, 1687.
St. Martin's, Ludgate, 1684.
St. Mary Abchurch, Abchurch-lane, 1686.
St. Mary's-at-hill, St. Mary's-hill, 1672.

St. Mary's Aldermary, Bow-lane, 1672.
St. Mary Magdalen, Old Fish-street, 1685.
St. Mary Somerset, Queenhithe, Thames-street, 1683.
St. Mary le Bow, Cheapside, 1683.

This church was built on the wall of a very ancient one in the early time of the Roman colony; the roof is arched, and supported with ten Corinthian columns; but the principal ornament is the steeple, which is deemed an admirable piece of architecture, not to be paralleled by that of any other parochial church. It rises from the ground a square tower, plain at bottom, and is carried up to a considerable height in this shape, but with more ornament as it advances. The principal decoration of the lower part is the door case; a lofty, noble arch, faced with a bold and well-wrought rustic, raised on a plain solid course from the foundation. Within the arch, is a portal of the Doric order, with well-proportioned columns; the frieze is ornamented with triglyphs, and with sculpture in the metopes.

There are some other slight ornaments in this part, which is terminated by an elegant cornice, over which rises a plain course, from which the dial projects. Above this, in each face, there is an arched window, with Ionic pilasters at the sides. The entablature of the order is well wrought; it has the swelling frieze, and supports on the cornice an elegant balustrade, with Attic pillars over Ionic columns. These sustain elegant scrolls, on which are placed urns with flames, and from this part the steeple rises circular. There is a plain course to the height of half the scrolls, and upon this is raised an elegant circular series of Corinthian columns. These support a second balustrade with scrolls; and above there is placed another series of columns of the Composite order; while, from the entablature, rises a set of scrolls supporting the spire, which is placed on balls, and terminated by a globe, on which is fixed a vane.

St. Mary Woolnoth's, Lombard-street, repaired in 1677.
St. Mary, Aldermanbury, rebuilt 1677.
St. Matthew, Friday-street, 1685.

St. Michael, Basinghall-street, 1679.
St. Michael Royal, College-hill, 1694.
St. Michael, Queenhithe, Trinity-lane, 1677.
St. Michael, Wood-street, 1675.
St. Michael, Crooked-lane, 1688.
St. Michael, Cornhill, 1672.
St. Mildred, Bread-street, 1683.
St. Mildred, Poultry, 1676.
St. Nicholas, Cole-abbey, Old Fish-street, 1677.
St. Olive's, Old Jewry, 1673.
St. Peter's, Cornhill, 1681.
St. Sepulchre's, Snow-hill, 1670.
St. Stephen's, Coleman-street, 1676.
St. Swithin's, Cannon-street, 1673.
St. Vedast, Foster-lane, 1697.

St. Stephen's, Walbrook, behind the Mansion-house, 1676, many encomiums *(A speech or piece of writing that praises someone or something highly.)* have been bestowed on this church for its interior beauties. The dome is finely proportioned to the church, and divided into small compartments, decorated with great elegance, and crowned with a lantern; the roof is also divided into compartments, and supported by noble Corinthian columns raised on their pedestals. This church has three aisles and a cross aisle, is 75 feet long, 36 broad, 34 high, and 58 to the lantern. It is famous all over Europe, and justly reputed the master-piece of Sir Christopher Wren. There is not a beauty, of which the plan would admit, that is not to be found here in its greatest perfection.

(Earl-Henry Bennet)

While these churches, and other public buildings, were going forward under the direction of Sir Christopher Wren, king Charles did not confine his improvements to England alone, but commanded Sir William Bruce, bart. Grand Master of Scotland, to rebuild the palace of Holyrood-house at Edinburgh; which was accordingly executed by that architect in the best Augustan stile.

During the prosecution of the great works above described, the private business of the Society was not neglected, but lodges were held at different places, and many new ones constituted, to which the best architects resorted.

In 1674, the Earl of Rivers resigned the office of Grand Master, and was succeeded by George Villiers, Duke of Buckingham. He left the care of the brethren to his wardens, and Sir Christopher Wren, who still continued to act as deputy. In 1679, the Duke resigned in favor of Henry Bennett, Earl of Arlington. Though this nobleman was too deeply engaged in state affairs to attend to the duties of masonry, the lodges continued to meet under his sanction, and many respectable gentlemen joined the fraternity.

On the death of the king in 1685, James II succeeded to the throne; during whose reign the fraternity was much neglected. The Earl of Arlington dying this year, the lodges met in communication, and elected Sir Christopher Wren Grand Master, who appointed Gabriel Cibber and Mr. Edward Strong his wardens. Masonry continued in a declining state for many years, and a few lodges only occasionally met in different places.

At the Revolution, the Society was so much reduced in the south of England, that no more than seven regular lodges met in London and its suburbs, of which two only were worthy of notice; the old lodge of St. Paul's, over which Sir Christopher had presided during the building of that structure; and a lodge at St. Thomas's-hospital, Southwark, over which Sir Robert Clayton, then Lord mayor of London, presided during the rebuilding of that hospital.

King William having been privately initiated into masonry in 1695, approved the choice of Sir Christopher Wren as Grand Master, and honored the lodges with his royal sanction; particularly one at Hampton Court, at which it is said his majesty frequently presided during the building of the new part of that palace. Kensington palace was built during this reign, under the direction of Sir Christopher; as were also Chelsea hospital, and the palace of Greenwich; the latter of which had been recently converted into a hospital for seamen, and finished after the design of Inigo Jones.

At a general assembly and feast of the masons in 1697, many noble and eminent brethren were present; and among the rest, Charles Duke of Richmond and Lenox, who was at that time master of a lodge at Chichester. His grace was proposed and elected Grand Master for the following year, and having engaged Sir Christopher Wren to act as his deputy, he appointed Edward Strong senior and Edward Strong junior his wardens. His grace continued in office only one year, when he was succeeded by Sir Christopher, who continued at the head of the fraternity till the death of the king in 1702.

During the following reign, masonry made no considerable progress. Sir Christopher's age and infirmities drawing off his attention from the duties of his office, the lodges decreased, and the annual festivals were entirely neglected. The old lodge at St. Paul, and a few others, continued to meet regularly, but consisted of few members. To increase their numbers, a proposition was made, and afterwards agreed to; THAT THE PRIVILEGES OF MASONRY SHOULD NO LONGER BE RESTRICTED TO OPERATIVE MASONS, BUT EXTEND TO MEN OF VARIOUS PROFESSIONS, PROVIDING THEY WERE REGULARLY APPROVED AND INITIATED INTO THE ORDER. In consequence of this resolution, many new regulations took place, and the Society once more rose into notice and esteem.

History of the Revival of Masonry in the South of England

On the accession of George I., the masons in London and its environs, finding themselves deprived of Sir Christopher Wren, and their annual meetings discontinued, resolved to cement under a new Grand Master, and to revive the communications and annual festivals of the Society. With this view, the lodges at the Goose and Gridiron in St. Paul's Church-yard, the Crown in Parker's-lane near Drury-lane, the Apple-tree tavern in Charles-street Covent-garden, and the Rummer and Grapes Tavern in Channel-row Westminster, the only four lodges in being in the south of England at that time, with some other old brethren, met at the Apple-tree tavern above mentioned in February 1717;

(King George I)

and having voted the oldest master-mason then present into the chair, constituted themselves a Grand Lodge pro tempore in due form. At this meeting it was resolved to revive the quarterly communications of the fraternity; and to hold the next annual assembly and feast on the 24th of June, at the Goose and Gridiron in St. Paul's Church-yard, (in compliment to the oldest lodge, which then met there), for the purpose of electing a Grand Master among themselves, till they should have the honor of a noble brother at their head. Accordingly, on St. John the Baptist's day 1717, in the third year of the reign of king George I. the assembly and feast were held at the said house; when the oldest Master-mason, and Master of a lodge, having taken the chair, a list of proper candidates for the office of Grand Master was produced: and the names being separately proposed, the brethren, by a great majority of hands, elected Mr. Anthony Sayer Grand Master of masons for the ensuing year; who was forthwith invested by the said oldest Master, installed by the Master of the oldest lodge, and duly congratulated by the assembly, who paid him homage. The Grand Master then entered on the duties of his office, appointed his wardens, and commanded the brethren of the four lodges to meet him and his wardens quarterly in communication, enjoining them at the same time to recommend to all the fraternity a punctual attendance on the next annual assembly and feast.

Amongst a variety of regulations which were proposed and agreed to at this meeting, was the following: "That the privilege of assembling as masons, which had hitherto been unlimited, should be vested in certain lodges or assemblies of masons convened in certain places; and that every lodge to be hereafter convened, except the four old lodges at this time existing, should be legally authorized to act by a warrant from the Grand Master for the time being, granted to certain individuals by petition, with the consent and approbation of the Grand Lodge in communication; and that without such warrant no lodge should be hereafter deemed regular or constitutional." In consequence of this regulation, some new lodges were soon after convened in different parts of London and its environ, and the masters and wardens of these lodges were commanded to attend the meetings of the Grand Lodge, make a regular report of their proceedings, and transmit to the Grand Master, from time to time, a copy of any bye-laws they might form for their own government; that no laws established among them might be contrary to, or subversive of, the general regulations by which the fraternity had been long governed.

(Anthony Sayer)

In compliment to the brethren of the four old lodges, by whom the Grand Lodge was then formed, it was resolved, "That every privilege which they collectively enjoyed by virtue of their immemorial rights, they should still continue to enjoy; and that now law, rule, or regulation to be hereafter made or passed in Grand Lodge, should deprive them of such privilege, or encroach on any landmark which was at that time established as the standard of masonic government." When this resolution was confirmed, the old masons in the metropolis, agreeably to the resolutions of the brethren at large, vested all their inherent privileges as individuals in the four old lodges, in trust that they would never suffer the old charges and ancient landmarks to be infringed. The four old lodges then agreed to extend their patronage to every new lode which should hereafter be constituted according to the new regulations of the Society; and while they acted in conformity to the ancient constitutions of the order, to admit their Masters and Wardens to share with them all the privileges of the Grand Lodge, excepting precedence of rank.

Matters being thus amicably adjusted, all the brethren of the four old lodges considered their attendance on the future communications of the Society as unnecessary, and therefore trusted implicitly to their Masters and Wardens, resting satisfied that no measure of importance would ever be adopted without their approbation. The officers of the old lodges, however, soon began to discover, that the new lodges, being equally represented with them at the communications, would, in process of time, so far out-number the old ones, as to have it in their power, by a majority, to subvert the privileges of the original masons of England, which had been centered in the four old lodges: they therefore, with the concurrence of the brethren at large, very wisely formed a code of laws for the future government of the Society, and annexed thereto a conditional clause, which the Grand Master for the time being, his successors, and the Master of every lodge to be hereafter constituted, were bound to preserve inviolable in all time coming. To commemorate this circumstance, it has been customary, ever since that time, for the Master of the oldest lodge to attend every Grand Installation; and taking precedence of all present, the Grand Master only accepted, to deliver the book of the original constitutions to the new installed Grand Master, on his promising obedience to the ancient charges and general regulations.

By the above prudent precaution of our ancient brethren, the original constitutions were established as the basis of all future masonic jurisdiction in the south of England; and the ancient land-marks, as they are emphatically styled, or the boundaries set up as checks to innovation, were carefully secured against the attacks of future invaders. The four old lodges, in consequence of the above compact, in which they considered themselves as a distinct party, continued to act by their original authority; and so far from surrendering any of their rights, had them ratified and confirmed by the whole fraternity in Grand Lodge assembled. No regulations of the Society which might hereafter take place could therefore operate with respect to those lodges, if such regulations were contrary to, or subversive of, the original constitutions by which they were governed; and while their proceedings were conformable to those constitutions, no power known in masonry could legally deprive them of any right which they had ever enjoyed.

(Theophilus Desaguliers)

The necessity of fixing the original constitutions as the standard by which all future laws in the Society are to be regulated, was so clearly understood by the whole fraternity at this time, that it was established as an unerring rule, at every installation, public and private, to make the Grand Master, and the Masters and Wardens of every lodge, engage to support these constitutions; to which also every mason was bound by the strongest ties at initiation. Whoever acknowledges the universality of masonry to be its highest glory must admit the propriety of this conduct; for were no standard fixed for the government of the Society, masonry might be exposed to perpetual variations, which would effectually destroy all the good effects that have hitherto resulted from its universality and extended progress.

During the administration of Mr. Sayer, the Society made no very rapid progress. Several brethren joined the old lodges; but only two new lodges were constituted.

Mr. Sayer was succeeded in 1718 by George Payne Esq., who was particularly assiduous in recommending a strict observance of the communications. He collected many valuable manuscripts on the subject of masonry, and earnestly desired that the brethren would bring to the Grand Lodge any old writings or records concerning the fraternity, to shew the usages of ancient times. In consequence of this general intimation, several old copies of the Gothic constitutions were produced, arranged, and digested.

On the 24th of June 1719, another assembly and feast was held at the Goose and Gridiron before mentioned, when Dr. Desaguliers was unanimously elected Grand Master. At this feast, the old, regular, and peculiar toasts or health's of the free-masons were introduced; and from this time we may date the rise of free-masonry on its present plan in the South of England. The lodges, which had considerably increased by the vigilance of the Grand Master, were visited by many old masons who had long neglected the craft, several noblemen were initiated, and a number of new lodges constituted.

(Sir William Robinson)

At an assembly and feast held at the Goose and Gridiron on the 24th June 1720, Theophilus Desaguliers was re-elected Grand Master, and under his mild but vigilant administration the lodges continued to flourish.

This year, at some of the private lodges, to the irreparable loss of the fraternity, several valuable manuscripts, concerning their lodges, regulations, charges, secrets, and usages, (particularly one written by Mr. Nicholas Stone, the warden under Inigo Jones,) were too hastily burnt by some scrupulous brethren, who were alarmed at the intended publication of the masonic constitutions.

At a quarterly communication held this year at the Goose and Gridiron on the festival of St. John the Evangelist, it was agreed, That, in future, the new Grand Master shall be named and proposed to the Grand Lodge some time before the feast; and if approved, and present, he shall be saluted as Grand Master elect: and that every Grand Master, when he is installed, shall have the sole power of appointing his deputy and wardens, according to ancient custom.

At a Grand Lodge held in ample form on Lady-day 1721, Brother Payne proposed for his successor, John, Duke of Montague, at that time master of a lodge. His grace, being present, received the compliments of the lodge. The brethren expressed great joy at the prospect of being once more patronized by the nobility; and unanimously agreed, that the next assembly and feast should be held at Stationers'-hall; and that a proper number of stewards should be appointed to provide the entertainment; but Mr. Josiah Villeneau, an upholder in the Borough, generously undertook the whole management of the business, and received the thanks of the Society for his attention.

While masonry was thus spreading its influence over the southern part of the kingdom, it was not neglected in the North. The General Assembly, or Grand Lodge, at York, continued regularly to meet as heretofore. In 1705, under the direction of Sir George Tempest bart., then Grand Master, several lodges met, and many worthy brethren were initiated in York and its neighborhood. Sir George being succeeded by the right hon. Robert Benson, Lord Mayor of York, a number of meetings of the fraternity was held at different times in that city, and the grand feast during his mastership is said to have been very brilliant. Sir William Robinson succeeded Mr. Benson in the office of Grand Master, and the fraternity seems to have considerably increased in the North under his auspices. He was succeeded by Sir Walter Hawkesworth bart., who governed the Society with great credit. At the expiration of his mastership, Sir George Tempest was elected a second time Grand Master; and from the time of his election in 1714 to 1725, the Grand Lodge continued regularly to assemble at York under the direction of Charles Fairfax Esq. Sir Walter Hawkesworth bart., Edward Bell Esq. Charles Bathurst Esq. Edward Thomson Esq. M. P. John Johnson M. D. and John Marsden Esq., all of whom, in rotation, during the above period, regularly filled the office of Grand Master in the North of England.

From this account, which is authenticated by the books of the Grand Lodge at York, it appears, that the revival of masonry in the South of England did not interfere with the proceedings of the fraternity in the North. For a series of years the most perfect harmony subsisted between the two Grand Lodges, and private lodges flourished in both parts of the kingdom under their separate jurisdiction. The only distinction which the Grand Lodge in the North appears to have retained after the revival of masonry in the South is in the title which they claim, viz., *The Grand Lodge of all England;* while the Grand Lodge in the South passes only under the denomination of *The Grand Lodge of England.* The latter, on account of its situation, being encouraged by some of the principal nobility, soon acquired consequence and reputation; while the former, restricted to fewer, though not less respectable, members, seemed gradually to decline. Till within these few years, however, the authority of the Grand Lodge at York was never challenged; on the contrary, every mason in the kingdom held it in the highest veneration, and considered himself bound by the charges which originally sprung from that assembly. To be ranked as descendants of the original York masons, was the glory and boast of the brethren in almost every country where masonry was established; and, from the prevalence and universality of the idea, that in the city of York masonry was first established by charter, the masons of England have received tribute from the first states in Europe.

History of Masonry from its Revival in the South of England till the Death of King George I

he reputation of the Society being now established, many noblemen and gentlemen of the first rank desired to be received into the lodges, which had increased considerably during the administration of Mr. Payne. The duties of masonry were found to be a pleasing relaxation from the fatigue of business; and in the lodge, uninfluenced by politics or party, a happy union was effected among the most respectable characters in the kingdom.

On the 24th of June 1721, Grand Master Payne and his wardens, with the former grand officers, and the masters and wardens of twelve lodges, met the Grand Master elect at the Queen's Arms Tavern in St. Paul's Church-yard, where the Grand Lodge was opened in ample form. Having confirmed the proceedings of the last Grand Lodge, several gentlemen were initiated into masonry at the request of the Duke of Montague; and, among the rest, Philip Lord Stanhope, afterwards Earl of Chesterfield. From the Queen's Arms the Grand Lodge marched in procession in their clothing to Stationers'-hall in Ludgate-street, where they joyfully received by one hundred and fifty brethren, properly clothed. The Grand Master having made the first procession round the hall took an affectionate leave of his brethren; and, being returned to his place, proclaimed the Duke of Montague his successor for the ensuing year. The general regulations compiled by Mr. Payne in 1721, and compared with the ancient records and immemorial usages of the fraternity, were read, and met with general approbation; after which Dr. Desaguliers delivered an elegant oration on the subject of masonry.

Soon after his election, the Grand Master gave convincing proofs of his zeal and attention, by commanding Dr. Desaguliers and James Anderson, men of genius and education, to revise, arrange, and digest the Gothic constitutions, old charges, and general regulations. This task they faithfully executed; and at the ensuing Grand Lodge held at the Queen's Arms St. Paul's Church-yard on the 27th of December 1721, being the festival of St. John the Evangelist, they presented the same for approbation. A committee of fourteen learned brothers was then appointed to examine the manuscript and to make their report; and on this occasion several very entertaining lectures were delivered and much useful information given by some old brethren.

At a Grand Lodge held at the Fountain Tavern in the Strand, in ample form, on the 25th March 1722, the committee reported, that they had perused the manuscript, containing the history, charges, regulations, Etc. of masonry, and, after some amendments, had approved thereof. The Grand Lodge ordered the whole to be prepared for the press, and printed with all possible expedition. This order was strictly obeyed, and in little more than two years the Book of Constitutions appeared in print, under the following title: "The Book of Constitutions of the Free Masons: containing the History, Charges, Regulations, Etc. of that Most Ancient and Right Worshipful Fraternity. For the Use of the Lodges" London, 1723.

In January 1722-3, the Duke of Montague resigned in favor of the Duke of Wharton, who was very ambitious to attain the office. His grace's resignation proceeded from the motive of reconciling the brethren to this nobleman, who had incurred their displeasure, by having convened, in opposition to the resolutions of the Grand Lodge, on the 25th of March, an irregular assembly of masons at Stationers'-hall, on the festival of St. John the Baptist, in order to get himself elected as Grand Master. The Duke of Wharton, fully sensible of the impropriety of his conduct, publicly acknowledged his error; and promising in future a strict conformity and obedience to the resolutions of the Society, was, with the general consent of the brethren, approved as Grand Master elect for the ensuing year. His grace was regularly invested and installed on the 17th of January 1722-3 by the Grand Master, and congratulated by upwards of twenty-five lodges, who were present in the Grand Lodge on that day. The diligence and attention of the Duke of Wharton to the duties of his office soon recovered and established his reputation in the Society; while under his patronage masonry made a considerable progress in the South of England. During his presidency, the office of Grand Secretary was first established, and William Cowper Esq., being appointed, that gentleman executed the duties of the department several years.

The Duke of Buccleugh succeeded the Duke of Wharton in 1723. This nobleman was no less attached to masonry than his predecessor. Being absent on the annual festival, he was installed by proxy at Merchant-taylors'-hall, in presence of 400 masons.

His grace was succeeded in the following year by the Duke of Richmond, under whose administration the Committee of Charity was instituted. Lord Paisley, afterwards Earl of Abercorn, being active in promoting this new establishment, was elected Grand Master in the end of the year 1725. Being in the country at the time, his Lordship was installed by proxy. During his absence, Dr. Desaguliers, who had been appointed his deputy, was very attentive to the duties of his office, by visiting the lodges, and diligently promoting masonry. On his Lordship's return to town, the Earl of Inchiquin was proposed to succeed him, and was elected in February 1726. The Society now flourished in town and country, and under the patronage of this nobleman the Art was propagated with considerable success. This period was rendered remarkable, by the brethren of Wales first uniting under the banner of the Grand Lodge of London. In Wales are some venerable remains of ancient masonry, and many stately ruins of castles, executed in the Gothic style, which evidently demonstrate that the fraternity must have met with encouragement in that part of the island in former times. Soon after this happy union, the office of Provincial Grand Master was instituted, and the first deputation granted by Earl Inchiquin, on the 10th of May 1727, to Hugh Warburton Esq. for North Wales; and on the 24th of June following, to Sir Edward Mansell bart., for South Wales. The lodges in the country now began to increase, and deputations were granted to several gentlemen, to hold the office of Provincial Grand Master in different parts of England, as well as in some places abroad where lodges had been constituted by

English masons. During the Earl of Inchiquin's mastership, a warrant was issued for opening a new lodge at Gibraltar.

Among the variety of noble edifices which were finished during the presidency of this nobleman, was that excellent structure the church of St. Martin in the Fields; the foundation stone of which, it being a royal parish church, was laid, in the king's name, on the 29th of March 1721, by brother Gibb the architect, in presence of the Lord Almoner, the surveyor general, and a large company of the brethren.

History of Masonry in England during the Reign of King George II

he first Grand Lodge after the accession of George II, to the throne was held at the Devil Tavern, Temple-bar, on the 24th of June 1727; at which were present, the Earl of Inchquin, Grand Master, his officers, and the Masters and Wardens of forty lodges. At this meeting it was resolved to extend the privilege of voting in Grand Lodge to Past Grand Wardens; that privilege having been heretofore restricted to Past Grand Masters, by resolution of 21st November 1724; and to Past Deputies, by another resolution of 28th February 1726.

The Grand Master having been obliged to take a journey into Ireland before the expiration of his office, his Lordship transmitted a letter to William Cowper Esq. his deputy, requesting him to convene a Grand Lodge for the purpose of nominating Lord Colerane Grand Master for the ensuing year. A Grand Lodge was accordingly convened on the 19th of December 1727, when his Lordship was regularly proposed Grand Master elect, and being unanimously approved, on the 27th of the same month was duly invested with the ensigns of his high office at a grand feast at Mercers'-hall in the presence of a numerous company of his brethren. His Lordship attended two communications during his mastership and seemed to pay considerable attention to the duties of his office. He constituted several new lodges and granted a deputation to hold a lodge in

St Bernard's Street in Madrid. At the last Grand Lodge under his Lordship's auspices, Dr. Desaguliers moved, that the ancient office of Stewards might be revived, to assist the Grand Wardens in preparing the feast; when it was agreed that their appointment should be annual, and the number restricted to twelve.

Lord Kingston succeeds Lord Colerane, and was invested with the ensigns of his high office on the 27th of December 1728, at a grand feast held a Mercer's-hall. his Lordship's zeal and attachment for the fraternity were very conspicuous, not only by his regular attendance on the communications, but by his generous present to the Grand Lodge, of a curious pedestal, a rich cushion with gold knobs and fringes, a velvet bag, and a new jewel set in gold for the use of the Secretary. During his Lordship's administration, the Society flourished at home and abroad. Many lodges were constituted and among the rest, deputation was granted to George Pomfret Esq. authorizing him to open a new lodge at Bengal. This gentlemen first introduced masonry into the English settlement in India, where it has since made such rapid progress, that, with these few years, upwards of fifty lodges, have been constituted there, eleven of which are now held in Bengal. The annual remittances to the charity and public funds of the Society from this and other factories of the East India Company amount to a considerable sum.

At the Grand Lodge held a Devil Tavern on the 27th of December 1729, Natheniel

(Lord Kingston)

Blackerby Esq., the Deputy Grand Master, being in the chair, in the absence of Lord Kingston, produced a letter from his Lordship, authorizing him to propose the Duke of Norfolk Grand Master for the ensuing year. This nomination meeting with general approbation, the usual compliments were paid to his grace, and he was saluted Grand Master elect. At an assembly and feast at Merchant-taylors'-hall on the 29th of January following his grace was duly installed, according to ancient form, in the presence of a numerous and brilliant company of masons. His grace's absence in Italy soon after his election, prevented him from attending more than one communication during his mastership; but the business of the Society was diligently executed by Mr. Blackerly his Deputy, on whom the whole management had devolved. Among other signal proofs of his grace's attachment to the Society, he transmitted from Venice to England the following noble patents for the use of the Grand Lodge:

1. Twenty pounds to the charity.

2. A Large folio book, of the finest writing paper, for the records of Grand Lodge, richly bound in Turkey and gilt, with a curious frontispiece in vellum, containing the arms of Norfolk, amply displayed, and a Latin inscription of the family titles, with the arms of masonry emblazoned.

3. A sword of state for the Grand Master, being the old trusty sword of Gustavus Adolphus king of Sweden, which was next wore by his brave successor in ware Bernard Duke of Saxe-Weimar, with both their names on the blade, and further enriched with the arms of Norfolk in silver on the scabbard. For these presents his grace was voted the public thanks of the Society.

It is not surprising that masonry should flourish under so respectable a banner. His grace appointed a Provincial Grand Lodge at New Jersey in America. A provincial patent was also made out under his auspices for Bengal. From this period we may date the commencement of the consequence and reputation of the society in Europe; as daily application were made for establishing new lodges, and the most respectable character of the age desired their names to be enrolled in our records.

The Duke of Norfolk was succeeded by Lord Lovel, afterwards Earl of Leicester, who was installed at Merchers'-hall on the 29th of March 1731. His Lordship being at the time much indisposed with an <u>ague</u> *(A fever or shivering fit.)*, was obliged to withdraw soon after his installation. Lord Colerane, however, acted as proxy during the feast. On the 14th of May, the first Grand Lodge after Lord Lovel's election was held at the Rose Tavern in Mary-le-bone, when it was voted that in future all past Grand Masters and their deputies shall be admitted members of the quarterly Committees of Charity, and that every committee shall have power to vote five pounds for the relief of any distressed mason; but no larger sum, without the consent of the Grand Lodge in Communication being first had and obtained. This resolution is still in force.

During the presidency of Lord Lovel, the nobility made a point of honoring the Grand Lodge with their presence. The Dukes of Norfolk and Richmond, the Earl of Inchiquin, and Lords Colrane and Montagu, with several other persons of distinction, seldom failed to give their attendance; and

(Viscount Montagu)

though the subscriptions from the lodges were inconsiderable, the Society was enabled to relieve many worthy objects with small sums. As an encouragement to gentlemen to accept the office of steward, it was ordered that in future each Steward should have the privilege of nominating his successor at every annual grand feast. The most remarkable event of Lord Lovel's administration was the initiation of Francis Duke of Lorraine, afterward emperor of Germany. By virtue of a deputation from his Lordship, a lodge was held at The Hague, where his highness was received into the first two degrees of masonry. At this lodge, Phillip Stanhope Earl of Chesterfield, then ambassador there, presided; Mr. Strickland, Esq., acted as Deputy and Mr. Benjamin Hadley with a Dutch brother as

Wardens. His highness coming to England in the same year was advanced to the third degree at an occasional lodge convened for the purpose at Houghton-hall in Norfolk, the seat of Sir Robert Walpole; as was also Thomas Pelham, Duke of Newcastle.

The Society being now in a very flourishing state, deputations were granted from England, for establishing lodges in Russia and Spain.

Lord Viscount Montagu was installed Grand Master at an assembly and feast at Merchant-Taylors'-hall on the 19th April 1732. Among the distinguished personages present on that Occasion were the Dukes of Montagu and Richmond; the Earl of Strathmore; and Lords Colerane, Teynham and Carpenter; Sir Francis Drake and Sir William Keith barts., and above four hundred other brethren. At this meeting it was first proposed to have a country feast and agreed that the brethren should dine together at Hampstead on the 24th June, for the purpose cards of invitation were sent to several of the nobility. On the day appointed, the Grand Master and his Officers, the Dukes of Norfolk and Richmond, Earl of Strathmore, Lord Carpenter and Teynham, and above a hundred other brethren, met at the Spikes at Hampstead, where an elegant dinner was provided. Soon after the dinner, the Grand Master resigned the chair to Lord Teynham, and from that time till the expiration of his office never attended another meeting of the Society. His Lordship granted a deputation for constituting a lodge a Valenciennes in French Flanders, and another for opening a new lodge at the Hotel de Buffy in Paris. Several other lodges were also constituted under his Lordship's auspices; but the Society was particularly indebted to Thomas Barton Esq. the Deputy Grand Master, who was very attentive to the duties of his office, and carefully superintended the government of the craft.

The Earl of Stratmore succeeded Lord Montagu in the office of Grand Master, and being in Scotland at the time, was installed by proxy at an assembly at Mercers'-hall on the 7th of June 1733. On the 13th December, a Grand Lodge was held at the Devil tavern, at which his Lordship and his officers, the Earl of Crawford, Sir Robert Mansel, a number of Past Grand

Officers, and the Masters and Wardens of fifty-three lodges were present. Several regulations were confirmed at this meeting respecting the Committee of Charity; and it was determined, that al complaints, in future to be brought before the Grand Lodge, previously be examined by the Committee, and from thence referred to the next Communication.

The history of the Society at this period afford no remarkable incident to record. Some considerable donations were collected, and distributed among distressed masons, to encourage the settlement of a new colony which had been just established in Georgia in America. Lord Strathmore showed every attention to the duties of his office, and regularly attended the meetings of Grand Lodge; under his auspices the Society flourished at home and aboard, and many genteel presents were received from the East Indies. Eleven German masons applied for authority to open a new lodge in Hamburgh under the patronage of the Grand Lodge of England, for which purpose his Lordship was pleased to grant a deputation; and soon after, several other lodges were constituted in Holland under the English banner.

The Earl of Strathmore was succeeded by the Earl of Crawford, who was installed at Mercers'-hall on the 30th March 1734. Public affairs attracting his Lordship's attention, the Communications during his administration were neglected. After eleven months' vacation, however, a Grand Lodge was convened, at which his Lordship attended and apologized for his long absence. To atone for past omission, he commanded two communications to be held in little more than six weeks. The Dukes of Richmond and Buccleugh, the Earl of Balcarras, Lord Weymouth, and other eminent persons, honored the Grand Lodge with their presence during the Earl of Crawford's presidency.

The most remarkable proceedings of the Society at this period related to a new edition of the Book of Constitutions, which Brother James Anderson was ordered to prepare for the press; and which made its appearance in January 1738, considerably enlarged and improved.

Among the new regulation which took place under the administration of Lord Crawford, was the following; that if any lodge with the bills of mortality shall cease to meet during twelve calendar months, the said lodge shall be erased out of the list, and if re-instated, shall lose its former rank. Some additional privileges were granted to the Stewards, in consequence of an application for that purpose; and to encourage gentlemen to serve the office, it was agreed, that in future all Grand Officers, the Grand Master excepted, shall be elected out of that body. A few resolutions also passed respecting illegal conventions of masons, at which it was reported many persons had been initiated into masonry on small and unworthy considerations.

(Duke of Richmond)

The Earl of Crawford seems to have made the first encroachment on the jurisdiction of the Grand Lodge in the city of York, by constituting two lodges within their district; and by granting, without their consent, three deputations, one for Lancashire, a second for Durham, and a third for Northumberland. This circumstance the Grand Lodge of York highly resented, and ever after viewed the proceeding of the brethren in the metropolis with a jealous eye. All friendly intercourse ceased, and the York masons from that moment considered their interest distinct from the masons under the Grand Lodge in London.

Lord Weymouth succeed the Earl of Crawford, and was installed at Mercers'-hall on the 17th April 1735, in presence of the Dukes of Richmond and Athol; the Earls of Crawford, Winchelsea, Balcarras, Wemys and Loudon; the marquis of Beamont; Lords Catheart and Vere Bertie; Sir Cecil Wray and Sir Edward Mansel barts., and a splendid company of other brethren. Several lodges were constituted during Lord Weymouth's presidency; and among the rest the Stewards' Lodges. His Lordship granted a deputation to hold a lodge at the seat of the Duke of Richmond at Aubigny in France; and, under his patronage masonry extended considerably in foreign countries. He issued warrants to open a new lodge at Lisbon, and another at Savannah in Georgia; and, by his special appointment, provincial patents were made out for South America, and Gambay in West Africa.

Lord Weymouth never honored any of the Communications with his presence during his presidency; but this <u>amission</u> (*Deprivation; loss*) was less noticed on account of the vigilance and attention of his deputy, John Ward, Esq., after Lord viscount Dudley and Ward, who applied with the utmost anxiety to every business which concerned the interest and well-being of the Society.

One circumstance occurred while Lord Weymouth was Grand Master; of which it may be necessary to take notice. The twelve Stewards, with Sir Robert Lawley, Master of the Stewards' Lodge, at their head, appeared for the first time in their new badges at a Grand Lodge held at the Devil Tavern on the 11th of December 1735. On this occasion they were not permitted to vote as individuals; but it being afterwards proposed that they should enjoy this privilege, and that the Stewards' Lodge should in future be represented in Grand Lodge by twelve members, many lodges objected to the measure as an encroachment on the privilege of every lodge which had been previously constituted. When the motion was put up for confirmation, such a disturbance ensued, that the Grand Lodge was obliged to be closed before the sentiments of the brethren could be collected on the subject. Of late years the punctilio has been waved, and the twelve Stewards are now permitted to vote in every Communication as individuals.

The Earl of Louden succeeded Lord Weymouth, and was installed Grand Master at Fishmongers'-hall on the 15th of April 1736. The Dukes of Richmond; the Earls of Albermarle and Crawford, Lords Harcout Erksine and Southwell; Mr Anstis garter king at arms, Mr. Brady lion king of arms, and a numerous company of other brethren, were present on the occasion. His Lordship constituted several lodges and granted three provincial deputation during his presidency, viz., one for

New England, another for South Carolina, and a third for Cape Coast Castle in Africa.

The Earl of Darnley was elected Grand Master, and duly installed at Fishmonger's-hall on the 28th of April 1737, in presence of the Duke of Richmond, the Earls of Crawford and Wemsys, Lord Gray, and many other respectable brethren. The most remarkable event of the his Lordship's administration, was the initiation of the late Frederick Prince of Wales, his present majesty's father, at an occasional lodge convened for the purpose at the palace of Kew, over which Dr. Desaguliers presided as Master. Lord Baltimore, Col. Lumley, the Hon. Major Madden, and several other brethren, were present. His royal highness was advanced to the second degree at the same lodge; and at another lodge, convened at the same place soon after, raised to the degree of a master mason.

(Fredrick the Great)

There cannot be a better proof of the flourishing state of the Society at this time, than by adverting to the respectable appearance of the brethren in Grand Lodge, at which that Grand Master never failed to attend. Upwards of sixty lodges were represented at every Communication during Lord Darnley's administration, and more Provincial patents were issued by him, than by any of his predecessors. Deputations were granted for Montserrat, Geneva, the Circle of Upper Saxony, the Coast of Africa, New York, and the Islands of America.

The Marquis of Carnarvon, afterwards Duke of Chanos, succeeded Lord Darnley in the office of Grand Master, and was duly invested and congratulated at an assembly and feast held at Fishmonger's-hall on the 27th of April 1738. At this assembly, the Duke of Richmond; the Earls of Inchiquin,

Loudon and Kintore; Lords Colerane and Gray; and a numerous company of other brethren, were present. The marquis showed every attention to the Society during his presidency, and in testimony of his esteem, presented to the Grand Lodge a gold jewel for the use of the Secretary; the device, two cross pens in a knot; the knot and points of the pens being curiously enameled. Two deputations for the office Provincial Grand Master were granted by his Lordship; one for the Caribbee Islands and the other for the West Riding of Yorkshire. This latter appointment was considered as another encroachment on the jurisdiction of the Grand Lodge of York, and so widened the original breach between the brethren in the North and the South of England, that from thenceforward all future correspondence between the Grand Lodges totally ceased.

On the 15th of August 1738, Frederick the Great afterwards King of Prussia, was initiated into masonry, in a lodge in Brunswick, under the Scots constitution, being at that time Prince Royal. So highly did he approve of the initiation, that, on his accession to the throne, he commanded a Grand Lodge to be formed at Berlin, and for that purpose obtained a patent from Edinburgh. Thus was masonry regularly established in Prussia, and under that sanction it has flourished there ever since.

No other remarkable occurrence is recorded to have happened during the administration of the marquis of Carnarvon, except a proposition for establishing a plan to appropriate a portion of the charity to place out the sons of masons apprentices, which, after a long debate in Grand Lodge, was rejected.

Some disagreeable altercations arose in the Society about this period. A number of dissatisfied brethren separated themselves from the regular lodges, and held meetings in different places for the purpose of initiating persons into masonry, contrary to the laws of the Grand Lodge. These seceding brethren taking advantage of the breach which had been made in the friendly intercourse between the Grand Lodges of London and York, on being censured for their conduct, immediately assumed, without authority, the character of York masons. The measures adopted to check them stopped their progress for some time; till, taking advantage of the general murmur spread abroad on account of innovations that had been introduced, and which seemed to authorize an omission of, and a variation in the ancient ceremonies, they rose again into notice. This imprudent measure of the regular lodges offended many old masons; but, through the mediation of John Ward Esq., afterwards Lord Viscount Dudley and Ward, matters were accommodated, and the brethren seemingly reconciled. This, however, proved only a temporary suspension of hostilities, for the same soon broke out anew, and gave rise to commotions, which afterward materially interrupted the peace of the Society.

Lord Raymond succeeded the Marquis of Carnarvon in May 1739, and under his Lordship's auspices the lodges were numerous and respectable. Notwithstanding the flourishing state of the Society, irregularities continued to prevail, and several worthy brethren, still adverse to the encroachments on the established system of the institution, were highly disgusted at the proceeding of the regular lodges. Complaints were preferred at every succeeding committee, and the communications fully employed in adjusting differences and reconciling animosities. More sessions taking place, it became necessary to pass votes of censure on the mist refractory and to enact laws to discourage irregular associations of the fraternity. This brought the power of the Grand Lodge in question; and in opposition to the laws which had been established in that assembly, lodges were formed with any legal warrant, and persons initiated into masonry for small and unworthy considerations. To disappoint the views of these deluded brethren, and to distinguish the persons initiated by them the Grand Lodge readily acquiesced in the imprudent measures which the regular masons had adopted, measures which even the urgency of the case could not warrant. Though this had the intended effect, it gave rise to a new subterfuge. The brethren who had seceded from the regular lodges immediately announced independency, and assumed the appellation of ancient masons. They propagated an opinion, that the ancient tenets and practices of masonry were preserved by them; and that the regular lodges, being composed of modern masons, had adopted new plans, and were not to be considered as acting under the old establishment. To counteract the regulations of the Grand Lodge, they instituted a new Grand Lodge in London, professedly on the ancient system, and under that assumed banner constituted several new lodges. There irregular proceeding they pretended to justify under feigned sanction of the *Ancient York Constitution* and many gentlemen of reputation were introduced among them, so that their lodges daily increased. Without authority for the Grand Lodge of York, or from any other established power of masonry, they persevered in the measures they had adopted, formed committees, held communications, and appointed annual feasts. Under the false <u>appellation</u> *(A name or title.)* of the York banner, they gained the countenance of the Scotch and Irish masons, who, placing implicit confidence in the representations made to them, heartily joined in condemning the measures of

(The Earl of Morton)

the regular lodges in London, as tending, in their opinion, to introduce novelties into the Society, and to subvert the original plan of the institution. The irregular masons in London, having acquired an establishment, noblemen of both kingdoms honored them with their patronage for some time, and many respectable names and lodges were added to this list. Of late years the fallacy has been detected, and they have not been so successful; several of their best members have renounced their banner and come under the patronage of the Grand Lodge of England. It is much to be wished, in that a general union among all the masons in the kingdom could be affected, and we are happy to hear that such a measure is likely soon to be accomplished, through the mediation of a Royal Brother at present abroad.

During the presidency of Lord Raymond, no considerable addition was made to the list of lodges and communications were seldom honored with the company of the nobility. His Lordship granted only one deputation for a provincial Grand Master during his presidency, viz., for Savoy and Piedmont.

The Earl of Kintore succeeded Lord Raymond in April 1740 and, in imitation of his predecessor, continued to discourage irregularities. His Lordship appointed several provincials: particularly, one for Russia; one for Hamburgh and the Circle of Lower Saxony; one for the West Riding of York, in the room of William Horton Esq., deceased; and one for the island of Barbadoes.

The Earl of Morton was elected on the 19th of March following, and installed with great solemnity the same day at Haberdashers'-hall, in preference of a respectable company of the nobility, foreign ambassadors, and others. Several seasonable laws were passed during this Lordship's mastership, and some regulations made concerning procession and other ceremonies. His Lordship presented a staff of office to the Treasurer, of neat workmanship, blue and tip't with gold; and the Grand Lodge resolved, that this officer should be annually elected, and, with the Secretary and Sword-breaker, *(These weapons were used as off-hand weapons in conjunction with a single-handed sword such as a rapier. As the name implies they were designed to parry, or defend, more effectively than a simple dagger form, typically incorporating a wider guard, and often some other defensive features to better protect the hand as well.)* be permitted to rank in future as a member of Grand Lodge. A large cornelian seal, with the arms of masonry, set in gold, was presented to the Society, at this time, by Brother Vaughan, the Senior Grand Warden; and William Vaughan Esq. was appointed by his Lordship, Provincial Grand Master for North Wales.

Lord Ward succeeded the Earl of Morton in April 1742. His Lordship was well acquainted with the nature and government of the Society having served every office from the Secretary in a private lodge to that of Grand Master. His Lordship lost no time in applying effectual remedies to reconcile the animosities which prevailed; he recommended to his officers, vigilance and care in their different departments; and by his own conduct, set a noble example how the dignity of the Society ought to be supported. Many lodges, which were in a declining state, by his advice, coalesced with other in better circumstances; some, which had been negligent in their attendance on the Communications, after proper admonitions were restored to favor; and others, which persevered in their contumacy, were erased out of the list. Thus his Lordship manifested his regard for the interests of the Society, while his lenity and forbearance were universally admired.

The unanimity and harmony of the lodges seemed to be perfectly restored under his Lordship's administration. The freemasons at Antigua built a large hall in that island for their meetings, and applied to the Grand Lodge for liberty to be styled the Great Lodge of St John's in Antigua, which favor was granted to them in April 1744.

Lord Ward continued two years at the head of the fraternity, during which time he constituted, many lodges, and appointed several Provincial Grand Masters; viz. one for Lancaster, one for North America, and three for the island of Jamaica. He was succeeded by the Earl of Strathmore, during whose administration, being absent the whole time, the care and management of the Society devolved on the other Grand Officers, who carefully studied the general good of the fraternity. His Lordship appointed a Provincial Grand Master for the island of Bermuda.

Lord Cranstoun was elected Grand Master in April 1745, and presided over the fraternity with great reputation two years. Under his auspices masonry flourished, several new lodges were constituted, and one Provincial Grand Master was appointed for Cape Breton and Louisburg. By a resolution of the Grand Lodge at this time it was order, that public procession on feast-days should be discontinued; occasioned by some mock processions, which a few disgusted brethren had formed, in order to burlesque those public appearances.

Lord Byron succeeded Lord Cranstoun, and was installed at Drapers'-hall on the 30th of April 1747. The laws of the Committee of Charity were, by his Lordship's order, revised, printed, and distributed among lodges, and a handsome, contribution to the general charity was received from the lodge at Gibraltar. During five years that is Lordship presided over the fraternity. No diligence was spared to preserve the privileges of masonry inviolate, to redress grievances, and to relieve distress. When business required his Lordship's attendance in country, Fotherly Baker Esq., his Deputy and Secretary Revis, were particularly attentive to the business of the Society. The former was distinguished by his knowledge of the laws and regulations; the latter, by his long and faithful services. Under the auspices of Lord Byron, provincial patents were issued for Denmark and Norway, Pennsylvania, Minorca, and New York.

On the 20th March, 1752, Lord Carysfort accepted the office of Grand Master. The good effects of his Lordship's application to the real interests of the fraternity soon became visible, by the great increase of the public fund. No Grand Officer ever took more pains to preserve, or was more attentive to recommend, order and decorum. He was ready, on all occasions, to visit the lodges in person, and to promote harmony among the members. Dr. Manningham, his Deputy, was no less vigilant in the execution of his duty. He constantly visited the lodges in his Lordship's absence, and used every endeavor to cement union among the

(Lord Byron)

brethren. The whole proceedings of this active officer were conducted with prudence, and his candor and affability gained him universal esteem. The Grand Master's attachment to the Society was so obvious, that the brethren, in testimony of their gratitude for his Lordship's great services, re-elected him on the 3d of April 1753; and during his presidency, provincial patents were issued for Gibraltar, the Bahama Islands, New York, Guernsey, Jersey, Alderney, Sark, and Mann; also for Cornwall, and the counties of Worcester, Gloucester, Salop, Monmouth, and Hereford.

The Marquis of Carnarvon (afterward Duke of Chandos) succeeded Lord Carysfort in March 1754. He began his administration by ordering the Book of Constitutions to be reprinted, under the inspection of a committee, consisting of the Grand Officers, and some other respectable brethren. The Grand Master's zeal and attention to the true interests of the Society were shown on every occasion. He presented to the Grand Lodge, a large silver jewel, gilt, for the use of the Treasurer, being cross keys in a knot, enameled with blue; and gave several other proofs of his attachment.

Soon after the election of the Marquis of Carnarvon, the Grand Lodge took into consideration a complaint against certain brethren, for assembling, without any legal authority, under the denomination of ancient masons; who, as such, considered themselves independent of the Society, and not subject to the laws of Grand Lodge, or to the control of the Grand Master. Dr. Manningham, the Deputy Grand Master, pointed out the necessity of discouraging their meetings, as being contrary to the laws of the Society, and openly subversive of the allegiance due to the Grand Master. On this representation the Grand Lodge resolved, that the meeting of any brethren under the denomination of masons, other than as brethren of the ancient and honorable Society of Free and Accepted Masons established upon the universal system, is inconsistent with the honors and interest of the craft, and a high insult on the Grand Master and the whole body of masons. In consequence of this resolution, fourteen brethren, who were members of a lodge held at the Ben Jonson's head in Pelham-street, Spitalfields, were expelled the Society, and that lodge was ordered to be erased out of the list.

No preceding Grand Master granted so many provincial deputations as the marquis of Carnarvon; in less than two years the following patents were issued;

1. for South Carolina;
2. for South Wales;
3. for Antigua;
4. for all North America where no former provincial was appointed;
5. for Barbadoes, and all other his majesty's islands to the windward of Guadaloupe;
6. for St. Eustatius, Cuba, and St. Martin's, Dutch Caribbean islands in America;
7. for Sicily, and the adjacent islands;
8. for all his majesty's dominions in Germany, with a power to choose their successors; and
9. for the County Palatine of Chester, and the City and County of Chester.

The greater part of these appointments appear to have been mere honorary grants in favor of individuals, few of them having been attended with advantage to the Society.

The marquis of Carnarvon continued to preside over the fraternity till the 18th of May 1757, when he was succeeded by Lord Aberdour; during whose mastership the Grand Lodge voted, among other charities, the sum of fifty pounds to be sent to Germany, to be distributed among such of the soldiers as were masons in prince Ferdinand's army, whether English, Hanoverians, or Hessians. This sum was soon after remitted to General Kingsley for the intended purpose.

Such was the state of masonry during the reign of George II. On the 5th of October 1760, his majesty expired at his palace at Kensington, in the 77th year of his age, and the 34th of his reign. It may be truly said, that this period was the golden era of masonry in England; the sciences were cultivated and improved, the royal art was diligently propagated, and true architecture clearly understood; the fraternity were honored and esteemed; the lodges patronized by exalted characters; and charity, humanity, and benevolence, were the distinguishing characteristics of masons.

History of Masonry in the South of England from the Accession of George III, to the end of the year 1779

n the 6th of October 1760, his present majesty George III was proclaimed. No prince ever ascended the Throne, whose private virtues and amiable character had so justly endeared him to his people. To see a native of England the sovereign of these realms, afforded the most glorious prospect of fixing our happy constitution in church and state on the firmest base. Under such a patron the polite arts could not fail of meeting with every encouragement; and to the honors his majesty it is to be observed, that, since his accession to the throne, by his royal munificence no pains have been spared to explore distant regions in pursuit of useful knowledge, and to diffuse science throughout every part of his dominions.

Masonry now flourished at home and aboard under the English Constitution and Lord Aberdour continued at the head of the fraternity five years, during which time the public festivals and quarterly communications were regularly held. His Lordship equaled any of his predecessors in the number of appointments to the office of Provincial Grand Master, having granted the following deputations:

1. for Antigua and the Leeward Caribbean Islands;
2. for the town of Norwich and county of Norfolk;
3. for the Bahama Islands, in the room of the governor deceased;
4. for Hamburgh and Lower Saxony;
5. for Guadaloupe;
6. for Lancaster;
7. for the province of Georgia;
8. for Canada;
9. for Andalusia, and places adjacent;
10. for Bermuda;
11. for Carolina;
12. for Mosquito Shore;
And 13. for East India.

The second of these appointments, viz. for Norwich, is that by which the Society has been most benefited. By the diligence and attention of the late Edward Bacon Esq. to whom the patent was first granted, the lodges in Norwich and Norfolk considerably increased, and masonry was regularly conducted in that province under his inspection for many years.

Lord Aberdour held the office of Grand Master till the 3d of May 1762, when he was succeeded by Earl Ferrers, during whose presidency nothing remarkable occurred. The Society seems at this time to have lost much of its consequence; the general assemblies and communications not having been honored with the presence of the nobility as formerly, and many lodges erased out of the lift for non-attendance on the duties of the Grand Lodge. By the diligence and attention, however, of the late general John Salter, then Deputy Grand Master, the business of the Society was carried on with regularity, and the fund of charity considerably increased. Provincial patents were made out during Earl Ferrers's presidency;

1. for Jamaica;
2. for East India, where no particular provincial was before appointed;
3. for Cornwall;
4. for Armenia;
5. for Westphalia;
6. for Bombay;
7. for the Dukedom of Brunswick;
8. for the Grenades, St. Vincent, Dominica, Tobago, Etc.; and
9. for Canada.

From these appointments no considerable emoluments have resulted to the Society, excepting from the third and sixth; George Bell for Cornwall; and James Todd for Bombay. Both these gentlemen were particularly attentive to the duties of their respective offices, especially the former, to whom the Society is in a great measure indebted for the flourishing state of masonry in Cornwall.

(Lord Blaney)

On the 8th of May 1764, at an assembly and feast at Vintners'-hall, Lord Blaney was elected Grand Master. Lord Ferrers invested John Revis Esq., late Deputy Grand Master, as proxy for his Lordship, who continued in office two years, during which time, being chiefly in Ireland, the business of the Society was faithfully executed by his deputy, general Salter, an active and a vigilant officer. The scheme of opening a subscription for the purchase of furniture for the Grand Lodge was agitated about this time, and some money collected; but the design dropped for want of encouragement. A new edition of the Book of Constitutions was ordered to be printed under the inspection of a committee, with a continuation of the proceedings of the Society since the publication of the last edition.

During Lord Blaney's presidency, the Dukes of Gloucester and Cumberland were initiated into the Order; the former, at an occasional lodge assembled at the Horn Tavern Westminster, on the 16th of February 1766, at which his Lordship resided in person; the latter, at an occasional lodge assembled at the Thatched House tavern in St. James's-street, under the direction of general Salter.

The following deputations for the office of Provincial Grand Master were granted by Lord Blaney;

1. for Barbadoes;
2. for Upper Saxony;
3 for Stockholm:
4. for Virginia;
5. for Bengal;
6. for Italy;
7. for the Upper and Lower Rhine, and the Circle of Franconia;

8. for Antigua;
9. for the Electorate of Saxony;
10. for Madras, and its dependencies;
11. for Hampshire;
and
12. for Montserrat.

(Thomas Dunckerley)

The fifth, tenth, and eleventh of these appointments have been faithfully executed. By the indefatigable assiduity of that truly masonic luminary, Esq., in whose favor the appointment for Hampshire was first made out; masonry has made considerable progress in that province, as well as in many other counties in England. Since his appointment to this office, he has accepted the superintendence of the lodges in Dorsetshire, Essex, Gloucestershire, Somersetshire, and Herefordshire. The revival of the Bengal and Madras appointments have been also attended with success, as the late liberal remittances from the East Indies amply show.

Among several regulations respecting the fees of constitutions, and other matters which passed during Lord Blaney's administration, was the following; That as the Grand Lodge entertained the highest sense of the honor conferred on the Society by the initiation of the Dukes of Gloucester, and Cumberland; it was resolved, that each of their royal highnesses should be presented with an apron, lined with blue silk; and that, in all future processions, they should rank as Past Grand Masters, next to the Grand Officers for the time being.

The same compliment was also paid to their royal brother the late Duke of York, who had been initiated into masonry while on his travels.

The Duke of Beaufort succeeded Lord Blaney, and was installed by proxy at Merchant Taylors'-hall on the 27th of April 1767. Under the patronage of his grace the Society flourished.

In the beginning of 1768, two letters were received from the Grand Lodge of France, expressing a desire of opening a regular correspondence with the Grand Lodge of England.

(Duke of Beaufort)

This was cheerfully agreed to; and a Book of Constitutions, a list of the lodges under the constitution of England, with the form of a deputation, elegantly bound, was ordered to be sent as a present to the Grand Lodge of France.

Several regulations for the future government of the Society were made about this time, particularly one respecting the office of Provincial Grand Master. At a Grand Lodge held at the Crown and Anchor tavern in the Strand, on the 29th of April 1768, it was resolved that ten guineas should be paid to the fund of charity on the appointment of every Provincial Grand Master who had not served the office of Grand Steward.

The most remarkable occurrence during the administration of the, was the plan of an incorporation by royal charter. At a Grand Lodge held at the Crown and Anchor tavern on the 28th of October 1768, a report was made from the Committee of Charity held on the 21st of that month at the Horn tavern in Fleet-street, on the Grand Master's intentions to have the Society incorporated, if it met with the approbation of the brethren; the advantages of such a measure were fully explained, and a plan for the purpose was submitted to the consideration of the Committee. The plan being approved, the thanks of the Grand Lodge were voted to the Grand Master, for his attention to the interests and prosperity of the Society. The hon. Charles Dillon, then Deputy Grand Master, informed the brethren, that he had submitted to the Committee a plan for raising a fund to build a hall, and purchase jewels, furniture, Etc. for the Grand Lodge, independent of the general fund of charity; the carrying of which into execution, he apprehended, would be a proper prelude to an Incorporation, should it be the wish of the Society to obtain a charter. The plan being laid before the Communication, several amendments were made, and the whole referred to the next Grand Lodge for confirmation. In the mean time it was resolved, that the said plan should be printed, and transmitted to all the lodges on record. The Duke of Beaufort finding that the Society approved of Incorporation, contributed his best endeavors to carry the design into immediate execution: though at first he was opposed by a few brethren, who misconceived his good intentions, he persevered in promoting every measure that

(Crown & Anchor)

might facilitate the plan; and a copy of the intended charter was soon after printed, and dispersed among the lodges. Before the Society, however, had come to any determined resolution on the business, the members of a respectable lodge, then held at the Half Moon tavern Cheapside, entered a caveat in the attorney-general's office, against the Incorporation; and this circumstance being reported to the Grand Lodge, an impeachment was laid against that lodge, for unwarrantably exposing the private resolutions of the Grand Lodge; and it being determined that the members of the said lodge had been guilty of a great offence, in presuming to oppose the resolutions of the Grand Lodge, and endeavoring to frustrate the intentions of the Society, a motion was made, That it should be erased from the list of lodges; but, on the Master of the lodge acknowledging the fault, and, in the name of himself and his brethren, making a proper apology, the motion was withdrawn, and the offence forgiven. From the return of the different lodges it appeared, that one hundred and sixty-eight had voted for the Incorporation, and only forty-three against it; upon which a motion was made in Grand Lodge, on the 28th of April 1769 that the Society should be incorporated; which was carried in the affirmative by a great majority.

At a Grand Lodge held at the Crown and Anchor tavern on the 27th of October 1769, it was resolved, that the sum of £1300. Then standing in the names of Rowland Berkeley Esq., the Grand Treasurer, and Mr. Arthur Beardmore and Mr. Richard Nevis on his sureties, in the three percent bank consolidated annuities, in trust for the Society, be transferred into the names of the present Grand Officers; and at an extra-ordinary Grand Lodge on the 29th of November following, the Society was

(Lord Petre)

informed that Mr. Beardmore had refused to join in the transfer; upon which it was resolved that letters should be sent, in the name of the Society, signed by the acting Grand Officers, to Lord Blarney the Past Grand Master, and to his Deputy and Wardens, to whom the Grand Treasurer and his sureties had given bond, requesting their concurrence in the resolutions of the Grand Lodge of the 29th of October last. Mr. Beardmore, however, dying soon after, the desire of the Grand Lodge was complied with by Mr. Nevison, and the transfer regularly made.

At a Grand Lodge held at the Crown and Anchor tavern on the 25th of April 1770, the Provincial Grand Master for foreign lodges acquainted the Society, that he had lately received a letter from Charles, Baron de Boetzelaer, Grand Master of the National Grand Lodge of the United Provinces of Holland and their dependencies, requesting to be acknowledged as such by the Grand Lodge of England, whose superiority he confessed; and promising, that if the Grand Lodge of England would agree in future not to constitute any new lodge within his jurisdiction, the Grand Lodge of Holland would observe the same restriction with respect to all parts of the world where lodges were already established under the patronage of England. Upon these terms he requested that a firm and friendly alliance might be established between the Officers of both Grand Lodges, an annual correspondence carried on, and each Grand Lodge regularly made acquainted once in every year with the most material transactions of the other. On this report being made, the Grand Lodge agreed, that such an alliance or compact should be immediately entered into, and executed, agreeably to Baron de Boetzelaer's request.

In 1771, a bill was brought into parliament by the hon. Charles Dillon, then Deputy Grand Master, for incorporating the Society by act of parliament; but on the second reading of the bill, it having been opposed by Mr. Onslow, at the desire of several brethren, who had petitioned the house against it, Mr. Dillon moved to postpone the consideration of it _sine die_ (Without any future date being designated (as for resumption):indefinitely. The meeting adjourned sine die.); and thus the design of an Incorporation fell to the ground.

The Duke of Beaufort constituted several new lodges, and granted the following provincial deputations, during his presidency:

1. for South Carolina;
2. Jamaica;
3. Barbadoes;
4. Naples and Sicily:
5. the Empire of Russia;
and
6. the Austrian Netherlands.

The increase of foreign lodges occasioned the institution of a new officer, a Provincial Grand Master for foreign lodges in general; and his grace accordingly nominated gentleman for that office. He also appointed provincial Grand Masters for Kent, Suffolk, Lancashire, and Cumberland. Another new appointment likewise took place during his grace's administration, viz., the office of General Inspectors or Provincial Grand Masters for lodges within the bills of mortality; but the majority of the lodges in London disapproving the appointment, the authority was soon after withdrawn.

Lord Petre succeeded the Duke of Beaufort on the 4th of May 1772, when several regulations were made for better securing the property belonging to the Society. A considerable sum having been subscribed for the purpose of building a hall, a committee was appointed to superintend the management of that business. Every measure was adopted to enforce the laws for raising a new fund to carry the designs of the Society into execution, and no pains were spared by the committee to complete the purpose of their appointment. By their report to the Grand Lodge on 27th April 1774, it appeared that they had contracted for the purchase of a plot of ground and premises, consisting of two large commodious dwelling houses, and a large garden, situated in Great Queen street, Lincoln's-Inn-Fields, late in the possession Phillip Carteret Webb Esq., deceased, the particulars of which were specified in a plan then delivered; that the real value appeared to be £3,205 at the least, but that £3,180 was the sum contracted to be paid for the premises; that the front house might produce £90 per annum, and the back house would furnish commodious committee-rooms, offices, kitchens, Etc., and that the garden was sufficiently large to contain a complete hall for the use of the Society, the expense of the which was calculated not to exceed £3,000. This report met with general approbation. Lord Petre, the Dukes of Beaufort and Chandos, Earl Ferrers, and Lord Viscount Dudley and Ward, were appointed trustees for the Society, and the conveyance of the premises purchased was made in their names.

On the 22nd of February 1775, the hall-committee reported to approved for raising £5,000 to complete the designs of the Society, and granting annuities for lives, with benefit of survivorship; a plan now known under the name of Tontine. It was accordingly resolved, that there should be one hundred lives at a £50 each; that the whole premises belonging to the society in Great Queen-street, with the hall to be built thereon, should be vested in trustees, as a security to the subscribers, who should be paid 5 percent for their money advanced amounting to £250 per annum; that this interest should be divided among the subscribers, and the survivors or survivor of them; and, upon the death of the last survivor, the whole to determine for the benefit of the Society. The Grand Lodge approving of the plan, the subscription immediately commenced, and in less than three months was complete; upon which the trustees of the Society conveyed the estate to the trustees of the tontine, in pursuance of a resolution of the Grand Lodge for that purpose.

On 1st May 1775, the foundation-stone of the new hall was laid in solemn form in the presence of a numerous company of the brethren. After the ceremony, the company proceeded in carriages to Leathersellers'-hall, where an elegant entertainment was provided on the occasion; and at the meeting the office of Grand-Chaplain was first instituted.

The building of the hall went on so rapidly that it was finished in little more than twelve months. On the 23rd of May 1776, it was opened, and dedicated, in solemn form to

MASONRY, VIRTUE and UNIVERSAL CHARITY and BENEVOLENCE, in the presence of a brilliant assembly of the brethren. A new Ode, was written and set to music on the occasion and was performed, before a number of ladies, who honored the Society with their company on that day. An exordium on masonry, not less elegant than instructive, was given by the Grand Secretary, and an excellent oration delivered by the Grand Chaplain. In commemoration of an event so pleasing to the Society, it was agreed, that the anniversary of this ceremony should be ever after regularly kept.

Thus was completed, under the auspices of a nobleman, whose amiable character as a man, and zeal as a mason may be equaled, but cannot be surpassed, that elegant and highly finished room on Great Queen-street, in which the annual assembly and quarterly communications of the fraternity are held; and to the accomplishment of which many lodges, as well as private individuals, have liberally subscribed. It is to be regretted, that the finances of the Society will not admit of its being solely reserved for masonic purposes.

The brethren of St John's Lodge in Newcastle, animated by the example set then in the metropolis, opened a subscription for the purpose of building, in the Low Friar Chair in that town, a new hall for their meetings; and on the 23rd of September 1776, the foundation stone of that building was laid by Mr. Francis Peacock, then Master of the lodge. This edifice was speedily completed, furnished and dedicated; but se since learn, that it has been sold, and appropriated to other purposes.

(Duke of Athol)

The flourishing state of the Society in England attracted the attention of the masons in Germany, who solicited our friendship and alliance. The Grand Lodge at Berlin, under the patronage of the prince of Hess-Darmstatd, requested a friendly union and correspondence with their brethren in England, which was agreed to, on the Grand Lodge of Germany engaging to remit an annual donation to the fund of charity.

The business of the Society having been now considerably increased, it was resolved, that the Grand Secretary should be permitted in future to employ a deputy or assistant, at an annual salary proportioned to his labor.

On the 14th February 1776, the Grand Lodge resolved, that in future all Past Grand Officers should be permitted to wear a particular gold jewel, the ground enameled in blue; and each officer to be distinguished by the jewel which he wore while in office; with this difference, that such honorary jewel should be fixed with a circle of oval; on the borders of which were to be inscribed his name, and the year in which he served the office. This jewel to be worn in Grand Lodge pendant to a broad blue ribbon, and on other occasions, to be fixed to the breast by a narrow blue ribbon.

Many regulations respecting the government of the fraternity were established during Lord Petre's administration. The meetings of irregular masons again attracted notice, and, on the 10th April 1777, the following law was enacted "That the persons who assemble in London, and elsewhere, in the character of masons, calling themselves Ancient Masons, and at present said to be under the patronage of the Duke of Athol, are not to be countenanced, or acknowledged, by any regular lodge, or mason, under the constitution of England: nor shall any regular mason be present be present at any of their proceedings, under the penalty of forfeiting the privileges of the Society: nor shall any person initiated at any of the irregular meetings, be admitted into any lodge, without being re-made. That this censure shall not extend to any lodge, or mason made in Scotland or Ireland, under the constitution of either of these kingdoms; or to any lodge, or mason made abroad, under the patronage of any foreign Grand Lodge in alliance with the Grand Lodge of England; but that such lodge and masons shall be deemed to be regular and constitutional."

An Appendix to the Book of Constitutions, containing all the principal proceedings of the Society since the publication of the last edition, was ordered to be printed; also a new annual publication, entitled THE FREE-MASONS CALENDAR; and the profits arising from the sale of both, were to be regularly brought to account in the charity fund. To preserve the consequence of the Society, the following law was enacted at this time: "That the fees for constitutions, initiations, Etc., should be advanced, and no person be initiated into masonry in any lodge in England for less sum that two guineas; and that the name, age profession, and place of residence of every person so initiated, and of every admitted member of a regular lodge since the 29th October 1768, should be registered, under the penalty of such mason made, or member admitted, being deprived of the privileges of the Society."

Lord Petre granted provincial deputations for Madras and Virginia, also for Hants, Sussex and Surrey. Though, during this presidency, some lodges were erased out of the list, for non-conformity to the laws, many new ones were added, so that under his Lordship's banner, the Society became truly respectable.

On the 1st of May 1777, Lord Petre was succeeded by the Duke of Manchester; during whose administration the tranquility of the Society was interrupted by private dissensions. An unfortunate dispute having arisen among the members of the lodge of Antiquity, on account for some proceedings of the brethren of that lodge on the festival of St John the Evangelist after his grace's election, the complaint was introduced into Grand Lodge, where it occupied the attention of every committee and communication for twelve months. It originated from the Master, Wardens and some of the members, having, in consequence of a resolution of the lodge, attended divine service at St Dunstan's Church in Fleet-street, in the clothing of the Order; and walked back to the Mitre-tavern in their regalia Grand Lodge determined the measure to be a violation of the general regulations respecting public processions. Various opinions were formed on the subject, and several brethren highly disgusted. Another circumstance tended still farther to widen the breach. This lodge, having expelled three members for misbehavior, the Grand Lodge interfered and, without proper investigation, ordered them to be reinstated. With this order the lodge refused to comply, conceiving themselves competent judges in the choice of their members. The privileges of the lodge of Antiquity were then set up, in opposition to the supposed uncontrollable authority of the Grand Lodge; and in the investigation of this important point, the original case of dispute was totally forgotten. Matters were agitated to the extreme on both sides. Resolutions were precipitately entered into, and edicts inadvertently issued. Memorial and <u>remonstrance's</u> *(A forcefully reproachful protest.)* were presented; at last a rupture ensued. the lodge of Antiquity supported its immemorial privileges; applied to the old lodge in York city, and to the lodges in Scotland and Ireland, for advice, entered a protest against, and peremptorily refused to comply with, the resolutions of the Grand Lodge, discontinued the attendance of its master and wardens at the committees of charity and quarterly communications as its representatives; published a manifesto in its vindication; notified its separation from the Grand Lodge; avowed an alliance with the Grand Lodge of all England, held in the city of York, and every lodge and mason who wished to act in conformity to the original constitutions. The Grand Lodge enforced its edicts, and extended protection to the brethren whose cause it had espoused. Anathemas *(Is something or someone that is detested or shunned.)* were issued, several worthy men in their absence expelled from the Society, for refusing to surrender the property of the lodge to three persons who had been regularly expelled from it; and printed letters were circulated, with the Grand Treasurer's accounts, highly derogatory to the dignity of the Society. This produced a schism, which subsisted for the space of ten years. To justify the proceeding of the Grand Lodge, the following resolution of the Committee of Charity held in February 1779, was printed and dispersed among the lodges:

"Resolved, that every private lodge derives its authority from the Grand Lodge, and that no authority but the Grand

Lodge can withdraw or take away that power, that thought the majority of a lodge may determine to quite the Society, the constitution, or power of assembling, remains with and is vested in, the rest of the members who may be desirous of continuing their allegiance; and that if all the members withdraw themselves, the constitution is extinct and the authority reverts to Grand Lodge."

This resolution, it was argued, might operate with respect to a lodge with derived its constitution from the Grand Lodge, but could not apply to one which derived its authority form another channel. Long before the establishment of the Grand Lodge, and which authority had been repeatedly admitted and acknowledged. Had it appeared upon record, that after the establishment of the Grand Lodge, and original authority had had been surrendered, forfeited, or exchanged for a warrant from the Grand Lodge, the lodge of Antiquity must have admitted the resolution of the Grand Lodge its full force. But as no such circumstance appeared on record, the members of the lodge of Antiquity were justified in considering their immemorial constitution sacred, while, they chose to exist as a lodge and act in obedience to its ancient constitutions.

Considering the subject in this point of view, it evidently appears that the resolution of the Grand Lodge could have no effect on the lodge of Antiquity; especially after the publication of the manifesto avowing its separation. The members of the lodge continued to meet regularly as heretofore, and to promote the laudable purposes of masonry on their old independent foundation. The lodge of Antiquity it was asserted could not be dissolved, while the majority of its members kept together, and acted in conformity to the original constitutions; and no edict of the Grand Lodge, or its committees could deprive the members of that lodge of a right which had been admitted to be vested in themselves collectively from time immemorial; a right which had never been derived from, or ceded to, any Grand Lodge whatever.

To understand more clearly the nature of that constitution by which the lodge of Antiquity is upheld, we must have recourse to the usages and customs which prevailed among masons, at the end of the last, and the beginning of the present century. The fraternity then had a discretionary power to meet as masons, in certain numbers, according to their degrees, with the approbation of the master of the work where any public building was carrying on, as often as they found it necessary so to do; and when so met, to receive into the Order brothers and fellows and practice the rites of masonry. the idea of investing Masters and Wardens of lodges in Grand Lodge assembled, or the Grand Master himself, with a power to grant warrants of constitution to certain brethren to meet as masons on the observance of certain conditions, at certain hours, had no existence. The fraternity was under no such restrictions. The ancient charges were the only standard for the regulation of conduct, and no law was known in the Society which those charges did not inculcate. To the award of the fraternity at large, in general meeting assembled, once of twice in a year, all brethren were subject, and the authority of the Grand Master never extended beyond the bounds of that general meeting.

When a lodge was fixed at any particular place for a certain time, an attestation from the brethren present entered on record, was a sufficient proof of its regular constitution; and this practice prevailed for many years after the revival of masonry in the South of England. By this authority, which never proceeded from the Grand Lodge, unfettered by any other restrictions than the constitutions of masonry, the lodge of Antiquity has always been, and still continues to be governed.

While I have endeavored to explain the subject of the unfortunate dispute, I rejoice in the opportunity which the proceedings of the grand feast in 1790 have afforded, of promoting harmony, by restoring to the privileges of the Society, all the brethren of the lodge of Antiquity who had been falsely and unjustly expelled in 1779. By the operation of our professed principles, and through the mediation of that true friend to genuine masonry, William Birch Esq., unanimity has been happily restored; the manifesto published by that lodge in 1779, revoked; and the Master and Wardens of that truly ancient association, the first lodge under the English constitution, have resumed their seats in Grand Lodge as heretofore; while the brethren who had received the sanction of the Society, as nominal members of the lodge of Antiquity, during the separation, have been reunited with the original members of the real lodge, and all privileges of that venerable body now center in one channel.

I have considerably abridged my observations on this subject in the last as well as the present edition, but think it proper still to record my sentiments, in justice to the gentlemen with whom I have long associated; and to convince my brethren, that our re-union with the Society has not induced me to vary a well-grounded opinion or deviated from the strict line of consistency which I have hitherto pursued.

History of the most remarkable Events in the Society from 1779 to 1791 inclusive

midst these disagreeable altercations, intelligence arrived of the rapid progress of the Society in India, where many new lodges had been constituted, which were amply supported by the first characters in the East. Omdit-ul-Omrah Bahauder, eldest son of the Nabob *(A provincial governor of the Mogul empire in India.)* of the Carnatic, had been initiated into masonry in the lodge of Trichinopoly near Madras; and had expressed the highest veneration for the institution. This news having been transmitted to England officially, the Grand Lodge determined to send a congratulatory letter to his highness on the occasion, accompanied with a blue apron elegantly decorated, and a copy of the Book of Constitutions superbly bound. To Sir John Day, advocated general of Bengal, the execution of the commission was entrusted. In the beginning of 1780, an answer was received from his highness, acknowledging the receipt of the present, and expressing the warmest attachment and benevolence to his brethren in England. This letter, which is written in the Persian language, was enclosed in an elegant cover of cloth of gold, and addressed To the Grand Master and Grand Lodge of England.

This flattering mark of attention from so distinguished a personage abroad, was peculiarly grateful to the Grand Lodge; who immediately resolved, that a letter should be prepared and transmitted to his highness, expressing the high opinion which the brethren in England entertained of his merits, and requesting the continuance of his friendship and protection to the masonic institution in the East. The thanks of the Grand Lodge were voted to Sir John Day; and a translation of his highness's Letter was ordered to be copied on vellum, and, with the original, elegantly framed and glazed, hung up in the hall at every public meeting of the Society.

Under the auspices of this celebrated chief, there is every reason to expect that masonry will flourish in the East; and it cannot fail of giving pleasure to every zealous brother, to find that the venerable principles of the institution pervade the most distant regions.

The first test testimony which Odmit-ul-Omrah gave of his regard to the institution was by the initiation of his brother Omur-ul-Omrah, who seems equally attached with himself to promote the welfare of the Society.

Another event has also taken place at Madras, which must be very satisfactory to the brethren of England. The division and secessions, which had originated in London in 1738, having unfortunately reached India, by the intervention of brigadier general Horne, who had been appointed, by patent from the Duke of Cumberland, Provincial Grand Master on the Coast of Cormomandel, an union of the brethren in that part of the world has been affected, and the lodge No. 152, styling themselves Ancient York Masons, joined a lodge under his auspices and voluntarily surrendered the constitution under which they had formerly acted. This desirable object being accomplished, and the wishes of the brethren fulfilled, the General requested their assistance to form a Grand Lodge, when the following Officers were appointed, and installed in due form.

Brigadier Gen. Horne, Prov. Grand Master.

Ter. Gahagan Esq. Deputy Grand Master.

Jos. Du Pre Porcher Esq. Acting Grand Master.

Lieut. Col. Rofs. Grand Architect.

Lieut. Col. J Campbell, Sen, Grand Warden.

Lieut. Col. Hamilton Esq. Junior Grand Warden.

James Grierson Esq. Grand Secretary.

James Amos Esq. Grand Treasurer.

Lieutenant-colonel Moorhouse, and Colonel L. Lucas Esq.

Grand Stewards.

Major Maule, Grand Orator.

Charles Bromley Esq. Grand Sword Bearer.

The Grand Lodge having been regularly established, a proposal was made, that a new lodge should be formed in Madras, under the name of Perfect Unanimity, No. 1. This being unanimously agreed to, the Provincial Grand Master gave notice, that he should perform the ceremony of consecration on Saturday the 7th of October 1787, in commemoration of the union which had been so amicably formed that day; and requested the proper officers to attend the occasion. Accordingly, on the morning of the day appointed upwards of fifty brethren assembled at the house of Choulty Plain, in which the public rooms are held, and at half past eleven o'clock the ceremony commenced, After the preparatory business had been gone through in Grand Lodge, a procession was formed and marched three times round the lodge; after which the business of consecration was entered on, and completed in a manner suitable to the solemnity of the occasion. Several old masons, who were present, declared they never saw a ceremony conducted with more dignity and propriety.

The following brethren were installed as Officers of this new lodge, viz., Colly Lyons Lucas Esq. Master; Pullier Spencer Esq. Senior Warden; George Robert Latham Esq., Junior Warden; George Maule Esq., Secretary; John Robins Esq. Treasurer.

At two o'clock, the brethren sat down at an excellent dinner, provided by the Grand Lodge; after which many masonic and loyal toasts were drank; and the day was concluded with that pleasing festivity, harmony, and good fellowship, which has always distinguished the Society of Free and Accepted Masons.

During the presidency of the Duke of Manchester, new lodges were constituted in different parts of the kingdom, and considerable additions made to the general funds of the Society. The sums voted to distressed brethren far exceeded those of any former period; and among other instances of liberality may be specified, a very generous contribution, of one hundred pounds, toward the relief of the brethren in America, who had suffered great losses in consequence of the rebellion there, and whose situation was very feelingly described in a letter from the lodge No. 1 at Halifax Nova Scotia.

A singular proposition was made in Grand Lodge on the 8th of April 1778, that the Grand Master and his Officers should be distinguished in future at all public meetings by robes to be provided at their own expense; and that Past Grand Officers should have the privilege of being distinguished in a similar manner. This measure was at first favorably received; but, on further investigation in the Hall Committee, to whom it was referred, it was found to be so diametrically opposite to the original plan of the institution, that it was very properly laid aside.

The finances of the Society occupied great part of the proceedings of the Committees and communications during his grace's administration. The debts due on account of the hall appearing to be very considerable, it was determined to make an application to the lodges to raise £2,000 to pay them off. For this purpose in consequence of a plan offered to the consideration of the Grand Lodge in June 1779, it was resolved, that a subscription should be opened, to raise money by loan, without interest, at the discretion of the subscribers; that £25 should be the sum limited for each subscriber, and the number of subscribers to be one hundred; and that the monies so subscribed should be repaid, in equal proportions, among the subscribers, at such times as the hall fund would admit. It was also determined, that an honorary medal should be presented to every subscriber, as a mark of distinction for the service which he had rendered the Society; and that the bearer of such medal, if a master mason, should have the privilege of being present at, and voting in, all the future meetings of the Grand Lodge. This mark of attention prompted some lodges, as well as individuals, to contribute and the greatest part of the money was speedily raised and applied for the purpose intended.

The Stewards Lodge, finding their finances much reduced be several members having withdrawn the annual subscriptions, applied to the Grand Lodge for relief; upon which it was resolved, that in future no Grand Officer should be appointed, who was not at the time a subscribing member of the Stewards Lodge.

A measure of more importance attracted the attention of the Society at this period. It had been observed with regret, that a number of worthy brethren in distress had been subjected to much inconvenience and disappointment from a want of relief during the long summer recess, as there was seldom any Committee of Charity held from the beginning of April to the end of October. To remedy this complaint, the Grand Lodge unanimously resolved that an Extraordinary Committee should meet annually in the last week of August, to administer temporary relief to such distressed objects as might regularly apply, not exceeding five pounds to one person.

This increase in the business of the Society induced the Grand Lodge to appoint pro tempore, an assistant to the Grand

Secretary, who should hold equal rank and power with himself in Grand Lodge. Among many regulations which were now established, it was determined, that in future no person should hold two offices at the same time in Grand Lodge.

The Grand Lodge of Germany applied for liberty to send a representative to the Grand Lodge of England, in order more effectively to cement the union and friendship of the brethren of both countries, and Brother John Leonhardi was appointed to the office. This request being complied with, a resolution passed, that, in compliment to the Grand Lodge of Germany, Brother Leonhardi should wear the clothing of a Grand Officer and rank next to the Past Grand Officers in all public meetings of the Society.

This additional cement was highly pleasing; and led the brethren to regret, that no intercourse or correspondence should have subsisted nearer home, between the Grand Lodge of England and the Grand Lodges of Scotland and Ireland, thought all the members were subjects of the same sovereign. At the communication in April 1782, this important business came under consideration; when, after a variety of opinions had been delivered, it was unanimously resolved, that the Grand Master should be requested to adopt such means as his wisdom might suggest, promoting a good understanding among the brethren of the three united kingdoms. Notwithstanding this resolution, the wished for union has not yet been accomplished; we trust, however, that the event is not far distant.

At this meeting also, the pleasing intelligence was communicated, of the intention to accept the government of the Society. This having been regularly stated in Grand Lodge, his highness was proposed Grand Master elect; and it was resolved, in compliment to him, that he should have the privilege of nominating a peer of the realm as Acting Grand Master, who should be empowered to superintend the Society in his absence; and that, at any future period, when the fraternity might be honored with a Prince of the blood at their head, the same privilege should be granted.

At the annual grand feast on the 1st of May 1782, the Duke of Cumberland was unanimously elected Grand Master; and it being signified to the Society that his highness meant to appoint the Earl of Effingham Acting Grand Master, that the appointment was confirmed, and his Lordship presided as proxy for his royal highness during the feast.

On the 8th of January 1783, a very singular motion was made in Grand Lodge, and afterward confirmed, that the interest of five percent on £1,000 which had been advanced for the purposes of the hall from the charity fund, should cease to be paid; and further, that the principal should be annihilated, and sunk into the hall fund. However extraordinary it may appear, this event took place; and the money has been regularly brought to account in the hall expenditures. A number of other regulations were confirmed at this meeting, to render the hall fund more productive, and to enforce obedience to the laws respecting it. How far some of the regulations are consistent with the original plan of the masonic institution must be left to abler judges to determine. In Earlier periods of our history, such compulsory regulations were unnecessary.

At the Grand Lodge held on the 23rd of November 1783, an addition was made to the Grand Officers, by the appointment of a Grand Portrait Painter; and, at the request of the Duke of Manchester, that honor was conferred on the rev. William Peters, in testimony of the service which he had rendered to the Society, by his elegant portrait of Lord Petre.

(Duke of Cumberland)

During the remainder of the year, there was scarcely any further business of importance transacted. On the 19th of November, information was given in Grand Lodge, that two brethren, under sanction of the Royal Military lodge at Woolwich, which claimed the privilege of an itinerant lodge, had lately held an irregular meeting in the King's Bench prison, and had there unwarrantably initiated sundry person into masonry. The Grand Lodge, conceiving this to be a violent infringement of the privileges of every regular constituted lodge, ordered the said lodge to be erased from the list; and determined, that it was inconsistent with the purposes of making, passing and raising masons, in a prison or place of confinement.

At this Grand Lodge also, it was resolved, to enact certain regulations, subjecting the Deputy Grand Master and Grand Wardens to fines, in case of non-attendance on the public meetings of the Society; and these regulations were confirmed on the 11th February following.

While those proceedings were carrying on in England, the brethren in Scotland were prosecuting their labors also for the good of the craft. The vast improvements made in the city of Edinburgh, afforded ample room for ingenious architects to display their masonic talent and abilities; and there the operative part of the fraternity were fully occupied, in rearing stately mansions, and planning elegant squares.

On the 1st of August 1785, a very pleasing sight was exhibited to every well-wisher to the embellishment of that city, in the ceremony of laying the foundation stone of the South Bridge, being the first step to farther improvement. In the morning of that day, the right hon. the Lord Provost and Magistrates, attended by the Grand Master Mason of Scotland, and a number of nobility and gentry, with the masters, office-bearers, and brethren of the several lodges; walked from the parliament-house to the bridge in procession. The streets were lined by the 58th regiment and the city guard.

Lord Haddo, Grand Master, having arrived at the place, laid the foundation stone with the usual solemnities. His Lordship standing on the east, with the Substitute on his right hand, and the Grand Wardens on the west, the square, the plumb, the level, and the mallet, were successively delivered by an operative mason to the Substitute, and by him to the Grand Master, who applied the square to that part of the stone which was square, the plumb to the level edges, the level above the stone in several positions, and then with the mallet gave three knocks, saying' "May the Grand Architect of the Universe grant a blessing on this foundation stone, which we have now laid; and by his providence enable us to finish this, and every other work which may be undertaken for the embellishment and advantage of this city." On this the brethren gave the honors.

The cornucopia and two silver vessels were then brought from the table, and delivered, the cornucopia to the Substitute, and the two vessels to the Wardens, which were successively presented to the Grand Master, who, according to ancient form, scattered the corn, and poured the wine and oil, which they contained, on the stone saying, "May the All-bounteous Author of Nature bless this city with an abundance of corn, wine and oil; and with all the necessaries, conveniences, and comforts of life! And may the same Almighty power preserve this city from ruin and decay to the latest posterity!"

The Grand Master, being supported on the right hand by the Duke of Buccleugh and on the left by the Earl of Balcarras, addressed himself to the Lord Provost and the Magistrates in a suitable speech for the occasion. The coins of the present reign, and a silver platter, with the following inscription, was deposited within the stone.

ANNUETE DEO OPTIMO MAXIMO,

REGNANTE GEORGIO III, PATRE PATRIA,

HUJUS PONTIS

QUO VICI EXTRA MOENIA EDINBURGH,

URBI COMMODE ADJUNGERENTUR,

ADITUMQUE NON INDIGNUM TANTA

URBS HABERET,

PRIMUM LAPIDEM POSUIT

NOBLIS VIR GEORGIUS DOMINUS HADDO,

ANTIQUISSIMI SODALITH ARCHITECTONICI

APUD SCOTOS CURIO MAXIMUS,

PLAUDENTE AMPLISSIMA FRATRUM CORONA,

IMMEMSAQUE POPULI FREQUENTIA OPUS

UTILE CIVIBUS GRATUM ADVENIS,

URBI DECORUM PATRIAE HONESTUM,

CONSULE JACOBO HUNTER BLAIR,

INCEPTI AUCTORE INDEFESSO,

SANCCIENTE REEGE, SENATUQUE BRITANNIAE,

APPROBANTIBUS OMNIBUS,

TANDEM INCHOATUM EST

IPSIS KALENDIS AUGUSTI

A.D. MDCCLXXXV

AERAE ARCHITECTONICAE 5785

Q.F.F.Q.S.

Translation

"By the blessing of Almighty God, in the reign of George the Third, the Father of his country, the right hon. George, Lord Haddo, Grand Master of the Most ancient Fraternity of Free Masons in Scotland, amidst the acclamation of a Grand Assembly of the brethren, and a vast concourse of people, laid the first stone of this bridge, intended to form a convenient

communication between the city of Edinburgh and its suburbs, and an access not unworthy of such a city."

This work, so useful to the inhabitants, so pleasing and convenient to strangers, so ornamental to the city, so creditable to the country, so long and much wanted and wished for, was at last begun, with the sanction of the king and parliament of Great Britain, and with universal approbation, in the provostship of James Hunter Blair, the author and indefatigable promoter of the undertaking, August the 1st, in the year of our Lord, 1785, and of the era of Masonry 5785. Which may God prosper."

An anthem was then sung, and the procession returned, reversed, to the Parliament-house. After which the Lord Provost and Magistrates gave an elegant entertainment at Dunn's rooms to the Grand Lodge, and the nobility and gentry who had assisted in the ceremony. The net public ceremony, in which the society bore a principal share, was in laying the foundation stone of that valuable seminary of learning, the new College of Edinburgh. This University has for many years been esteemed one of the most celebrated in Europe, and has attracted a great number of students of physic and other branches of science, from all parts of the world. The eminence of its professors in every branch of learning is universally admitted; and it is most fervently so be wished, for the honors of the kingdom, that the whole plan may be completely executed agreeably to the intention of the original promoters. As this is an event worth of record in the annals of masonry, I shall describe minutely the ceremony observed on that remarkable occasion.

(Lord Haddo)

On the 13th of October 1789, Mr. Robert Adam, architect, presented the plans of the intended building, at a public breakfast given by the Lord Provost, to the Magistrates, the Principal and the Professors of the University, of Edinburgh, on the occasion; and explained their uses for the various schools, halls, and houses. The whole company expressed the highest satisfaction at the design; and it was immediately resolved, that a subscription should be opened to carry the plan into execution. Monday the 16th of November was then fixed for laying the foundation stone of the new structure.

On the morning of the day appointed for performing the ceremony, the brethren assembled at eleven o'clock in the Parliament-house, to meet Lord Napier, at that time Grand Master of Scotland. When the lodges were arranged, the Grand Master sent notice to the Lord Provost and Magistrates, who had assembled in the Council-chamber; and to the Principal, Professors and Student of the University, who had met in the High Church. At half past twelve, the procession began to move in the following order:

1st. The Principal, Professors, and Students of the University, with their mace carried before them. Principal Robertson being supported on the right hand by the rev. Dr. Hunter, professor of divinity; and on the left, by Dr. Handy, professor of church history. The Professors were all robed, and each of the Students had a sprig of laurel in his hat.

2nd. The Lord Provost, Magistrates, and Council, in their robes, preceded by the sword, mace, etc. The Lord Provost being supported on the right and left by the two eldest Baillies.
(Baillies is a civic officer in the local government of Scotland.)

3rd. A complete choir of Singers, under the direction of Signor Scherky, singing anthems as the procession moved.

4th. The Lodges, according to seniority, juniors preceding, with their different insignia.

5th. A complete band of instrumental music.

6th. The Grand Stewards, properly clothed, with white rods.

7th. The Noblemen and Gentlemen attending the Grand

Master.

8th. A large drawing of the East Front of the New College, carried by two operative masons.

9th. The grand jewels, borne by Past Masters of lodges.

10th. Officers of the Grand Lodge, properly clothed.

11th. Past Grand Masters.

12th. Lord Napier, present Grand Master, supported on the right hand by Sir William Forbes bart. Past Grand Master; and on the left, by the Duke of Buccleugh.

A detachment of the 35th regiment from the castle, together with the city guard, lined the streets.

At one o'clock, the Grand Master reached the site of the College, when the foundation stone was laid with the usual ceremonies. After which the Grand Master addressed himself to the Lord Provost and Magistrates as follows:

"My Lord Provost, and Magistrates, of the City of Edinburgh.

In compliance with your request, I have now had the honor, in the capacity of Grand Master Mason of Scotland, to lend my aid towards laying that stone on which it is your intention to erect a new College. I must ever consider it a sign of the fortunate events in my life, that the Craft of Free and Accepted Masons should be called forth, to assist at an undertaking so laudable; and so glorious, during the time that, from their affections, I have the honor of sitting in the chair of the Grand Lodge.

The attention to the improvement of this city, manifested by the Magistrates, your predecessors in office, has for many years, excited the admiration of their fellow-citizens. The particular exertions of your Lordship and your Colleagues have merited, and it gives me infinite satisfaction to say, have obtained, the universal approbation of all ranks of men.

The business of, this day, equally to be remembered in the annals of this city and of masonry, will transmit your name with luster to posterity. Thousands yet unborn, learning to admire your virtues, will thereby be stimulated to follow the great example you have set them, of steady patriotism, love of your country, and anxious desire to advance the welfare, and increase the fame of the city of Edinburgh.

In the name of the Craft of Free and Accepted Masons, and in my own, I sincerely implore the protection of the Supreme Architect of the Universe on your Lordship and your brethren in the Magistracy! May you long continue here the ornaments of civil society; and may you hereafter be received into those mansions, those lodges, prepared in heaven for the blessed."

To this address the Lord Provost, in the name of the Magistrates and Town Council of the City of Edinburgh, mad a suitable reply.

The Grand Master next addressed the Principal as representing the University of Edinburgh, as follows:

"Reverend Sir,

Permit me to congratulate you, as Principal, and your brethren, as Professors, of the University of Edinburgh, on the work which we have this day been engaged. A work, worthy of your Patrons, who (ever considering the public good) will not permit the seat of learning, established in this ancient metropolis, to bear the appearance of decay, at a time when so much attention is bestowed on the elegance and convenience both of public and private edifices.

Permit me, likewise, to congratulate my country, on the probability of seeing the different chairs of the magnificent structure now to be erected, filled by men so distinguished for their piety, so eminent for their learning, and so celebrated for their abilities, as those to whom I now have the honor to address myself.

Any <u>panegyric</u> *(A eulogistic oration or writing; also : formal or elaborate praise.)* that I can pronounce, must fall so far short of what is due to you, Sir, and your honorable and learned brethren, that it would be presumption in me to attempt to express my sense of your deserts. Suffice it to say that the Grand Lodge of Scotland and the lodges depending on it, are most happy, in having this opportunity of assisting at, and witnessing, the laying of the foundation, whence it is their earnest wish a building may arise, which, in future ages may be renowned for the excellence of its teachers, and as much respected for the propriety of conduct in its students, as the University now is, over which you have the peculiar satisfaction of presiding.

May the Almighty Architect, the Sovereign Disposer of all events, grant that the Principal and Professors of this College may continue to deliver their instructions, and the Students to receive their admonitions, in such a manner as may rebound to the glory of God, the promoting of science, and the extension of all useful learning."

To which the rev. Principal made the following reply:-

"My Lord,

From very humble beginnings, the University of Edinburgh has attained to such eminence, as entitles it to be ranked among the most celebrated seminaries of learning. Indebted to the bounty of several of our Sovereigns - distinguished particularly by the gracious Prince now seated on the British throne, whom with gratitude, we reckon among the most munificent of our royal benefactors - and cherished by the continued attention and good offices of our honorable Patrons, this University can no boast of the number and variety of its institutions for the instruction of youth in all the branches of literature and science.

With what integrity and discernment persons have been chosen to preside in each of these departments, the character of my learned colleagues affords the most satisfying evidence. From confidence in their abilities, and assiduity in discharging the duties of their respective offices, the University of Edinburgh has become a seat of education, not only to the youth in every part of the British dominions, but, to the honor of our country, students have been attracted to it from almost every nation in Europe, and every state in America.

One thing still was wanting, the apartments appropriate for the accommodation of Professors and Students were so extremely unsuitable to the flourishing state of the University, at it has long been the general wish to have buildings more decent and convenient erected. What your Lordship has now done, gives a near prospect of having this wish accomplished; and we consider it as a most auspicious circumstance, that the foundation stone of this new mansion of science is laid by your Lordship, who, among your ancestors, reckon a man, whose original and universal genius places him high among the illustrious persons who have contributed most eminently to enlarge the boundaries of human knowledge.

Permit me to add, what I regard as my own peculiar felicity, that of having remained in my present station much longer than any of my predecessors, I have lived to witness an event so beneficial to this University, the prosperity of which is near to my heart, and has ever been the object of my warmest wishes.

May Almighty God, without invocation of whom no action of importance should be begun, bless this undertaking, and enable us to carry it on with success! May he continue to protect our University, the object of whose institution is to instill into the minds of youth, principles of sound knowledge; to inspire them with the love of religion and virtue; and to prepare them for filling the various situations in society, with honor to themselves, and with benefit to their country!

All this we ask, in the name of Christ; and unto the Father, the Son, and the Holy Spirit, we ascribe the kingdom, power and glory! Amen!"

After the Principal had finished his speech, the brethren again gave the honors, which concluded the ceremony. Two crystal bottles, cast on purpose at the glass-house of Leith, were deposited in the foundation-stone. In one of these were put different coins of the present reign, each of which were previously enveloped in crystal, in such an ingenious manner that the legend on the coins could be distinctly read without breaking the crystal., In the other bottle were deposited seven rolls of vellum, containing a short account of the original foundation and present state of the University, together with several other papers; in particular, the different newspapers, containing advertisements relative to the college, Etc. and a list of the names of the present Lord Provost and Magistrates, and Officer of the Grand Lodge of Scotland. The bottles being carefully sealed up, were covered with a plate of copper wrapped in block-tin; and, upon the underside of the copper, were engraved the arms of the city of Edinburgh, and of the University; likewise the arms of the right hon. Lord Napier, Grand Master Mason of Scotland. Upon the upper side, a Latin inscription, of which the following is a copy:

ANNUENTE DEO OPT. MAX

REGNANTE GEORGIO III, PRINCIPE MUNIFICER

TISSIMO,

ACADEMIA EDINBURGENIS/EDIBUS

INITO QUIDEM HUMILLIMIS

ET JAM, POST DUO SECLA, PENE RUINOS

NOVI HUJUS /EDIFICH,

UBI COMMODITATI SIMEL ET ELGANTI/E

TANTODUCTINARUM DOMICILIO DIGN/E,

CONSULERETUR,

PRIMUM LAPIDEM POSUIT

FLAUDENTE INGENTI OMNIUM ORDIUNIUM

FREQUENTIA

VIR NOBILISSIUMUS FRANCISCUS DOMINUS NAPIER,

REIPUB ARCHITECTONIC/E APUD SCOTOS

CURIO

MAXIMUS.

XVI KAL DECEMB

ANNO SALUTIS HUMAN /E MDCCLXXXIX

/ER/E ARCHITECTIONIC/E IOOIDCCLXXIX

CONSULE THOMA ELDER,

ADAMIE/E PR/EFECTO GULIELMO ROBERTSON ARCHITECTO ROBERTO ADAM

Q.F.F.Q.S.

TRANSLATION

"By the Blessing of Almighty God, In the reign of the most munificent Prince George III, The buildings of the University of Edinburgh, being originally very mean, And now, after two centuries, almost a ruin. The Right Hon. Francis Lord Napier, Grand Master of the Fraternity of Free Masons of Scotland, Amidst the acclamations of the people, laid the foundation stone of this new fabric, In which an union of elegance with conveniences, suitable to the dignity of learning, Has been studied; On the 16th day of November in the year of our Lord 1789 And in the era of Masonry 5789.

Thomas Elder being the Lord Provost of the City; William Robertson, the Principal of the University; and Robert Adam the Architect.

ay the undertaking prosper and be crowned with success. An anthem having been sung, the brethren returned, the whole procession being reversed, and when the junior lodge arrived at the door of the Parliament-house, it fell back to the right and left, within the lines of soldiers; when the Principal, Professors and Students; the Lord Provost, Magistrates, and Town Council; and the Grand Lodge; passed though, with their hats off.

The procession on this occasion was one of the most brilliant and numerous that ever was exhibited in the city of Edinburgh. The Provost and Magistrates had very properly invited many of the Nobility and Gentry from all parts of the country, to witness the solemnity of laying the foundation-stone of a college, the architecture of which, it is agreed by all who have seen the plan, will not only do honor to the city, but to the nation of Europe. But the number of persons invited was far exceeded by the immense multitude of all ranks, who, desirous of viewing so magnificent a spectacle, filled the streets, windows, and even roofs of the houses, all the way from the Parliament-close, down the High-street and Bridge-street, near the fourth end of which the foundation-stone was laid. Above 20,000 were supposed to be witnesses of this ceremony. It is, however, worthy of notice, that, notwithstanding so immense a crowd, the greatest order and decency were observed; nor did the smallest accident happen.

On the 7th of January 1795, the brethren in Scotland had another opportunity of exemplifying their skill in the practical rules of the Art, at opening the new bridge for carriages at

Montrose. This undertaking had been long deeded impracticable, on account of the extent being near half a mile across a rapid influx and reflux of the sea. The important work, however, was happily accomplished under the superintendence of the fraternity, and the great post road from the fourth to the north of Scotland is now united. A public procession was formed on this occasion when the Grand Master, amidst an immense concourse of people, critically examined the work and declared it well built and ably executed.

Having described the principal works in which the brethren in Scotland have been employed, we shall now resume the history of masonry in England, and trace the occurrences that have taken place there, under the auspices of the Duke of Cumberland, and his successor the prince of Wales.

On the 4th of January 1787, was opened in London, the grand chapter of Harodim. Though this order is of ancient date, and had been patronized in different parts of Europe, previous to this period there appears not on record the regular establishment of such an association in England. For some years it was faintly encouraged, but since its merit has been further investigated, it has received the patronage of the most exalted masonic characters; and, under the patronage of Lord Macdonald, meets regularly at Free-Masons tavern on the 3rd Monday of January, February, March, April, October, November, and December; at which meetings any member of a regular lodge may be admitted by ticket as a visitor, to hear the lectures of masonry judiciously illustrated.

The mysteries of this order are peculiar to the institution itself, while the lectures of the Chapter include every branch of the masonic system, and represent the art of masonry in a finished and complete form.

Different classes are established, and particular lectures restricted to each class. The lectures are divided into sections, and the sections into clauses. the sections are annually assigned by the Chief Harod, to a certain number of his skillful companions in each class, who are denominated SECTIONISTS; *(Excessive regard for sectional or local interests; regional or local spirit, prejudice, etc.)* and they are empowered to distribute the clauses of their respective sections, with the approbation of the Chief Harod and General Director, among certain private companions of the Chapter, who are denominated CLAUSE-HOLDERS. Such companions as by assiduity become possessed of all the sections in the lecture are called LECTURERS; and out of these the General Director is always chosen.

Every Clause holder, on his appointment, is presented with a ticket, signed by the Chief Harod, specifying the clause allotted to him. This ticket entitles him to enjoy the rank and privileges of a Clause-holder of the Chapter; and no Clause-holder can transfer his ticket to the another Companion, unless the consent of the Council has been obtained for that purpose, and the Director General shall have approved the Companion to whom it is to be transferred, as qualified to hold it. In case of the death, sickness, or non-residence in London, of any Lecturer, Sectionist or Clause-holder, another Companion is immediately appointed to fill up the vacancy, that the lectures may be always complete; and once in every month, during the session, a public lecture is delivered, in a masterly manner, in open Chapter.

The Grand-Chapter is governed by a Grand Patron, two Vice Patrons, a Chief Ruler, and two Assistants, with a Council of twelve respectable Companions, chosen annually at the Chapter nearest to the festival of St John the Evangelist.

On the 25th of March 1788, another event worthy of notice in the annals of masonry took place, by the institution of the Royal Cumberland Free-mason school, for maintaining, clothing and educating female orphans, the children of indigent brethren. To the benevolent exertions of chevalier Bartholomew Ruspini, the fraternity was first indebted for this establishment. Under the patronage of her royal highness the duchess of Cumberland, the school was originally formed; and to her softening hand is owning its present flourishing state, by here recommendation of it to the Royal Family as well as to many of the nobility and gentry of both sexes. On the 1st of January 1789, fifteen children were taken into the house provided for the purpose at Somers Town, St. Pancras; but since that time, by the liberal encouragement which the Charity has received from the fraternity in India as well as in England, the Governors have been enabled to augment the number of children at different periods to thirty-four.

The object of this Charity is to train up children in the knowledge of virtue and religion; in an early detestation of vice, and its unhappy consequences, in industry, as necessary to their condition; and to impress strongly on their minds, a due sense of subordination, true humility, and obedience to their superiors.

In 1793, the Governors, anxious still farther to extend the benefits of this Institution, hired on lease a piece of ground in St. George's Fields belonging to the City of London, on which they have erected as commodious and spacious school-house at the expense of upwards of £2500 into which the children are now removed. This building is sufficiently extensive to accommodate an hundred children; and from the exertions of the fraternity at home and abroad, there is every reason to hope that the Governors will soon have it in their power to provide for that number.

The following are some of the general regulations for the management of the school:

very child who is admitted in to the school must be the daughter of a mason who has been initiated into the Society three years, and registered in the books of the Grand Lodge; and such child, at the time of application; must be between the age of five and nine years; not weak, sickly, or afflicted with any disorder or infirmity; must have had the smallpox, and be free from any defect in her eyes or limbs. There is no restriction as to her parochial settlement, whether it be in town or country.

Children continue in the school till they attain the age of fifteen years, during which time they are carefully instructed in every domestic employment; and when they quit the school, are placed out as apprentices, either to trades, or as domestic servants, as may be found mist suitable to their respective capacities.

A quarterly General Court of the Governors is held on the second Thursday in January, April, July, and October, to receive the reports of the General Committee, order all payments admit and discharge children, and transact all general business relative to the Charity.

A General Committee, consisting of perpetual and life Governors, and thirty annual Governors, meet on the last Friday in every month, to receive the reports of the Sub-Committee, and give such directions as they judge proper, subject to the confirmation or rejection of the succeeding Quarterly Court.

A House Committee, consisting of twelve members of the General Committee, meet on the Friday preceding each meeting of that Committee, (or oftener, if any matter require their attendance,) to whom the internal management is specially delegated; for which purpose they visit the school in weekly rotation, examine the provision and stores sent in for the use of the Charity, and see that the several regulations are strictly complied with, and report their proceedings to the General Committee.

A Committee of Auditors, consisting of twelve members of the General Committee, meet previous to every Quarterly Court, to examine the vouchers and accounts of the Treasurer and Collector, see that the same are properly entered by the Secretary, and prevent any payments being made, which have not been approved and by the House and General Committees.

This Charity is under the immediate supervision of her royal highness the duchess of Cumberland, the patroness; their royal highnesses the prince of Wales, the Duke of York, and the Duke of Gloucester, the Patrons; Chevalier Bartholomew Ruspini, the Institutor; the right hon. Lord Macdonald, James Heseltine, James Galloway, William Birch, William Addington Esqs., the Trustees; and Sir Peter Parker, bart., the Treasurer.

To the benevolent and indefatigable exertion of William Forsteen, Anthony Ten Broeke, Adam Gordon, Henry Spicer, Esq's., and a few other respectable brethren, the Society are principally indebted for the complete establishment if this truly laudable Institution; and such have been the care and pains bestowed on the education of the children, that the sum arising from their work for the last year has exceeded £200.

On the 10th of February 1790, the Grand Lodge voted a subscription to this Charity, and particularly recommended it to the lodges as deserving encouragement; in consequence of which considerable sums have been raised for its support, and the annual contributions have of late years so increased, that an Institution, which reflects so much honor on the fraternity, promise fair to have a permanent establishment.

The Duke of Cumberland continued in the office of Grand Master till his death in September, 1790; and it may be truly said, that such a valuable acquisition was made to the Society during his highness's administration, as is almost unparalleled in the annals of masonry.

On Thursday the 9th of March 1786, his royal highness prince William Henry, now Duke of Clarence, was initiated into masonry at the lodge No. 86, held a the Prince George inn at Plymouth.

On Thursday the 6th of February 1787, his royal highness the Prince of Wales was made a mason, at an occasional lodge convened for the purpose at the Star and Garter, Pall-Mall, over which the Duke of Cumberland presided in person.

On Friday the 21st of November following, his royal highness the Duke of York was initiated into masonry, at a special lodge convened for the purpose at the same place, over which the Grand Master presided in person. His highness was introduced by his royal brother the Prince of Wales, who was present on the occasion and assisted at the ceremony.

On the 10th of February 1790, regular notice was given in Grand Lodge, that his Royal Highness Prince Edward, while on his travels had been regularly initiated into masonry in the Union Lodge of Geneva.

The Grand Lodge, highly sensible of the great honor conferred on the Society by the initiation of so many royal personages, unanimously resolved, that each of them should be presented with an apron, lined with blue silk, the clothing of a Grand Officer, and that they should be placed, in all public meetings of the Society, on the right hand of the Grand Master, and rank in the processions as Past Grand Masters.

On the 2nd of May 1790, the grand feast was honored with the presence of the Duke of Cumberland, the Grand Master in the chair; attended by his royal nephews, the Prince of Wales, and the Dukes of York and Clarence, with about five hundred other brethren. This Grand Assembly confirmed the re-instatement of the members of the lodge of Antiquity in all their masonic privileges, after an unfortunate separation of ten years; and among those who were re-instated, the Author of this treatise had the honor to be included.

On the 2nd of November 1790, his royal highness the Prince of Wales was elected to the high and important office of Grand Master of Masons, and was pleased to appoint Lord Rawdon (now Earl Moria) Acting Grand Master, who had previously filled that office under his late royal uncle, on the resignation of the Earl of Effingham, who had gone abroad, having accepted the governorship of Jamaica.

On the 9th of February 1791, the Grand Lodge resolved, on the motion of Lord Petre, that, in testimony of the high sense of the fraternity entertained of the honor done to the Society by his royal highness the Prince of Wales's acceptance of the office of Grand Master, three elegant chairs and candlesticks should be provided for the use of the Grand Lodge; and at the grand feast in May following, these elegant chairs and candlesticks were presented to public view; but unfortunately the Grand Master's indisposition at that time prevented him from honoring the Society with his presence. Lord Rawdon, however, officiated as proxy for his royal highness, who was re-elected with the most joyful acclamations.

History of Masonry from the Installation of the Prince of Wales as Grand Master, to the Grand Feast in 1795 inclusive

t the Grand Feast held at Freemason's Hall on the 2d of May 1792, his royal highness the Prince of Wales was installed Grand Master, to the inexpressible joy of the fraternity, in the presence of his royal brother, the Duke of York, the right hon. Lord Rawdon, now Earl of Moria and above 500 other respectable brethren. The repeated applause bestowed by the company upon the royal brothers were highly grateful to their feelings, while the affability and heartfelt satisfaction of the Grand Master at the head of his brethren were particularly noticed. His highness performed the duties of his office in a style superior to most of his predecessors. His observations were clear, acute and distinct; his expression was fluent, manly and pertinent; and his eulogium on his deceased uncle, the last Grand Master, pathetic, graceful, and elegant. The compliment he conferred

(Prince of Wales)

on Earl Moira as Acting Grand Master was truly masonic; and to all his Officers, on their appointments, he paid a proper tribute to their respective merits. In short, during the whole ceremony, his demeanor was courteous, pleasing and dignified.

An era so important in the annals of masonry must be recorded with peculiar satisfaction. Under the auspices of so illustrious a patron, as the heir apparent to the Crown of Great Britain, the Society must necessarily extend its influences, and the fraternity derives great encouragement in their zealous endeavors to promote the principles of the institution. Testimonies of loyalty and attachment to the family on the throne, and to the happy constitution of the country, were therefore transmitted to his highness in every quarter. The lodges in town and country vied with each other in their expressions of duty and affection to the Grand Master, and in various addresses testified submission and obedience to the laws, and an ardent will to support that well-regulated form of government, from which they and their ancestors had derived the invaluable blessings of liberty, so truly essential to the happiness of his majesty's subjects in general, and to the propagation of those principles which distinguish the Craft of masons in particular - universal charity, brotherly love, and peace.

On the 21st of June, the brethren in the county of Lincoln transmitted their grateful acknowledgements to his highness in a column of heart of oak, which was presented by the rev. William Peters, their Provincial Grand Master. Stimulated by the same motive several other lodges copied the example; and on the 7th January 1793, the Freemasons of Cornwall unanimously voted an address to his highness, which was presented by Sir John St. Aubyn, their Provincial Grand Master, and most graciously received. One spirit seemed to animate the whole fraternity, who joyfully hailed the rising splendor and prosperity of the Craft.

The unhappy dissension which had brought about the revolution in France, having spread their contagion among some of the inhabitants of this island, it became necessary to counteract the measure of a few mistaken individuals, who were endeavor to sow the seeds of anarchy, and to poison the minds of the people, against his majesty's government, and the excellent constitution under which they enjoyed the invaluable blessings of liberty and prosperity. This induced most of the corporate bodies in the kingdom, and all the true friends of the constitution, to stem the torrent of opposition, and promote their different departments a just sense of the advantages enjoyed under the present government. Hence addresses to the throne were daily presented, with assurances of a determination to support the measures of administration; and among the rest, it was deemed proper that the Society of Masons, by adding their mite to the number, should shew that attachment to the King and Constitution which the laws of the Order enjoined. Accordingly, on the 6th of February 1793, the Grand Lodge unanimously resolved, that the following address should be presented to his Royal Highness; who in compliance with the request of his brethren, condescended to present it in person to his Royal Parent, by whom it was most graciously received.

To the King's Most excellent Majesty

The humble address of the Grand Lodge of the Ancient Fraternity of Free and Accepted Masons under the constitution of England

Most Gracious Sovereign

At a time when nearly the whole mass of the people anxiously press forward, and offer with one heart, and one voice, the most animated testimonies of their attachment to your Majesty's Person and Government, and of their unabated zeal, at this period of innovation and anarchy in other countries, for the unequaled Constitution of their own, permit a body of men, Sire, which, though not unknown to the laws, has been ever obedient to them:- Men who do not yield to any description of your Majesty's subjects, in the love of their country, in true allegiance to their Sovereign, or in any other of the duties of a good citizen, to approach you with the public declaration of their political principles. The Times, they think demand it of them; and they wish not to be among the last, in such times, to throw their weight, whatever that may be, into the scale of Order, Subordination, and good Government.

It is written, Sire, in the Institute of our Order, that we shall not, at our meetings, go into religious or political discussion; because, composed (as our fraternity is) of men of various nations, professing different rules of faith, and attached to opposite systems of government, such discussions, sharpening the mind of man against his brother, might offend and disunite. A crisis, however, so unlooked for as a present, justifies to our judgment a relaxation of that rule; and our first duty as Britons superseding all other considerations, we add, without farther pause, our voice to that of our fellow-subjects, in declaring one common and fervent attachment to a government by King, Lords, and Commons, as established by the glorious revolution of 1688.

The excellence of all human institutions is comparative and fleeting: positive perfection, or unchanging aptitude to its object, we know, belongs not to the work of man: but, when we view the principles of government which have recently obtained in OTHER NATIONS, and then look upon OUR OWN, we exult in possessing, at this time, the wisest and best posed system the world has ever known:- a system which affords EQUAL protection (the only EQUALITY we look for, or that indeed is practicable) and impartial justice to all.

I may be thought, perhaps, that being what we are, a private society of men - connected by invisible ties - professing secrecy, - mysterious in our meetings, - stamped by no Act of Prerogative, - and acknowledged by no law; we assume a post and hold a language on this occasion, to which we can urge no legal or admitted right. We are the free citizens, Sire, of a free state, and number many thousands of our body. The Heir Apparent of the empire is our Chief, - We fraternize for the purpose of social intercourse, of mutual affection, of charity to the distressed, and good will to all; and fidelity to a trust, reverence to the magistrates, and obedience to the laws, are sculptured in capitals upon the pediment of our Institution. And let us add, that, pervading as we do, every class of the community, and every walk of life, and disseminating our principles wherever we strike root, this address may be considered as speaking, in epitomes, the sentiments of a people.

Having thus attested our principles, we have only to implore the Supreme Architect of the Universe, whose almighty hand hath laid in the deep the firm foundations of this country's greatness and whose protecting shield hath covered her amidst the crush of nations, that he will continue to shelter and sustain her. May her sons be contented and her daughters happy; and may your Majesty - the immediate instrument of her present prosperity and power. to whom unbiased posterity shall this inscribed the column:

TO GEORGE, the Friend of the People and Patron of the Arts, which brighten and embellish life. With your amiable Queen, and your Royal Progeny, Long, long continue to be the blessing and the boast of a grateful, happy and united people!

Given, unanimously, in Grand Lodge, at Freemason's Hall, this 6th day of February, 1793

Signed Rawson, A. G. M.

Counter signed

William White, G. S. Peter Parker, D.G.M.

For the Grand Master's attention to the interests of the Society, in presenting the above loyal and affectionate Address, the Grand Lodge unanimously voted the following Address

To his Royal Highness the Prince of Wales, Grand Master of the most Ancient and Honorable Society of Free and Accepted Masons

Most Worshipful and Royal Sir,

Accustomed as we have been, from the hour in which your name first adorned the roll of our Order, to the manly vigor of your mind, and the winning benignity of your manners, we did not look for any event which could raise you in our estimation, or draw you nearer to our affections. With you at our head, we have seen our reputation advanced in the opinion of our fellow subjects, our system expand itself, and added honor and increasing prosperity lie in unclouded prospect before us. These things we ascribe to you, Sir, as to their proper source and yet the silent homage of the heart has been hitherto the only return we have made you. Such, however, has been the generous alacrity with which your Royal Highness has offered to present his Majesty the accompanying tribute of our fervent loyalty to him, and of our unshaken attachment to the Constitution, which (happily for these nations) at once confirms his position and your inheritance, and all the rights of all the people, and such the sense we entertain of the proud distinction you have thus conferred upon our Body. That it were inconsistent with our honor, we think, as well as irksome to our feelings to continue longer silent.

Accept then, Royal Sir, our warmest and most dutiful acknowledgments for your gracious condescension upon this (to us) most momentous occasion. May he, by whom kings govern and empires prosper, shower upon your royal parents, yourself, and the whole of your illustrious line his choice of blessings! May you all long exist in the hearts of a brave and generous people; and Britain triumphant; her enemies be abased! Nay her acknowledged superiority, returning peace and the grateful reverence of rescued nations, perpetuate the fame of her virtues, the influence of her example, and the weight and authority of her dominion!

By the unanimous order of the Grand Lodge.

Signed Rawdon A.G.M.

Counter signed William White, G. S. Peter Parker, D. G. M.

While these proofs of the prosperity of the Society in England were universally spread throughout the kingdom, accounts were daily transmitted of the rapid progress of the Institution in different parts of the world. Many dignified and respectable characters had enrolled their names among the fraternity, and it is with some degree of satisfaction, that among then we have to record the name of the present king of Sweden, who was initiated into the Order at the Grand Lodge of Stockholm on the 22nd of March 1793, under the auspices of Charles Duke of Sudermainia, regent of the kingdom, who presided as Grand Master on the occasion.

The brethren in America at this period also seem to have been no less zealous in expressing a dutiful attachment to their patrons and protectors; for the Grand Lodge of the Commonwealth of Massachusetts in North America having newly arranged their Constitutions, transmitted a copy of them to General Washington with the following Address.

Address of the Grand Lodge of Free and Accepted Masons of the Commonwealth of Massachusetts, to their Brother George Washington

hilst the historian is describing the career of your glory, and the inhabitants of an extensive empire are made happy in your unexampled exertions; whilst some celebrate the Hero, so distinguished in liberating United America, and other the Patriot who presides over her councils; a band of brothers, having always joined the acclamations of their countrymen, now testify their respect for those milder virtues which have ever graced the man.

Taught by the precepts of our Society, that all its members stand upon a LEVEL, we venture to assume; this station, and to approach you with that freedom which diminishes our diffidence, without lessening our respect. Desirous to enlarge the boundaries of social happiness, and to vindicate the ceremonies of their Institution, this Grand Lodge has published "A Book of Constitutions," (and a copy for your acceptance accompanies this,) which, by discovering the principles that actuate, will speak the eulogy of the Society, thought they fervently wish the conduct of its members may prove its highest commendation.

Convinced of his attachment to its cause, and readiness to encourage its benevolent designs, they have taken the liberty to dedicate this work to one, the qualities of whose heart, and the actions of whose life, have contributed to improve personal virtue, and extend throughout the world the most endearing cordialities; and they humbly hope he will pardon this freedom, and accept the tribute of their esteem and homage.

May the Supreme Architect of the Universe protect and bless you, give you length of days and increase of felicity in this world, and then receive you the harmonious and exalted Society in Heaven

John Cutler, G.M.   Josiah Bartlet, S. G. W. Mungo Mackay, J. G. W.   Bolton, Dec 27, A. L. 5792

To this Address General Washington returned the following Answer.

Answer to the Grand Lodge of Free and Accepted Masons of Massachusetts

Flattering as it may be to the human mind, and truly honorable as it is, to receive from our fellow-citizens testimonies of approbation for exertions to promote the public welfare; it is not less pleasing to know, that the milder virtues of the heart are highly respected by a Society whose liberal principles are founded in the immediate laws of truth and justice.

To enlarge the sphere of social happiness is worthy, the benevolent design of a Masonic Institution; and it is most fervently to be wished, that the conduct of every member of the fraternity, as well as those publications that discover the principles which actuate them, may tend to convince mankind, that the grand object of Masonry is to promote the happiness of the human race.

While I beg your acceptance of my thanks for "the Book of Constitutions" which you have sent me, and for the honor you have done me in the Dedication, permit me to assure you, that I feel all those emotions of gratitude which your affectionate Address and cordial wishes are calculated to inspire; and I sincerely pray that the Great Architect of the Universe may bless you here, and receive you hereafter in his immortal temple.

Geo. Washington.

The extended progress of the Society in England under the royal auspices, far exceeds that of any former period; and as the fraternity have increased in numbers; it is but justice to add that the principles of the Institution seem equally to predominate. The lodges in general are well regulated, and the masonic Lectures more clearly understood.

On Monday the 25th of November 1793, the Prince of Wales laid the first stone of the New Chapel at Brighthelmstone. His Highness was accompanied from the pavilion to the appropriated place by the Rev. Mr. Hudson the vicar, Mr. Saunders, Etc. On coming to the ground, Mr. Saunders addressed his royal highness as follows: That, as constructor of the building the high honor was allotted to him of pointing out to the Prince the situation where the stone was intended to be placed, and he respectfully requested that, as Grand Master of the Masons, he would be pleased to signify if it met his approbation. On receiving an assurance that it did, the stone, with the following inscription was laid:

"This stone was laid by his Royal Highness GEORGE, PRINCE OF WALES, November 25, 1793."

On Mr. Saunders covering it with a plate of metal, he desired leave to say. That however late the period might be before it was again exposed to the face of day, and he sincerely wished that it might be a very distant one, he hoped that the descendants of his royal highness's august family would be found, as now, happily governing a happy people.

Mr. Hudson then respectfully addressed the Prince, and desired permission to return his most sincere and grateful thanks to his highness for the honor that day done, not only to him in particular as the proprietor, but to the town at large; and he hoped that God would give his blessing to the undertaking those begun, and long preserve his highness, their majesties, and every branch of the royal family, to superintend our invaluable, unequaled and long envied Constitution in church and state.

The day proved fine, and the acclamations of the surrounding crowd showed how much they were gratified with such an instance of goodness in the Prince, who, at the same time was both a resident in, and a protector of, their town and liberties.

The Prince ordered a handsome distribution to the workmen, Etc.

The promenade gardens were laid open, and the company entertained with refreshments.

A party of gentlemen dined at the Castle, and some lines were composed and sung on the occasion.

Among the other masonic occurrences of the year 1793, it may be proper to mention the publication of a new periodical Miscellany, entitled The Freemason's Magazine; or, General and Complete Library: the first number of which appeared in June 1793, and a number has continued to be published monthly since that time. Independent of its being a general repository for everything curious and important in masonry, it contains a choice selection of miscellaneous and literary articles, well calculated for the purpose of general instruction and improvement. This Magazine has been honored with the sanction of the Grand Lodge, and while it is so ably conducted, will certainly merit the approbation of the public.

On the 4th of June 1793, the Shakespeare Lodge at Stratford on Avon was opened and dedicated in solemn form, in the presence of a numerous assembly of brethren from different lodges. The ceremony was conducted under the direction of Mr. James Timmins, D.P.G.M. for the county of Warwick.

On the 31st of July 1794, the Lodge of Apollo at Alcester was constituted in due form in the presence of 121 brethren. At ten in the morning, a procession was made to the church, where a sermon was preached before the Lodge by the rev. brother Green. After which the brethren returned to the Hall, when the ceremonies of consecration and dedication took place, according to ancient usage.

On the 28th of July 1794, the Royal Brunswick Lodge at Sheffield was also constituted in due form. The brethren made a very elegant procession to St. James's church, where an excellent sermon was preached by the rev brother Chadwick; after which the procession was resumed to the Lodge, when the ceremony of dedication took place. Several anthems and psalms were sung, and the while was concluded with a liberal subscription to the poor girls Charity School.

His royal highness the Grand Master's marriage to Princess Caroline of Brunswick took place on the 8th of April 1795, when the Grand Lodge on the 15th of April following unanimously voted the following Address to his royal highness on the occasion:

To his Royal Highness the Prince of Wales, Grand Master of the most Ancient and Honorable Society of Free and Accepted Masons under the Constitution of England.

Upon an event so important to your own happiness, and to the interests of the British empire, as the late nuptials of your royal highness, we feel ourselves peculiarly bound to testify our joy, and offer our humble congratulations.

To affect a degree of gratification superior to that professed by others, when all his majesty's subjects exhibit such heartfelt satisfaction at the union which you have formed, would, perhaps, be in us an undue pretension; we cannot, however, but be proudly conscious, Sir, that we possess a title beyond what any other class of men can advance, to approach you upon an occasion like the present with a tender of our particular duty. When your royal highness deigned so far as to honor the Craft as to accept the trust of presiding over us, the condescension not only authorized but demanded from all and each of us a peculiar sensibility to whatever might concern your welfare; and the ties of brotherhood, with which you invested yourself in becoming one of our number, entitle us to express, without fear of incurring any charge of presumption, the satisfaction we feel in contemplating such an accession to the prospects of the nation, an those of your own felicity. That the interests of your royal highness and those of the British people may ever continue as strictly united as we feel them in this most auspicious occurrence, is the warmest with, and, at the same time, the confident trust, of those who hold it the highest honor to have your name enrolled in the records of their Institution.

To the obligation, which the brethren already owe to you, Sir, it will be a material addition, if you will render acceptable to you royal Consort, the humble homage of our veneration, and of our prayers for every possible blessing upon your union.

By the unanimous Order of the Grand Lodge.

Signed   Moria, A.G.M.

Counter signed   William White, G. S.

Most Worshipful and Royal Grand Master

Upon an event so important to your own happiness, and to the interests of the British empire, as the late nuptials of your royal highness, we feel ourselves peculiarly bound to testify our joy, and offer our humble congratulations.

To affect a degree of gratification superior to that professed by others, when all his majesty's subjects exhibit such heartfelt satisfaction at the union which you have formed, would, perhaps, be in us an undue pretension; we cannot, however, but be proudly conscious, Sir, that we possess a title beyond what any other class of men can advance, to approach you upon an occasion like the present with a tender of our particular duty. When your royal highness deigned so far as to honor the Craft as to accept the trust of presiding over us, the condescension not only authorized but demanded from all and each of us a peculiar sensibility to whatever might concern your welfare; and the ties of brotherhood, with which you invested yourself in becoming one of our number, entitle us to express, without fear of incurring any charge of presumption, the satisfaction we feel in contemplating such an accession to the prospects of the nation, an those of your own felicity. That the interests of your royal highness and those of the British people may ever continue as strictly united as we feel them in this most auspicious occurrence, is the warmest with, and, at the same time, the confident trust, of those who hold it the highest honor to have your name enrolled in the records of their Institution.

To the obligation, which the brethren already owe to you, Sir, it will be a material addition, if you will render acceptable to you royal Consort, the humble homage of our veneration, and of our prayers for every possible blessing upon your union.
By the unanimous Order of the Grand Lodge.
Signed   Moria, A.G.M.

Counter signed William White, G. S.

(Earl of Moira)

The Right hon. the Earl of Moira having, at the request of the Grand Lodge, presented the Address to the Prince of Wales, his Royal Highness was graciously pleased to return the following Answer.

he Grand Master has received with great satisfaction the Address of the Craft, which he regards as not indicating solely their sentiments towards him, but as also repeating those declarations of devotion to the Sovereign and attachment to the House of Brunswick, hereforto so becomingly expressed by them.

He has had peculiar pleasure in explaining to the Princess of Wales their loyal congratulations; and he desires to convey to the brethren the sincere thanks of the Princess for their generous wishes.

At the grand feast at Freemason's Hall on the 13th of May 1795, his royal highness being in the chair, was accompanied by the Duke of Clarence and prince William of Gloucester, who had been initiated at an occasional lodge convened for the purpose on the preceding evening. Five hundred brethren were present on this occasion. Happiness was visible in every countenance while the benevolent principles of Freemasonry cheered the heart. His royal highness thanked the brethren for the repeated instances of their attachment and for the affectionate reception which he had met with; and after expressing his warmest attachment to the Society, concluded with a handsome compliment to the Acting Grand Master, Earl Moira, whom he styled "the man of his heart, and the friend he admired" sincerely hoping that e might long live to superintend the government of the Craft, and extend the noble principles of the Art.

Having thus traced the progress of Masonry from its Early dawn in England to a recent period, I shall conclude with a sincere wish that an abler hand may prosecute this work; that, the nature of the institution being more clearly understood, all narrow prejudices may cease to operate; and that, the universality of the system being firmly established, the Society at large may be regulated according to its original principles.

Ode 1

Hail to the Craft! at whose serene command

The gentle Arts in glad obedience stand:

Hail, sacred Masonry, of source divine,

Unerring sovereign of the unerring line:

Whose plumb of truth, with never failing sway,

Makes the join'd parts of symmetry obey:

whose magic stroke bids confusion cease,

And to the finished Orders gives a place:

Who rears vast structures from the womb of earth,

and gives imperial cities glorious birth.

To work of Art Her merit not confined,

She regulates morals, squares the mind;

Corrects with care the sallies of the soul,

And points the tide of passions where to roll;

On virtue's tablet marks Her moral rule,

And forms her Lodge an universal school;

Where Nature's mystic laws unfolded stand,

and Sense and Science joined go hand in hand.

O may Her social rules instructive spread,

Till Truth erect Her long neglected head!

Till thought deceitful night She dare her ray,

and beam full glorious in the blaze of day!

Till men by virtuous maxims learn to move,

Till all the peopled world Her laws approve,

and Adam's race are bound in brother's love,

Ode II

Written by a Member of the ALFRED Lodge at Oxford set to Music by Dr. Fisher, and performed at the Dedication of Freemason's HALL.
STROPHE.

A I R

WHAT solemn sounds on holy Sinai rung.

When heavenly lyres by angel fingers strung,

Accorded to th' immortal lay,

That hyrnn'd Creation's natal day

RECITATIVE, accompanied.

Trwas then the shouting sons of morn

Bl,ess'd the great omnific word.;

Abash'ld hoarse jarring atoms heard,

Forgot their pealing strife, And softly crowded into life,

When Order, Law, and Harmony were born

CHORUS.

The mighty Master's pencil warm,

Trac'd out the shadowy form,

And bid each fair proportion grace,

Smiling Nature's modest face.

AIR

Heaven's rarest gifts were seen to join

To deck a finish'd form divine,

And fill the Sovereign Artist's plan;

The Almighty's image stampt the glowing frame

And sealed him with the noblest name,

Archetype of beauty, Man.

ANTISTROPHE.

SEMI-CHORUS AND CHORUS.

Ye spirits pure, that roused the tuneful throng.

And loosed to rapture each triumphant tongue

Again with quick instinctive fire,

Each harmonious lip inspire:

Again bid every vocal throat

Dissolve in tender, votive strain.

AIR

Now while yonder white-rob'd train

Before the mystic shrine.

 In lowly, adoration join

Now sweep the living lyre and swell the melting note

RECITATIVE

Yet ere the holy rites begin,

The conscious shrine within

Bid your magic song impart.

AIR.

How within the wasted heart

Shook by passion's ruthless power,

Virtue, trimmed her faded flower

To opening buds of fairest fruit:

How from majestic Nature's glowing face

She caught each animating grace,

And planted there the immortal root.

EPODE

RECITATIVE, accompanied,'

Daughter of gods, fair Virtue, if to thee

And thy bright sister Universal Love,

Soul of all good, e'er flow'd the soothing harmony

Of pious gratulation; from above

To us, thy duteous votaries impart

Preference divine.

AIR.

The sons of antique Art,

In high mysterious jubilee,

With Paean loud, and solemn rite,

Thy holy step invite,

And court thy listening ear,

To drink the cadence clear

That swells the choral symphony.

CHORUS.

To thee, by foot profane untrod

Their votive hands have rear'd the high abode.

RECITATIVE.

Here shall your impulse kind,

Inspire the tranced mind:

AIR'

And lips of Truth shall sweetly tell

What heavenly deeds befit,

The soul by Wisdom's lesson smit;

What praise he claims, who nobly spurns,

Gay vanities of life, and tinsel joys.

For which unpurged fancy burns.

CHORUS.

What pain he shuns, who dares be wise

What glory wins, who dares excel!

Anthem I

Grant us, kind Heaven! what we request,

In masonry let us be blest;

Direct us to that happy place

Where Friendship smiles in every face:

Where Freedom and sweet Innocence

Enlarge the mind and cheer the sense.

Where sceptered Reason, from her throne,

Surveys, the Lodge, and makes us one;

And Harmony's delightful sway

For ever sheds ambrosial day:

Where we blest Eden's pleasures taste,

While balmy joys are our repast.

No prying eye can view us here;

No fool or knave disturb our cheer:

Our well-formed laws set mankind free,

And give relief to misery:

The poor, oppressed with woe and grief,

Gain form our bounteous hands relief.

Our Lodges the social Virtues grace,

And Wisdom's rules we fondly trace;

Whole Nature open to our view,

Points out the paths we should persue

Let us subsist in lasting peace,

And may our happiness increase!

Anthem II

By Mason's Art the aspiring dome

On stately columns shall arise,

All climates are their native home,

Their godlike actions reach the skies.

Heroes and kings revere their name

While poets sing their lasting fame.

Great, noble, generous, good, and brave;

All virtues they must justly claim;

Their deeds shall live beyond the grave,

And those unborn their praise proclaim,

Time shall their glorious acts enrol,

While live and friendship charm the soul.

Anthem II

 Let there be light - the Almighty spoke,

Resulgent streams from chaos broke,

To illume the rising earth!

Well pleased the Great Johavah stood

The Power Supreme pronounced it good,

And gave the planets birth!

In choral numbers Masons join,

To bless and praise this light divine.

Parent of light! accept our praise!

Who sheddest on us thy brightest rays,

The light that fills his mind

By choice selected, lo! we stand.

By friendship joined, a social band!

That love, that aid mankind!

In choral numbers Masons join,

To bless and praise this light divine.

The widow's tear - the orphan's cry -

All wants our ready hands supply,

As far as power is given

The naked clothe - the prisoner free -

These are thy works, Sweet Charity!

Revealed to us from Heaven.

In choral numbers Masons join,

To bless and praise this light divine.

Song 1

tune, Attic Fire.

Arise, and blow thy trumpet, Fame!

Free-masonry aloud proclaim,

To realms and worlds unknown:

Tell them 'twas this, great David's son

The wise, the matchless Solomon,

Pris'd far above his throne.

The solemn temple's cloud-capt towers,

The aspiring domes are works of ours

By us those piles were raisd,.

Then bid mankind with songs advance,

And through the ethereal vast expanse,

Let masonry be praised

We help the poor in time of need,

The naked clothe, the hungry feed.

William Preston

'Tis our foundation stone;

We build upon the noblest plan

For friendship rivets man to man.

And makes us all as one.

Still louder, Fame! they trumpet blow;

Let all the different regions know

Free-masonry is this;

Almighty Wisdom gave it birth,

And Heaven has fixed it here on earth

A type of future bliss

Song II

tune, He comes &c

Unite, unite, your voices raise,

Loud, loudly sing Free-masons' praise;

Spread far and wide their spotless fame,

And glory in the sacred name.

Behold, behold, the upright band,

In Virtue's paths go hand in hand;

They shun each ill, they do no wrong,

Strict honor does to them belong.

How just, how just are all their ways,

Superior far to mortal praise!

Their worth, description far exceeds,

For matchless are Free-mason's deeds.

Go on, go on, ye just and true,

Still, still the same bright paths pursue;

The admiring world shall on ye gaze,

And Friendship's altar ever blaze.

Begone, begone, fly discord hence!

With party rage, and insolence!

Sweet Peace shall bless this happy band.

And Freedom smile throughout the land.

Song III

Tune, Rule Britannia

When earth's foundation first was laid,

By the almighty Artist's hand,

'Twas then our perfect, our perfect laws were made;

Established by his strict command.

CHORUS

Hail, mysterious; Hail, glorious Masonry

That makes us ever great and free.

In vainm mankind for shelter sought,

In vain from place to place did roam,

Until from heaven, from heaven he was taught

To plan, to build, to fix his home.

Illustrious hence we date our Art,

Which now is beauteous piles appear;

And shall to endless, to endless time impart,

How worthy and how great we are.

Nor we less famed for every tie

By which the human thought is bound;

Love, truth, and friendship, and friendship socially,

Unite our hearts and hands around.

Our actions still be virtue bless,

And to our precepts every true;

The world admiring, admiring shall request.

To learn, and our bright paths pursue.

In memory of: William St. Clair
1410-1482

About the Editor

Darrell Jordan has written and edited several books, the latest are; "Surviving Documents of the Widows Son" and "Jefferson's Bibles - *A Comparative Study*." He is an acolyte of the August Fraternity, Freemason, Past Noble Grand – IOOF, and is a **M**ember of the **P**hilalethes **S**ociety, Masonic Philosophical Society and the Theosophical Society.

NOTES

NOTES

NOTES

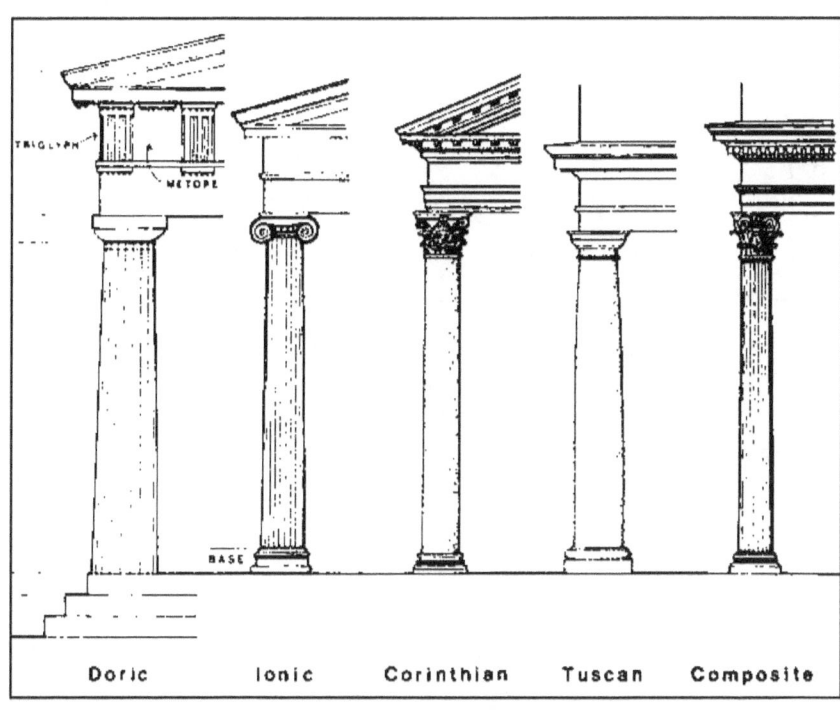

Triumphal Arch

Cathedral of Rochester

St. Peter's, Westminster

Abbey of Coventry

Reconstruction of old London Bridge

Templar church on Fleet St.

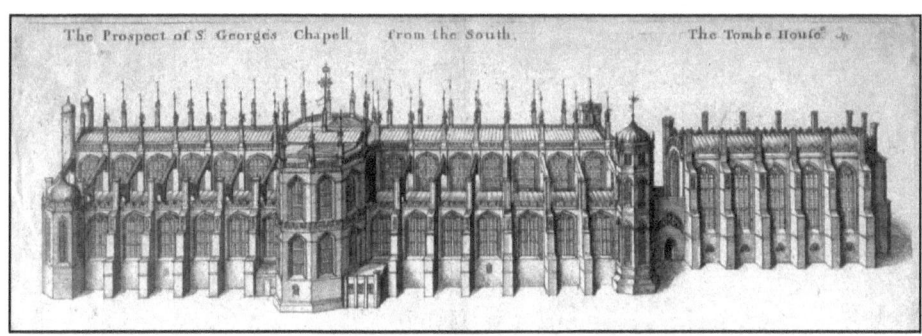

St. George's chapel at Windsor

Queenborough castle

New College, Oxford

Battle Abbey

Christ's college, Cambridge

Palace of Richmond

Somerset-House

Banqueting-House

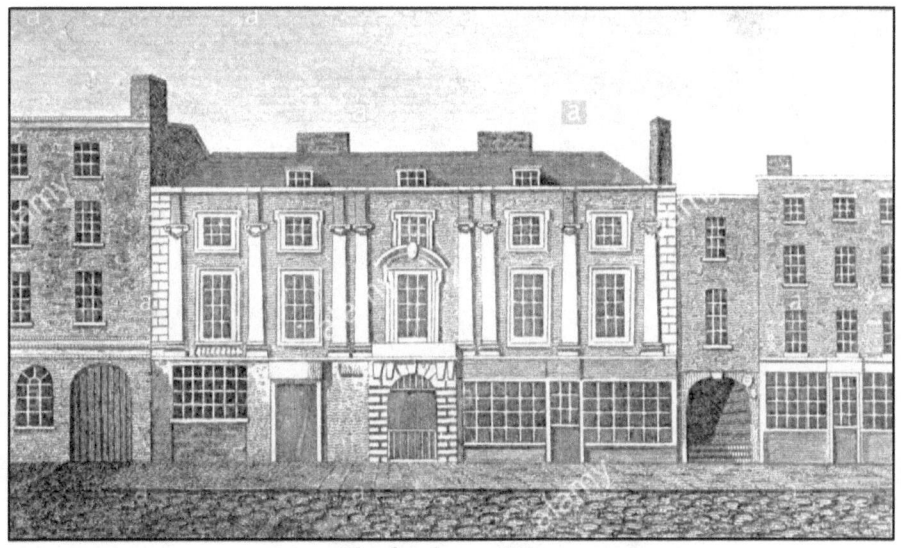

Shaftesbury-House

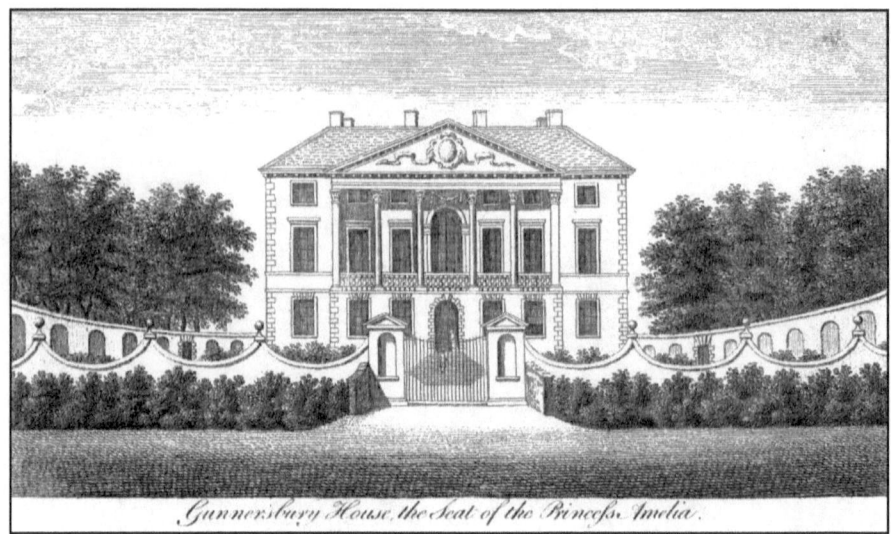
Gunnersbury-House

Wilton-House in Wiltshire

Charlton-House

Cobham-Hall

Coles-hill in Berkshire

Grange, in Hampshire

New Royal Exchange

Gresham College

Winchester College

Custom House

College of Physicians

Selection of Christopher Wren Churches

All Hallows Church-Bread St

All Hallows the Great, Thames-street

All Hallows, Lombard-street

St. Alban, Wood-street

St. Anne and Agnes, St.

St. Andrew's, Wardrobe

St. Andrew's, Holborn

St. Anthony's, Watling-street

St. Augustin's, Watling-street

St. Benedict, Grace-Church-street

St. Benedict's, Threadneedle-street

St. Bennet's, Paul's Wharf

Christ-church, Newgate-street

St. Christopher's, Threadneedle-street

St. Clement Danes, in the Strand

St. Clement's, East Cheap

St. Dennis Back, Lime-street

St Dunstan's in the East, Tower-street

St. Edmond's, Lombard-street

St George Botolph Lane

St. James, Garlick-hill

St. James, Westminster

St. Lawrence Jewry

St. Magnes, London-bridge

St. Margaret, Lothbury

St. Margaret Pattens

St. Martin's, Ludgate

St. Mary Abchurch, Abchurch-lane

St. Mary's-at-hill

St. Mary's Aldermary

St. Mary Magdalen

St. Swithin's, Cannon-street

St. Sepulchre's, Snow-hill

St. Paul's

The "topping out" of the cathedral (when the final stone was placed on the lantern) took place on 26 October 1708, performed by Wren's son Christopher Jr and the son of one of the masons. The cathedral was declared officially complete by Parliament on 25 December 1711. At 365 feet (111 m) high, St Paul's was the tallest building in London from 1710 to 1965. St Paul's is the second-largest church building by area in the United Kingdom. Cast in 1878, the 12-change ringing bells hanging in the north west tower of St Paul's form the second largest ring of bells in the world. St Paul's is also home to the second largest bell ever cast in the British Isles: Great Paul, which weighs 16-and-a-half tons. The crypt of St Paul's actually serves a structural purpose. Although it is extensive, half the space of the crypt is taken up by massive piers which spread the weight of the much slimmer piers of the church above. Look out for the tomb of Horatio Nelson in the crypt, striking with its shiny, black marble sarcophagus. The sarcophagus is actually one of the oldest things inside the cathedral; it was made in the 1520s for Cardinal Wolsey, Henry VIII's Lord Chancellor. When Henry and Wolsey fell out over Henry's divorce plans, the sarcophagus was never used. It's hard to believe, but the St Paul's Cathedral building is just so vast, and so complex, that there are still areas that remain unexplored by the people that work there. ~ londonist.com

INDEX

Dates

1

1041, 121
1066, 121
1087, 122
1135, 122
1155, 122
1199, 122
1209, 122
1220, 123
1272, 123
1307, 123
1350, 123
1357, 123
1375, 123
1377, 124
1413, 124
1422, 124
1425, 124, 126
1437, 126
1442, 126, 128
1447, 127
1471, 129
1485, 129
1500, 129
1502, 130
1509, 131
1530, 131
1534, 131
1540, 131
1552, 132
1553, 132
1567, 129, 132
1588, 133
1603, 133, 134
1607, 135
1618, 136
1625, 137
1630, 137
1633, 137
1635, 137
1646, 137
1663, 138
1666, 133, 138, 144
1667, 140
1668, 140
1669, 140, 142
1670, 154
1671, 142
1672, 152, 153, 154
1673, 145, 152, 154
1674, 152, 155
1675, 151, 152, 154
1676, 152, 154
1677, 142, 152, 153, 154
1679, 152, 154, 155
1680, 152
1682, 152
1683, 152, 153, 154
1684, 152
1685, 152, 153, 155
1686, 152
1687, 152
1688, 154, 229
1690, 152
1692, 152
1694, 9, 152, 154
1695, 152, 155
1696, 97, 152
1697, 150, 152, 156
1698, 152
1702, 156
1705, 97, 152, 162
1710, 150, 300
1714, 163
1717, 8, 157
1718, 161
1719, 161
1720, 161
1721, 162, 164, 165, 167
1722, 165
1723, 165, 166
1724, 167
1725, 163, 166
1726, 166, 167
1727, 166, 167
1728, 168
1729, 168
1731, 170
1732, 171
1733, 171

1734, 172
1735, 173, 174
1738, 172, 175, 176, 201
1739, 177
1740, 179
1742, 5, 179
1745, 180
1747, 181
1752, 181
1753, 181
1754, 182
1757, 183
1760, 183, 184
1764, 186
1766, 186
1767, 188
1768, 188, 196
1769, 190
1772, 7, 192
1774, 8, 192
1775, 193
1776, 193, 194, 195
1777, 8, 195, 196
1778, 203
1779, 8, 184, 197, 199, 200, 204
1780, 200
1782, 205
1783, 206
1785, 207, 210
1786, 223
1787, 9, 202, 219, 224
1788, 25, 220
1789, 210, 218, 220
1790, 199, 223, 224
1791, 225
1792, 226
1793, 221, 227, 228, 230, 231, 234, 235
1794, 235
1795, 22, 218, 226, 236, 239

2

26th of July 1437, 126

3

35th regiment, 212

5

557, 118
5785, 209, 210

6

600, 118
602, 118
604, 118
605, 118

8

856, 119
872, 119

9

900, 120
924, 120
926, 120, 131
960, 121

A

A. D. 303, 116
Abbey of Coventry, 121, 271
Abbot of Wirral, 119
ABRAC, 110
ABRACADABRA, 110
acroteria, 146
Adam, 102, 210, 218, 223, 243
Addington, 223
Africa, 174, 175
ague, 170
Albanus, 116
Alcmain, 122
Alderney, 182
Aldersgate-street, 137, 152
Alfred, 117, 119, 120
Almoner, 167
America, 9, 21, 148, 169, 172, 174, 175, 180, 183, 203, 215, 232
amission, 174
Amos, 202
Amphibalus, 116
Anathemas, 197
Anaxarchus, 109

Anchor tavern, 188, 190, 191
Ancient York Constitution, 178
Andalusia, 184
Anderson, 164, 172
Angerona, 110
annotator, 101
Anstis, 174
anthem, 82, 83, 91, 94, 95, 210, 218
antient, 76, 114
Antigua, 180, 183, 184, 187
appellation, 178
Apple-tree tavern, 157
April 1425, 126
archbishop of Canterbury, 118
architecture, 13, 16, 30, 31, 63, 64, 65, 66, 72, 75, 92, 118, 122, 130, 134, 136, 142, 144, 146, 153, 183, 218
Architecture, 64, 143
Arithmetic, 75
Armenia, 185
astronomy, 12, 76, 110, 112
Astronomy, 76
Athelstane, 117, 120, 121
Athenians, 109
Aubigny, 174
Audley, 131
Augustan, 155
Augustus, 136
Austin, 117, 118
Austrian Netherlands, 192

B

Bacon, 111, 185
Bahama Islands, 182, 184
Baillies, 211
Baker, 181
Balcarras, 173
Baltimore, 175
balustrade, 136, 147, 151, 153
Banqueting-house, 135
Baptist's day, 157
Barbadoes, 179, 183, 186, 192
Barbers-Hall, 137
Barnham, 123
Bartlet, 233
Barton, 171
basso relieve, 143
basso relievo, 148

Bathurst, 163
Battle-abbey, 124
Beardmore, 190
Beauchamp, 129
Beaufort, 125, 188, 189, 192, 193
Bedford-House, 137
Bell, 163, 185
Ben Jonson's head, 182
Bengal, 168, 169, 186, 187, 200
Benson, 162
Berkeley, 190
Berkley-House, 137
Berkshire, 137, 280
Berlin, 176, 194
Beverley, 121
Birch, 199, 223
Bird, 146
bishop of Exeter, 123
Bishop of Sarum, 129
Blackerly, 169
Blair, 210
Bloomsbury-Square, 137
Bodleian, 97
Boetzelaer, 191
Bolton, 233
Bombay, 185
Book of Constitutions, 165, 172, 182, 186, 188, 196, 200, 232, 233
Brachmans, 104
Brady, 174
Bray, 130, 131
Brazen-nose College, 131
Brentford, 137
Bridewell, 139
Britain, 113, 115, 116, 117, 118, 134, 210, 226, 231
Britannia, 148, 253
Broeke, 223
Bromley, 202
Brunswick, 176, 185, 235, 236, 239
Buccleugh, 172

C

Cæsarean, 140
Callimachus, 13, 65
Cambridge, 20, 120, 123, 129, 131, 275
Campbell, 202

Canada, 184, 185
Canterbury, 118, 121, 124, 142
Cape Breton, 180
capstone, 49, 130, 142
Carausius, 115, 117
Carnarvon, 176
Carpenter, 171
Carpetner, 171
Castle-Abbey, 137
Catheart, 173
caviller's, 113
Cecil, 173
Celtic, 114, 117
Ceremonies, 43, 80
ceremony, 43, 44, 45, 49, 50, 60, 76, 81, 82, 83, 86, 89, 91, 92, 95, 96, 135, 193, 194, 202, 207, 210, 211, 216, 218, 224, 226, 235, 236
Chadwick, 236
Channel-row, 157
Chapel at Brighthelmstone, 234
Chaplain, 90, 91, 93, 95, 193, 194
Charity, 37, 55, 170, 221, 222, 223, 236, 250
Charles I, 135, 136
Charlton-house, 137
Charter-house, 123
Chester, 116, 183
Chicheley, 124, 125
Chirurgions's Hall, 137
Choulty Plain, 202
Christ church college, 131
Christian, 97, 106, 116
Christianity, 106, 116, 118
Christians, 116
Christ's hospital, 131
Cibber, 143, 151, 155
City of Edinburgh, 212
Clare-hall, 123
Clarence, 223, 224, 239
Clayton, 155
Clergyman, 82
Cobham-Hall, 137, 279
Colerane, 167, 168, 170, 171, 176
Coles-hill, 137, 280
college of Physicians, 151
Committee of Charity, 166, 172, 181, 188, 197, 204
Composite order, 146, 153

Compton, 150
Consecration, 80, 81, 82
Constitution, 80, 81, 89, 91, 94, 178, 184, 228, 231, 234, 236
convivial, 38
Corinth, 65
Corinthian, 13, 63, 64, 65, 136, 145, 146, 147, 148, 153, 154
Cornwall, 182, 185, 227
Cowper, 166, 167
Cranstoun, 180, 181
Crawford, 172, 173, 174, 175
Crawford's, 172
Cromwell, 131
Crotona, 103, 104
Crotonian, 105
Cuba, 183
Cumberland, 186, 187, 192, 201, 205, 219, 220, 223, 224
Custom-house, 140
Custom-House, 139
Cutler, 233
Cylon, 104
Cyprus, 109

D

Damaris Masham, 97
Danvers, 137
Darnley, 175
Day, 8, 200, 201
Deacons, 87
Denham, 138
Denmark, 181
Deputy, 81, 83, 85, 91, 92, 93, 94, 96, 138, 142, 167, 168, 169, 170, 171, 174, 181, 182, 185, 186, 189, 191, 202, 207
Desaguliers, 161, 164, 166, 168, 175
devil tavern, 171
Devil Tavern, 167, 168, 174
Diana at Ephefus, 64
Dillon, 189, 191
Doric, 63, 64, 65, 142, 153
Dorsetshire, 187
Drake, 171
Drapers'-hall, 181
Druids, 113, 114
Du Pre Porcher, 202

duchess of Cumberland, 220
Dudley, 174, 177, 193
Duke of Athol, 195
Duke of Bedford, 125
Duke of Buccleugh, 166, 208, 212
Duke of Buckingham, 155
Duke of Chanos, 175
DUke of Cumberland, 224
Duke of Devonshire, 137
Duke of Gloucester, 102, 125, 126, 128, 223
Duke of Lancaster, 124
Duke of Lorraine, 170
Duke of Manchester, 196, 203, 206
Duke of Montague, 164
Duke of Newcastle, 171
Duke of Norfolk, 168, 170
Duke of Richmond, 156, 166, 174, 175
Duke of Saxe-Weimar, 169
Duke of Somerset, 132
Duke of Wharton, 165, 166
Duke of York, 226
Dukedom, 185
Dunn's rooms, 210
Dunstan, 8, 121, 152, 196, 292
Durham, 173
Dutch Caribbean, 183

E

Earl Ferrers, 185, 193
Earl Moira, 226, 239
Earl Moria, 224
Earl of Abercorn, 166
Earl of Arlington, 155
Earl of Arundel, 137
Earl of Balcarras, 172, 208
Earl of Bedford, 132, 137
Earl of Chesterfield, 164, 170
Earl of Crawford, 171, 172, 173
Earl of Danby, 137
Earl of Effingham, 206, 224
Earl of Essex, 131
Earl of Essingham, 133
Earl of Gloucester, 123
Earl of Huntingdon, 133
Earl of Inchiquin, 166, 167, 170
Earl of Inchquin, 167
Earl of Leicester, 170

Earl of Louden, 174
Earl of Moria, 226
Earl of Morton, 179
Earl of Pembroke, 97, 134, 135, 136, 137
Earl of Rivers, 138, 155
Earl of Strathmore, 171, 172, 180
Earl of Surrey, 124
East India, 168, 184, 185
East Indies, 172, 187
Edgar, 121
Edinburgh, 5, 155, 176, 207, 210, 212, 213, 214, 215, 216, 217, 218
Edward, 120, 121, 123, 124, 129, 131, 145, 155, 156, 163, 166, 173, 185, 224
Edwin, 120, 121
Egyptians, 55, 110
Elizabeth, 132, 133, 134
elucidation, 31, 55, 62, 74, 102
encomiums, 154
England, 8, 9, 10, 21, 113, 117, 118, 119, 120, 121, 122, 123, 126, 129, 132, 133, 134, 135, 136, 138, 140, 144, 154, 155, 157, 159, 161, 163, 164, 166, 167, 169, 171, 172, 175, 176, 178, 183, 184, 187, 188, 191, 194, 195, 196, 197, 199, 200, 201, 205, 207, 219, 221, 228, 231, 234, 236, 239
entablature, 63, 136, 142, 147, 153
entablement, 142
Erksine, 174
Essex, 187
Ethelbert, 118
Ethelward, 120
Ethelwolph, 119
Ethered, 120
Eton College, 129
Exeter, 123
exordium, 94
Extraordinary Committee, 204

F

Fairfax, 163
Feeling, 68
Ferdinand's, 183
Ferrers, 185, 186

First Degree, 58, 59
Fishmongers'-hall, 174
Fitz-Peter, 122
Flanders, 171
Fleet-street, 122, 152, 188, 196
Forbes, 212
Forsteen, 223
Fortitude, 57, 144
Fotheringay, 124
Fotherly, 181
Fountain Tavern, 165
France, 118, 125, 174, 188, 227
Franconia, 186
Frederick, 175, 176
Friedrich Krause, 4

G

Gahagan, 202
Gallia, 148
Galloway, 223
Gatrix, 139
Gauls, 114
Geneva, 175, 224
geometrician, 105
Geometrician, 70, 71
geometry, 61, 71, 75, 139
Geometry, 13, 61, 62, 70, 75
George I, 138, 157, 164
George II, 167, 183
George III, 184, 217
George Oliver, 4
Georgia, 172, 174, 184
Germany, 9, 170, 183, 194, 205
Gibbons, 140
Gibert de Clare, 123
Giffard, 123
Gloucester, 182, 186, 187, 239
Gloucestershire, 187
God, 29, 44, 52, 54, 59, 70, 73, 83, 97, 104, 106, 107, 209, 210, 214, 215, 217, 234
Goose and Gridiron, 157
Gordon, 223
Gothic, 18, 118, 130, 150, 161, 164, 166
Grammar, 16, 74
Grand Lodge, 6, 8, 9, 20, 81, 85, 89, 90, 92, 95, 120, 132, 157, 158, 159, 160, 161, 162, 163, 164, 165, 166, 167, 168, 169, 170, 171, 172, 173, 174, 175, 176, 177, 178, 179, 180, 182, 183, 185, 186, 187, 188, 189, 190, 191, 193, 194, 195, 196, 197, 198, 199, 200, 201, 202, 203, 204, 205, 206, 207, 210, 212, 214, 216, 218, 222, 223, 224, 225, 228, 230, 231, 232, 233, 235, 236, 237, 238, 239
Grand Master, 81, 82, 83, 84, 85, 86, 88, 89, 91, 92, 94, 95, 96, 116, 120, 122, 123, 124, 129, 131, 132, 133, 135, 136, 138, 139, 145, 155, 156, 157, 158, 159, 160, 161, 162, 164, 165, 166, 167, 168, 169, 171, 173, 174, 175, 176, 179, 180, 181, 182, 184, 185, 186, 188, 191, 192, 199, 201, 202, 203, 205, 207, 208, 209, 211, 212, 213, 216, 217, 219, 223, 224, 225, 226, 227, 230, 231, 234, 236, 237, 239
Grand Secretary, 82, 84, 88, 89, 90, 92, 93, 95, 96, 166, 194, 195, 202, 205
Grand Treasurer, 191
Grange, 137, 280
Gray, 175, 176
Great Queen-street, 193, 194
Grecian, 134
Greece, 103
Greenwich, 131, 156
Greenwich castle, 131
Grenades, 185
Gresham, 132, 133, 139, 281
Grierson, 202
Guadaloupe, 183, 184
Guernsey, Jersey, 182
Guildhall, 124, 139
Gundulph, 121
Gunnersbury-House, 137, 278
Gustavus Adolphus, 169

H

Haberdashers'-hall, 179
Haddo, 207, 209
Hague, 170
Half Moon tavern, 190
Hall Committee, 203
Hamburgh, 172, 179, 184

Hamilton, 202
Hampshire, 137, 187, 280
Hampstead, 171
Hampton court, 131
Hampton Court, 155
Handy, 211
Hanoverians, 183
Hants, 196
Harcout, 174
Harod, 219, 220
Harpocrates, 110
Hastings, 133
Hawkesworth, 163
hecatomb, 105
Henry I, 122
Henry II, 122
Henry III, 123
Henry V, 123, 124
Henry VI, 97, 123, 124
Henry VII, 129, 130
heptarchy, 118, 119
Herbert, 134, 135
Hereford, 182
Herefordshire, 187
Heseltine, 223
Hessians, 183
High Church, 211
Hill, 148
hoary, 36
Holland, 172, 191
Holyrood-house, 155
Hooke, 139
Horn tavern, 188
Horn Tavern, 186
Horne, 201
Hotel de Buffy, 171
House of Commons, 122
Howard, 133, 137
Hudson, 234
Hume, 5, 119
Humphrey,, 125

I

Inchiquin, 166, 175
infidelity, 108
Inigo Jones, 134, 136, 137, 156, 162
inveteracy, 127
invidious, 58

Ionic, 63, 64, 65, 136, 142, 153
Italy, 103, 134, 150, 169, 186

J

Jamaica, 180, 185, 192, 224
James, 131, 134, 135, 146, 150, 152, 155, 164, 172, 185, 186, 202, 210, 223, 235, 236, 293, 294
James I, 135
James II, 155
James VI, 134
Jerusalem, 72, 73
Jesus and St. Jon's colleges, 131
Johnson, 163
Justice, 57, 144

K

Karl Christian, 4
Keith, 171
Kenred, 119
Kensington, 156, 183
Kent, 118, 137, 192
King James, 135, 136, 137
King William, 155
King's Bench prison, 206
King's hall, 123
Kingsley, 183
Kingston, 168
Kintore, 176, 179
Knight of the Garter, 130

L

Lancashire, 173, 192
Lancaster, 20, 129, 130, 180, 184
Langham, 123
Lanthorns, 119
Latham, 203
Lawley, 174
Leathersellers'-hall, 193
Lecture, 49, 50, 58, 59, 61, 76
Lectures, 21, 24, 49, 234
Leeward, 184
Lenox, 156
Leofrick, 121
Leonhardi, 205
liberality, 38

Liberty, 144
licentiousness, 108
Lincoln's-Inn-Fields, 192
Lindsey-house, 137
Locke, 97, 98
lodge at Gibraltar, 167, 181
lodge of Antiquity, 196, 197, 198, 199, 224
Lodge of Antiquity, 8, 9, 138
lodge of Trichinopoly, 200
Logic, 75
London, 5, 6, 98, 118, 121, 122, 123, 124, 133, 134, 137, 138, 142, 143, 144, 150, 152, 155, 157, 158, 165, 166, 173, 176, 178, 192, 195, 201, 219, 220, 221, 272, 295, 300
Lord, 73, 74, 91, 97, 98, 111, 123, 125, 131, 140, 144, 145, 155, 162, 164, 166, 167, 168, 170, 171, 172, 173, 174, 175, 177, 179, 180, 181, 182, 183, 184, 185, 186, 187, 188, 191, 193, 195, 196, 206, 207, 208, 209, 210, 211, 212, 213, 214, 216, 217, 218, 219,223, 224, 225, 226, 300
Lord Aberdour, 183, 184, 185
Lord Blaney, 186, 187, 188
Lord Blarney, 191
Lord Byron, 181
Lord Carysfort, 181, 182
Lord Haddo, 207
Lord Napier, 211, 212, 216, 217
Lord Petre, 195
Lord Rawdon, 224, 225
Loudon, 173, 176
Louisburg, 180
love, 27, 41, 45, 49, 57, 101, 112, 115, 213, 215, 227, 228, 243, 250
Lovel, 170
Lovel's, 170
Lucas, 202, 203
Ludgate-street, 148, 164
Lumley, 175
Lycurgus, 103, 104, 110

M

Macdonald, 219, 223
Mackay, 233
Madden, 175

Madras, 187, 196, 200, 201, 202
Madrid, 168
Magdalene college, 131
Magdalene College, 129
Magi, 55, 103
Malta, 129
Mann, 182
Manningham, 181, 182
Mansel, 171, 173
Mantagues, 123
Margaret of Anjou, 129
marquis of Beamont, 173
marquis of Carnarvon, 175, 177, 182, 183
marquis of Suffolk, 127
Marsden, 163
MASONS CALENDAR, 196
Massachusetts, 20, 232, 233
Master, 23, 43, 44, 46, 47, 51, 54, 81, 82, 83, 84, 85, 86, 87, 88, 89, 90, 91, 92, 93, 94, 95, 96, 122, 123, 129, 130, 131, 133, 157, 158, 159, 162, 164, 165, 166, 167, 168, 171, 174, 175, 180, 182, 185, 186, 188, 189, 194, 196, 199, 203, 205, 206, 207, 211, 212, 224, 225, 226, 227, 244
Maule, 202, 203
meliorated, 123
Mercers'-hall, 167, 171, 172, 173
Merchant-taylors'-hall, 166, 169
Merchant-Taylors'-hall, 171
Merchers'-hall, 170
metempsychosis, 104
metopes, 64, 153
Milton, 111
Minorca, 181
Minos at Crete, 103
Mitre-tavern, 196
Monkwell-street, 137
Monmouth, 182
Montagu, 170, 171
Montague, 162, 164, 165
Montserrat, 175, 187
Monument, in memory, 142
Moore, 139
Moorhouse, 202
moral law, 52, 84, 106
Moses, 111
Mosquito Shore, 184

Mr. Locke, 101, 102, 105, 108, 109, 110, 113
Mr. Locke's, 108, 109, 113
munificence, 129
mysteries, 31, 33, 35, 50, 51, 52, 54, 55, 59, 70, 82, 102, 108, 116, 136, 219

N

Nevis, 190
Nevison, 191
New College, 124, 212, 274
New Jersey, 169
Newcastle, 194
Nicocreon, 109
Norfolk, 137, 169, 170, 171, 184, 185
Normans, 122
North Wales, 166
Northampton-shire, 137
Northumberland, 173
Norway, 181
Norwich, 184, 185

O

obsequies, 96
Ode, 194, 242, 243
Odmit-ul-Omrah, 201
Olympiad, 104
Omdit-ul-Omrah Bahauder, 200
Onslow, 191
Oriel, 123
Oxford, 120, 123, 124, 129, 131, 137, 142, 243, 274

P

pagan, 136
Paisley, 166
palace of Kew, 175
palace of Richmond, 131
Palatine, 183
Palladio, 134
panegyric, 214
Paris, 171
Parker, 157, 223, 230, 231
Parliament-house, 210, 211, 218
parterres, 25

Past Grand Masters, 91, 93, 167, 187, 212, 224
Past Grand Wardens, 167
Payne, 161, 162, 164
Peacock, 194
Pelham, 171, 182
Pennsylvania, 181
Perfect Unanimity, 202
Persia, 109
Peter de Rupibus, 122
petition, 81, 82, 158
Petre, 193, 195, 196, 206, 225
Petre's, 195
Pherecydes, 104
philosophy, 3, 4, 5, 10, 11, 14, 15, 16, 18, 29, 31, 49, 69, 71, 76, 97, 103, 106, 114
physics, 14, 76
Piccadilly, 137
Picts, 117
Plancus, 109
Pomfret, 168
Pope Gregory, 118
Popish faction, 144
Poynet, 132
præadamites, 102
præmunire, 126
precisians, 18
prelate, 126, 131
prince of Hess-Darmstatd, 195
Prince of Wales, 224
Princess Caroline, 236
Prudence, 57
Prussia, 176
Pudding-lane, 139
Pythagoras, 55, 102, 103, 104, 110, 114

Q

Queen's Arms, 164, 165
Queen's Arms Tavern, 164
Queensborough, 123
Queen-street, 137

R

Raymond, 177, 179
remonstrance's, 197

resolution, 57, 156, 158, 167, 170, 180, 182, 190, 193, 196, 197, 198, 205
RESURGAM, 146
revelation, 106
Revis, 181, 186
Revolution, 10, 144, 155
Rhetoric, 75
Rhine, 186
Rhodes, 129
Richard II, 123, 124
Richard III, 129
Richmond, 170, 171, 172, 173, 174, 276
Rivers, 145
Robins, 203
Robinson, 162
Rochester, 118, 121, 270
Rofs, 202
Romans, 65, 103, 110, 113, 115, 117
Royal Exchange, 139, 140, 152, 281
Royal Military lodge, 206
Rubens, 136
Rummer and Grapes Tavern, 157
Ruspini, 220, 223
Russel, 132, 137
Russia, 171, 179, 192
Ryswick, 150

S

Sackville, 132
Salop, 182
Salter, 185, 186
Samos, 103
Sark, 182
Saunders, 234
Savage, viii, 138
Savannah, 174
Saxon, 117
Saxons, 117
Saxony, 179, 184, 187
Sayer, 157, 161
Scherky, 211
Sciences, 143
Scotland, 6, 21, 117, 118, 134, 144, 155, 171, 195, 197, 205, 207, 209, 211, 212, 214, 216, 217, 218, 219
Second Degree, 59, 60, 76

secrets, 32, 33, 51, 109, 110, 114, 132, 162
SECTIONISTS, 219
Seymour, 132
Shaftesbury-house, 137
Sheldon, 142
Shrewsbury, 122, 124
Sicily, 183, 192
sine die, 191
Sir Christopher, 8, 138, 150, 152, 154, 155, 156, 157
Sisera, 111
Smelling, 69
Solomon, 31, 72, 73, 251
Somerset house, 132
Somersetshire, 187
soul, 25, 27, 28, 41, 70, 103, 104, 112, 242, 247, 249
souls, 104
South, 129, 133, 142, 157, 161, 163, 164, 166, 174, 175, 176, 183, 184, 192, 199, 207
South Carolina, 175, 183, 184, 192
south Wales, 166
Southwark, 155
Southwell, 174
Spain, 171
Spencer, 203
Spicer, 223
spirit, 11, 18, 27, 29, 37, 57, 60, 104, 107, 227
Spitalfields, 182
Spoulee, 123
St Aubyn, 227
St Bernard's Street, 168
St John the Evangelist, 196, 220
St John's, 180, 194
St Paul, 146, 300
St. Alban, 113, 116, 117, 138, 152, 285
St. Alban's, 116, 138
St. Edmondsbury, 127
St. Eustatius, 183
St. George, 123, 152, 273
St. James's, 131, 186, 236
St. John, 8, 129, 137, 146, 157, 162, 165
St. Luke,, 146
St. Martin, 152, 167, 183, 296
St. Matthew, 146, 153

St. Pancras, 220
St. Paul, 118, 138, 139, 144, 145, 148, 149, 151, 155, 156, 157, 164, 165
St. Paul's, 118, 138, 139, 144, 145, 149, 150, 151, 155, 157, 164, 165
St. Peter, 118, 145, 146, 149, 150, 154, 271
St. Peter's, 118, 145, 149, 150, 154, 271
St. Stephen's, 123, 154
St. Swithin, 119, 299
St. Thomas's-hospital, 155
St. Vincent, 185
stand upon a LEVEL, 232
Stanhope, 164, 170
Stapleton, 123
Stationers'-hall, 162, 164, 165
Stewards Lodge, 204
Stewards' Lodge, 90, 93, 174
Stoke-park, 137
Stone, 91, 92, 94, 135, 162
Strand, 132, 152, 165, 188, 290
Strathmore, 171, 172
Stratmore, 171
Strong, 145, 150, 155, 156
superfluous, 63
Surrey, 196
Sussex, 196
Sword-breaker, 179
symmetry, 70

T

Taciturnity, 109
Tasting, 69
Tavern in Mary-le-bone, 170
Tempest, 162
Temple-bar, 167
Teynham, 171
Thames, 137, 142, 152, 153, 284
Thatched House tavern, 186
the Crown, 157, 188, 190, 191, 226
The three lights, 94
third degree, 96, 171
Thomson, 163
Tobago, 185
Tontine, 193
Touchet, 131
Tower, 122, 152, 292

Trajan's pillar, 142
trammels, 35
Translation, 209
TRANSLATION, 217
Treasurer, 87, 90, 91, 92, 93, 179, 182, 190, 197, 202, 203, 223
triglyphs, 64, 153
triumphal
   triumphal arch, 91
triumphal arch, 91
Tuscan, 63, 64, 65, 142
Tyler, 88, 90, 92

U

Upper Saxony, 175, 186

V

Valenciennes, 171
Vaughan, 179
Vere Bertie, 173
Villeneau, 162
Vintners'-hall, 186
Virginia, 186, 196
virtue, 26, 27, 28, 31, 37, 40, 41, 45, 49, 55, 57, 58, 61, 69, 74, 82, 108, 110, 112, 158, 170, 215, 221, 232, 242, 254
volutes, 64, 65

W

Wales, 118, 166, 175, 179, 183, 219, 223, 224, 225, 226, 230, 234, 236, 239
Wanefleet, 129
Warburton, 166
Ward, 174, 177, 179, 180, 193
Warden, 46, 86, 87, 179, 202, 203
Wardens, 44, 46, 47, 81, 86, 87, 89, 90, 91, 92, 93, 94, 159, 160, 167, 168, 171, 172, 191, 196, 199, 207, 208
Warwick, 151, 235
Warwick-lane, 151
Washington, 20, 232, 233
Webb, 12, 138, 142, 192
Wemsys, 175
Wemys, 173

West Riding, 176, 179
Westminster, 118, 121, 122, 123, 124, 126, 130, 152, 157, 186, 271, 294
Westphalia, 185
Weymouth, 172, 173, 174
Weymouth's, 173
White, 230, 231, 237, 238
Whitehall, 131, 135
William III, 147
William Preston, iv, 3, 4, 5, 25
Wilton-house, 137
Wiltshire, 137, 278
Winchelsea, 173
Winchester, 101, 123, 124, 125, 126, 127, 129, 132, 282
Windsor, 123, 129, 150, 273

Wisdom, 39, 58, 247, 248, 252
Worcester, 121, 182
Wray, 173
Wren, 8, 138, 139, 142, 144, 145, 147, 149, 150, 152, 154, 155, 156, 157, 300
Wykeham, 123, 124

Y

Yeuele, 123
York, 9, 20, 120, 121, 123, 129, 132, 133, 137, 144, 162, 163, 173, 175, 176, 178, 179, 181, 182, 188, 197, 201, 223, 224, 226

www.ingramcontent.com/pod-product-compliance
Lightning Source LLC
Chambersburg PA
CBHW030230170426
43201CB00006B/165